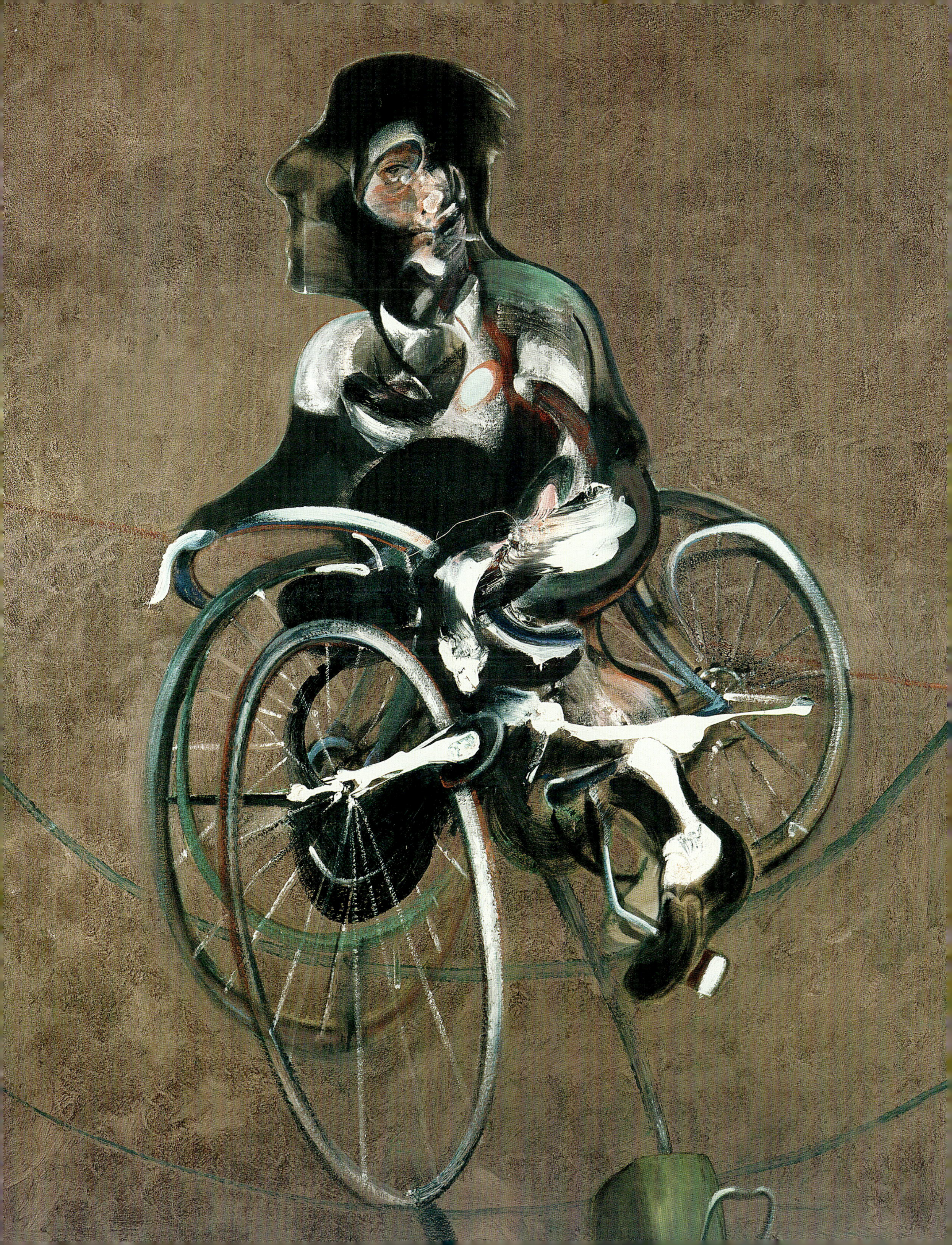

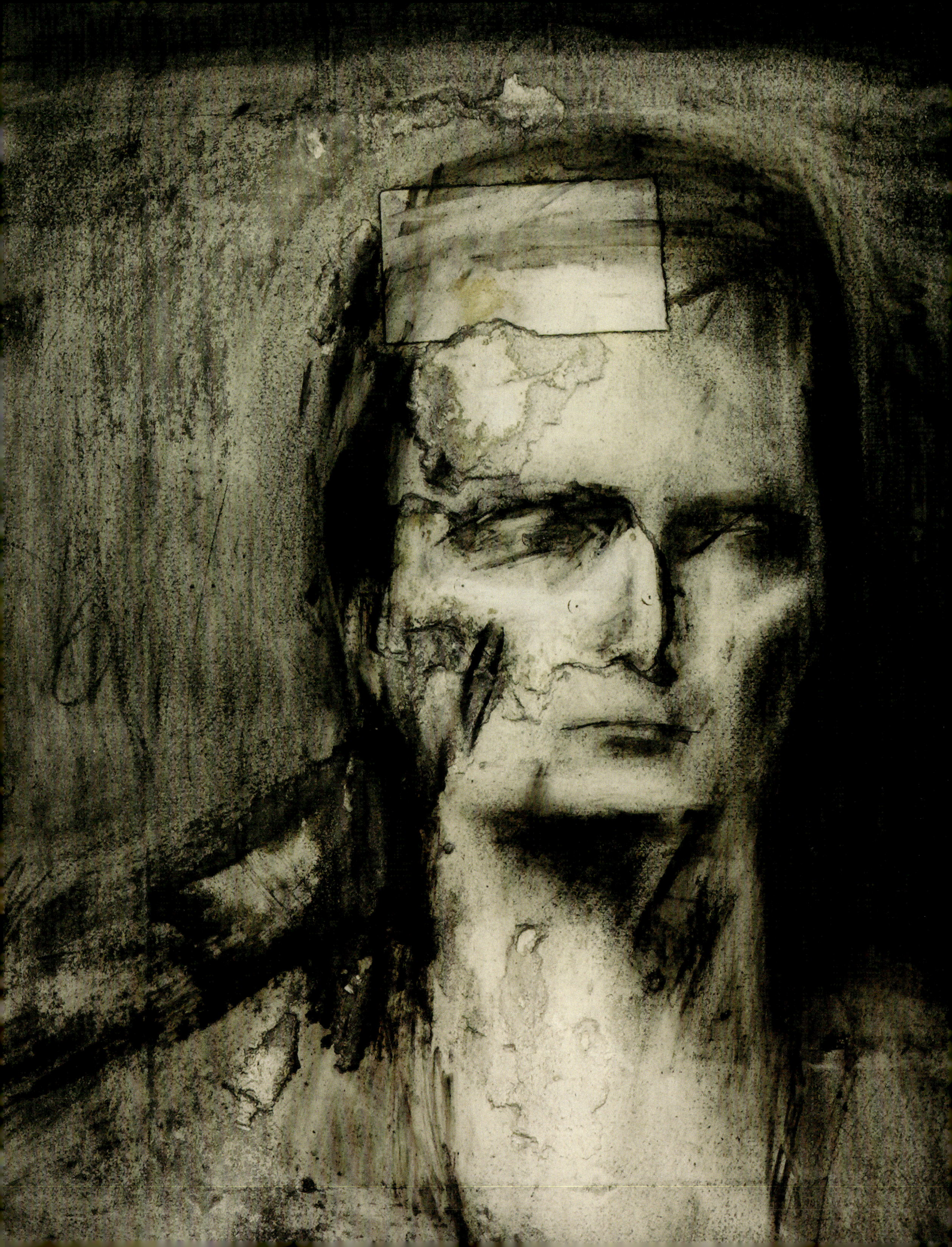

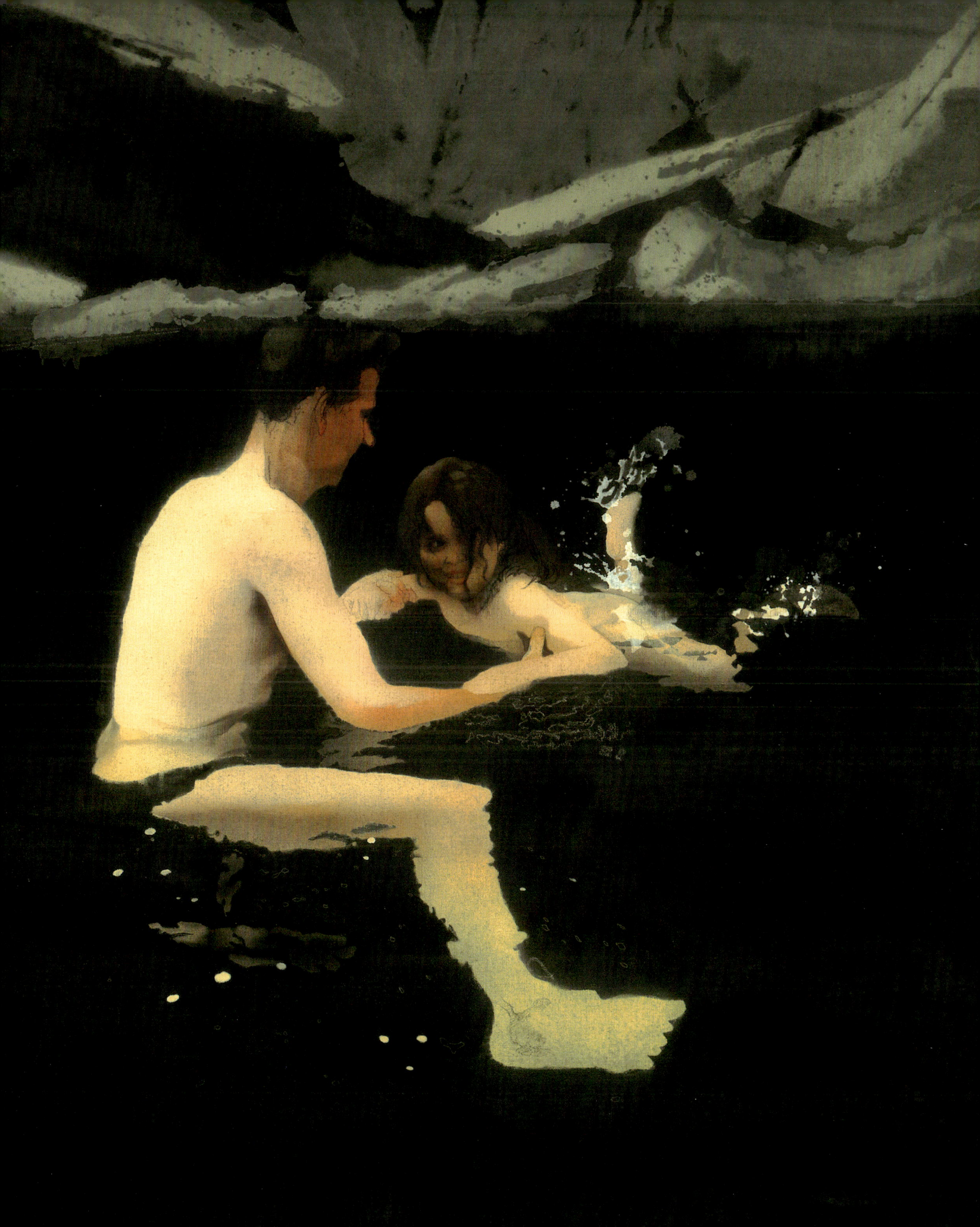

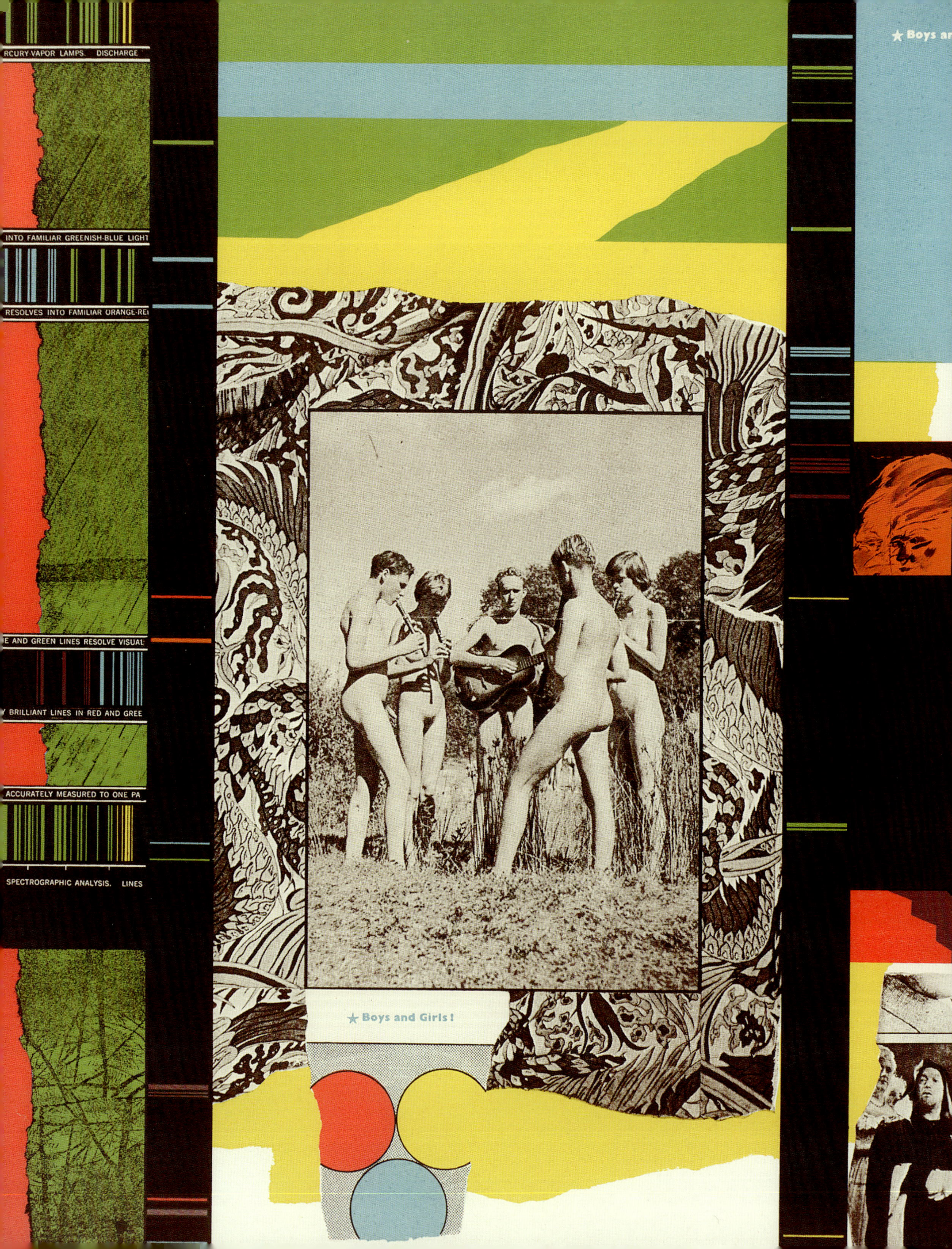
RCURY-VAPOR LAMPS. DISCHARGE
INTO FAMILIAR GREENISH-BLUE LIGHT
RESOLVES INTO FAMILIAR ORANGE-RE
E AND GREEN LINES RESOLVE VISUAL
BRILLIANT LINES IN RED AND GREE
ACCURATELY MEASURED TO ONE PA
SPECTROGRAPHIC ANALYSIS. LINES
★ Boys and Girls!
★ Boys an

LONDON CALLING
BACON, FREUD, KOSSOFF, ANDREWS, AUERBACH, AND KITAJ

ELENA CRIPPA AND CATHERINE LAMPERT

THE J. PAUL GETTY MUSEUM, LOS ANGELES, IN ASSOCIATION WITH TATE, LONDON

This publication accompanies the exhibition *London Calling: Bacon, Freud, Kossoff, Andrews, Auerbach, and Kitaj*, on view at the J. Paul Getty Museum at the Getty Center, Los Angeles, from July 26 to November 13, 2016. The presentation of this exhibition is a collaboration between Tate and the J. Paul Getty Museum.

Published by the J. Paul Getty Museum, Los Angeles
Getty Publications
1200 Getty Center Drive, Suite 500
Los Angeles, California 90049-1682
www.getty.edu/publications

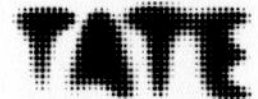

Tate
Millbank, London, SW1P 4RG
United Kingdom

Nola Butler, *Project Editor*
Karen Jacobson, *Manuscript Editor*
Catherine Lorenz, *Designer*
Suzanne Watson, *In-House Production*
Amanda Freymann, *Production*

Distributed in the United States and Canada by the University of Chicago Press

Distributed outside the United States and Canada by Yale University Press, London

Printed in Canada

Library of Congress Cataloging-in-Publication Data

Names: Crippa, Elena, author. | Lampert, Catherine, author. | J. Paul Getty Museum, host institution, issuing body, organizer. | Tate Modern (Gallery), organizer, sponsoring body.
Title: London calling : Bacon, Freud, Kossoff, Andrews, Auerbach, and Kitaj / Elena Crippa and Catherine Lampert.
Description: Los Angeles : J. Paul Getty Museum, [2016] | "This publication accompanies the exhibition London Calling: Bacon, Freud, Kossoff, Andrews, Auerbach, and Kitaj, on view at the J. Paul Getty Museum at the Getty Center, Los Angeles, from July 26 to November 13, 2016. The presentation of this exhibition is a collaboration between the Tate and the J. Paul Getty Museum."—ECIP galley. | Includes bibliographical references and index.
Identifiers: LCCN 2016013098 | ISBN 9781606064849 (hardcover)
Subjects: LCSH: School of London (Group of artists)—Exhibitions. | Figurative painting, English—England—London—20th century—Exhibitions.
Classification: LCC ND468.5.F55 C75 2016 | DDC 759.2074/79494—dc23
LC record available at https://lccn.loc.gov/2016013098

Front cover: Lucian Freud, *Girl with a Kitten*, 1947 (detail; see p. 52)
Back cover: (top row, from left) Francis Bacon, 1960; photo: Cecil Beaton. Lucian Freud, 1969; photo: Harry Diamond. Leon Kossoff, 1972; photo: Mark Gerson. (bottom row, from left) Michael Andrews, 1963; photo: Jorge Lewinski. Frank Auerbach, 1963; photo: Jorge Lewinski. R. B. Kitaj, 1963; photo: Jorge Lewinski
Page i: Francis Bacon, *Portrait of George Dyer Riding a Bicycle*, 1966 (detail; see p. 43)
Page ii: Frank Auerbach, *Head of E.O.W.*, 1959–60 (detail; see p. 100)
Page iii: Michael Andrews, *Melanie and Me Swimming*, 1978–79 (detail; see p. 92)
Page iv: R. B. Kitaj, *Boys and Girls!*, 1964 (detail; see p. 123)
Page viii: Leon Kossoff, *Christ Church, Spitalfields, Morning*, 1990 (detail; see p. 85)

CONTENTS

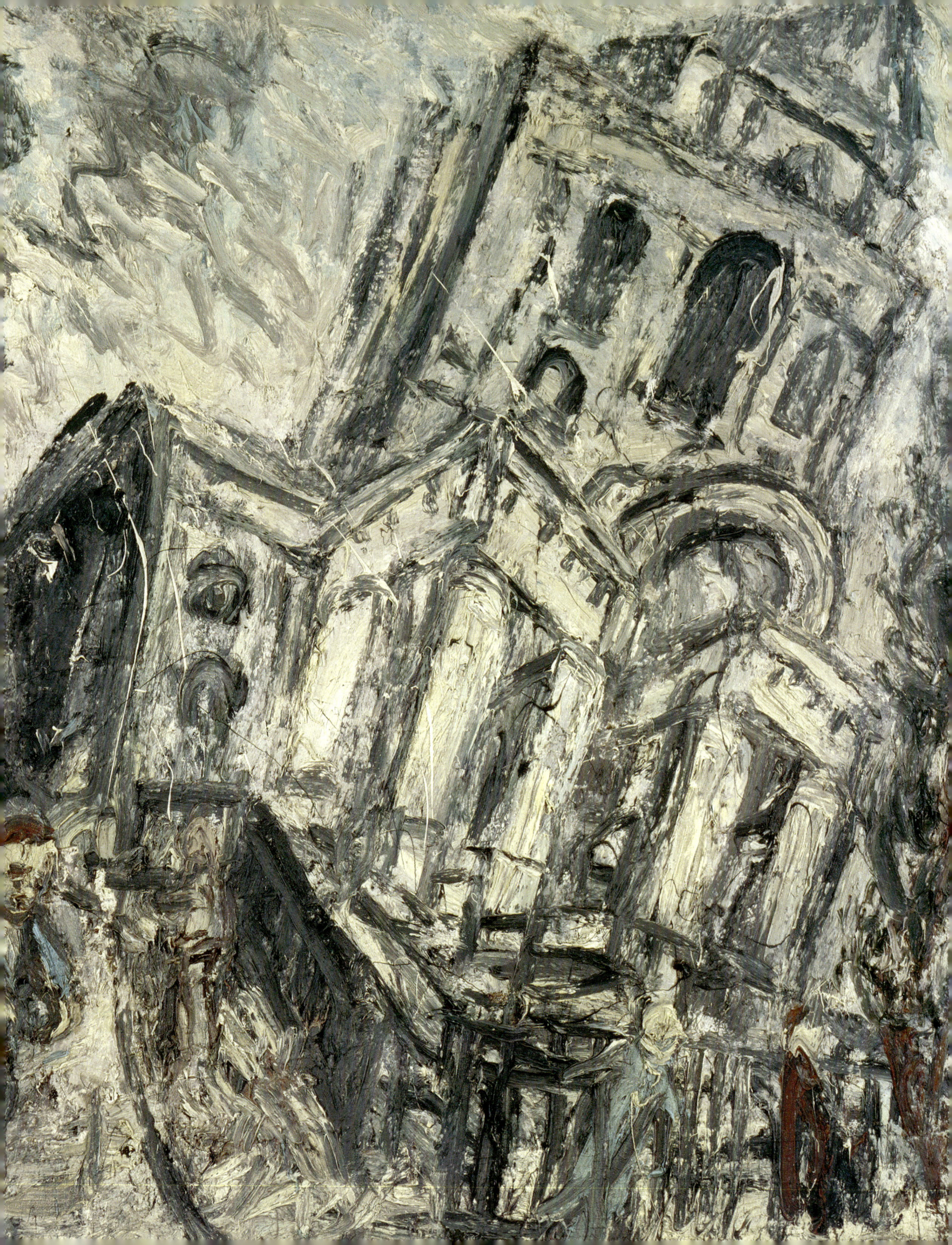

FOREWORD

When R. B. Kitaj adopted the term School of London in 1976, the "School" was an amorphous and disparate group of artists then working in the city. Even though he later retracted the designation, it has stuck, and as time has passed, the movement has become increasingly recognized and better defined, with some of the artists achieving huge international renown.

This exhibition presents the work of six key practitioners—by order of birth, Francis Bacon, Lucian Freud, Leon Kossoff, Michael Andrews, Frank Auerbach, and R. B. Kitaj—and explores the relationships between their practices with the benefit of hindsight that two generations of scholarship now provides. As the first major museum exhibition in the United States of these artists collectively, *London Calling* will for many of our visitors be their introduction to this powerful body of work. Despite their close friendships and a shared engagement with the people and landscapes around them, the artists adopted very different approaches. For example, while Bacon and Andrews embraced the use of photographs in their practices, Freud, Kossoff, and Auerbach prized study from the live model above all. Freud insisted on this direct encounter even when working directly on etching plates.

The exhibition marks a timely exploration of these artists, one in which almost the full arc of their careers can be considered, from their early achievements to full maturity. It is perhaps surprising that there have so far been few attempts to study them as a group. These six painters were the subject of an exhibition titled *From London*, which began at the Scottish National Gallery of Modern Art in 1995, but there has never before been a major museum exhibition of their work collectively in the United States, just an uneven representation of monographic shows. (The only recent US exhibition devoted to the same company of artists, with the exception of Bacon, was *The School of London and Their Friends*, drawn from a single private collection, which took place in 2000 at the Yale Center for British Art.) Los Angeles is a fitting place in which to right this imbalance, given that Kitaj made the city his home from 1997 and David Hockney, included in Kitaj's original "School of London," moved here in 1964, settling permanently in 1978.

The majority of works in the exhibition have been generously lent from the unparalleled holdings of Tate in London, with key additional loans from other public and private collections. Following our very successful collaboration on *J. M. W. Turner: Painting Set Free* last year, we have been delighted to partner with Tate again on this project. We are also extremely grateful to the other institutional and private lenders who, through their loans, have enabled us to represent these six artists at their very best: the Art Institute of Chicago; Fondation Beyeler; Los Angeles County Museum of Art; the Metropolitan Museum of Art; Pallant House Gallery, Chichester; Michael Moritz and Harriet Heyman; Daniel Katz Gallery; and several lenders who wish to remain anonymous. Finally, the generosity and support of Frank Auerbach and Leon Kossoff themselves has been much appreciated.

Our sincere thanks are due to Elena Crippa, curator of modern and contemporary British art at Tate, whose expertise on twentieth-century British painting has been crucial to the success of the project. Gemma Hollington, Tate's former exhibitions project manager, national/international partnerships, played an important role too in the early stages of the collaboration. I would also like to thank the large team at the Getty who have brought this exhibition to fruition, including my cocurator, Julian Brooks, curator, Department of Drawings; Quincy Houghton, associate director for exhibitions; and Amber Keller, principal project specialist, exhibitions. Beyond our campus, additional thanks are due to Peter Goulds and Elizabeth East at L.A. Louver, and to Barnaby Wright, the Daniel Katz Curator of Twentieth Century Art at the Courtauld Gallery.

Getty Publications has produced this splendid catalogue, with its insightful essays by Elena Crippa and Catherine Lampert. Thanks are due to Kara Kirk, publisher; Karen Levine, editor in chief; Nola Butler, editor; Catherine Lorenz, senior graphic designer; Pam Moffat, rights manager; Suzanne Watson, senior production coordinator; and the talented freelance professionals Karen Jacobson, editor, and Amanda Freymann, Glue + Paper Workshop.

With the notable exception of photography, the J. Paul Getty Museum collections are principally concerned with European figurative art up to 1900, a tradition admired and acknowledged by the School of London artists. With this exhibition, we explore a major strand of figurative art in the twentieth century that is an important part of "what happened next."

Timothy Potts
Director, J. Paul Getty Museum

FOREWORD

In the period since World War II, a small group of painters in Britain has consistently explored the appearance and frailty of the human form. At different times in their lives, Michael Andrews, Frank Auerbach, Francis Bacon, Lucian Freud, R. B. Kitaj, and Leon Kossoff have been connected by friendship and mutual admiration. Auerbach and Kossoff continue to make powerful paintings of the figure and of the city of London. All received critical acclaim during their lifetimes, some very early in their careers, and their presence in some of the most prominent collections is testament to the quality of their painting. All have responded to their experiences of London, the city where, following the devastation of war and the subsequent reconstruction, the artists met and measured themselves against one another.

All six artists have had monographic exhibitions at the Tate. Bacon—nearly a generation older than the other artists—has had three retrospectives, in 1962, 1985, and 2008. Kitaj had a retrospective in 1994, Kossoff in 1996, Andrews in 2001, and Freud in 2002. The timing of these exhibitions relatively late in their careers tells us that while critical praise came early on, public recognition was harder to win. Such recognition is now more widely shared, and we are delighted to present the exhibition *London Calling* in Los Angeles. Such an exhibition could not be more timely, as we recently closed a survey of Auerbach's work at Tate Britain. The Auerbach exhibition, lauded by the critics and popular among our visitors, provided a great opportunity to see and celebrate the work of one of our most prominent and wonderfully elusive painters. Several of these artists still await the broader international recognition they deserve. We hope that *London Calling* contributes to public awareness of their work in the United States.

London Calling is drawn largely from the Tate collection. Tate recognized early the merit of these artists. Works such as Andrews's painting *A Man Who Suddenly Fell Over* (1952), Auerbach's *Oxford Street Building Site I* (1959–60), and Bacon's *Reclining Woman* (1961) were acquired soon after they were made. Early and more recent purchases have been complemented by generous donations from a number of enlightened individuals whose gifts have strengthened the representation of these artists in the national collection. The collection has also benefited from the generosity of the Contemporary Art Society and government programs such as the

Acceptance in Lieu (AIL) scheme, which have brought preeminent works to Tate. Additionally, we are tremendously grateful to the artists and to their estates for their exceptional gifts, which have augmented their representation in our collection.

The exhibition is curated by Elena Crippa, curator of modern and contemporary British art at Tate; Julian Brooks, curator of drawings at the J. Paul Getty Museum; and Timothy Potts, director of the J. Paul Getty Museum. In the organization of this exhibition we could have not worked with more faithful partners, and their efforts have allowed us to add significant works from public and private collections to the exhibition. Our immense gratitude goes to Frank Auerbach and Leon Kossoff for their suggestions and support, as well as to Andrea Rose for her generous assistance. We would also like to thank Catherine Lampert for her essay, which brings new insights to the many national and international exchanges that have contributed to the development of the work of the painters represented in the exhibition, and also for her generous help with various aspects of the project.

I would like to acknowledge the dedicated team at Tate who managed this exhibition: Gemma Hollington, Daniel Slater, Rahila Haque, and Elodie Collin. Sarah Olivey has contributed to the research and writing for the exhibition catalogue and interpretation material. I would also like to thank Sanne Klinge and Alice Calloway in the Registrars department and colleagues in the Display, Conservation, and Art Handling teams for releasing, preparing, and coordinating such a large number of collection works—as well as Chris Stephens, for his essential contribution.

Nicholas Serota
Director, Tate

LENDERS TO THE EXHIBITION

Tate, London

The Art Institute of Chicago
Beyeler Museum AG, Riehen/Basel
Daniel Katz Family Trust, London
Daniel Katz Gallery, London
Los Angeles County Museum of Art
The Metropolitan Museum of Art, New York
Michael Moritz and Harriet Heyman
Pallant House Gallery, Chichester
And several private collectors who wish to remain anonymous

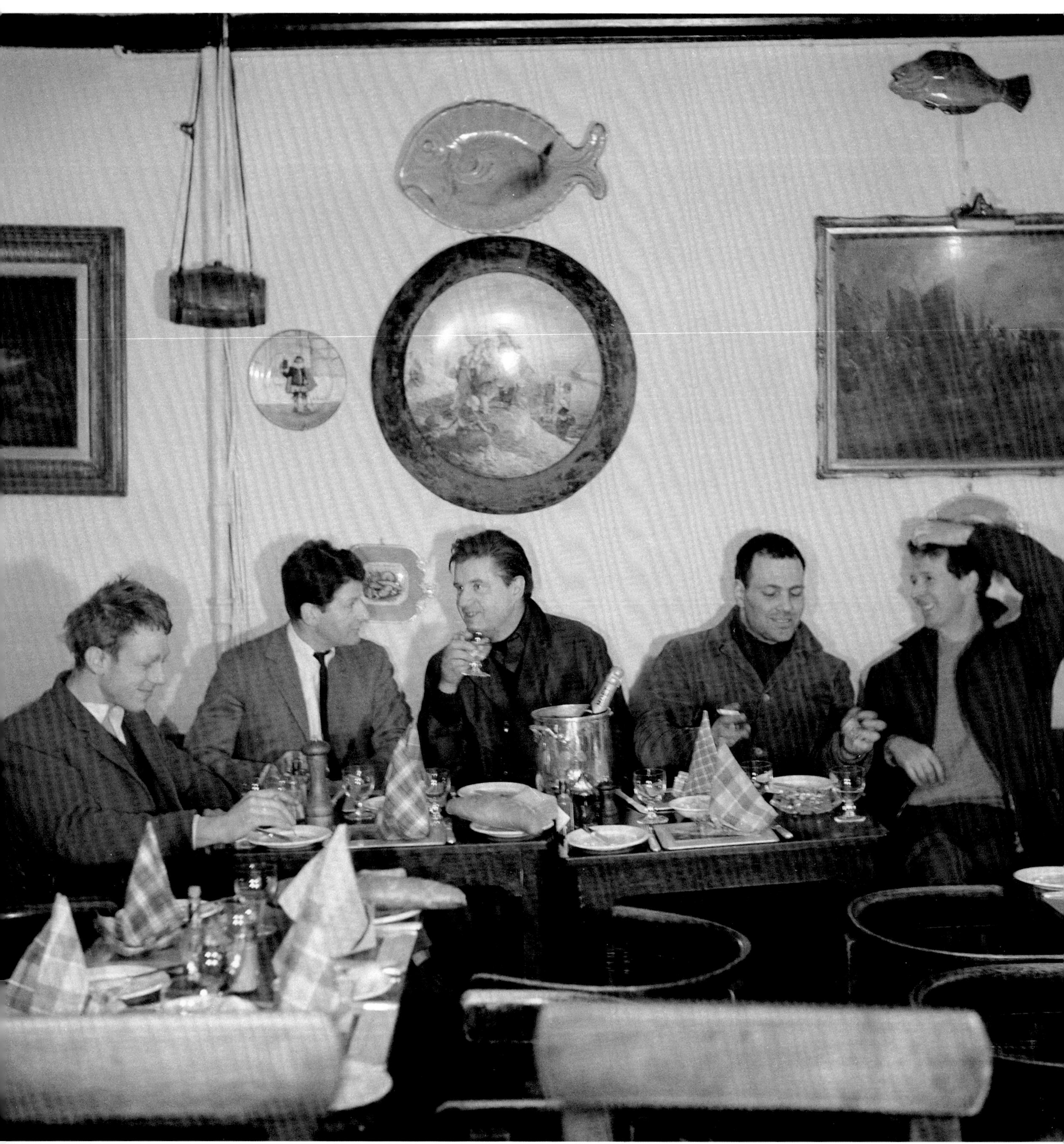

THE HUMAN CONDITION
SIX MODERN PAINTERS REINVENT REALITY

ELENA CRIPPA

Since the 1980s six prominent painters whose work is characterized by the central role granted to the human figure—Michael Andrews, Frank Auerbach, Francis Bacon, Lucian Freud, R. B. Kitaj, and Leon Kossoff—have been discussed collectively as the School of London.[1] Most of the six received critical praise early in their careers. Bacon, the oldest of the group, reached prominence later in his life—when he was in his mid-thirties—but gained considerable public recognition. Nonetheless, through the 1960s and 1970s and well into the 1980s, art focusing on the figure was typically underrated, seen as divorced from the avant-garde of its period.[2] In this context the expression School of London became key in an attempt to reconsider the history of postwar British art in relation to international developments. It aimed to give visibility to the continuity and strength of a figurative tradition that resisted the growing discourse of "high modernism."

There are a number of elements that link Andrews, Auerbach, Bacon, Freud, Kitaj, and Kossoff. Over periods of their lives and careers they were connected by friendships and mutual admiration and were featured in one another's paintings on numerous occasions (figs. 1, 2). They were united by the conjunctions of historical time and place and were all affected—directly or indirectly—by World War II. The notion of a School of London has, however, been criticized by art historians as well as by the artists involved.[3] As always, when it comes to groupings and movements, simplistic associations are an inadequate substitute for an exploration of complex and unique artistic visions, which in this case developed considerably over sustained careers.

In hindsight we can still identify shared qualities in the work of the six artists, most notably an overriding preoccupation with capturing and giving visual representation to the physical and emotional conditions that they inhabited. Focusing on the depiction of the figure, they all sought to represent the human condition in the intimacy of everyday life and encounters. As Andrews remarked, commenting on the existentialist approach that permeated the making and teaching of art at the time, "I think we thought our responses to people and circumstances and life were more important than nursing some systematic idea of what painting was all about."[4]

figure 1
Wheeler's, Old Compton Street, London, 1963. From left: Timothy Behrens, Lucian Freud, Francis Bacon, Frank Auerbach, and Michael Andrews. Photo: John Deakin

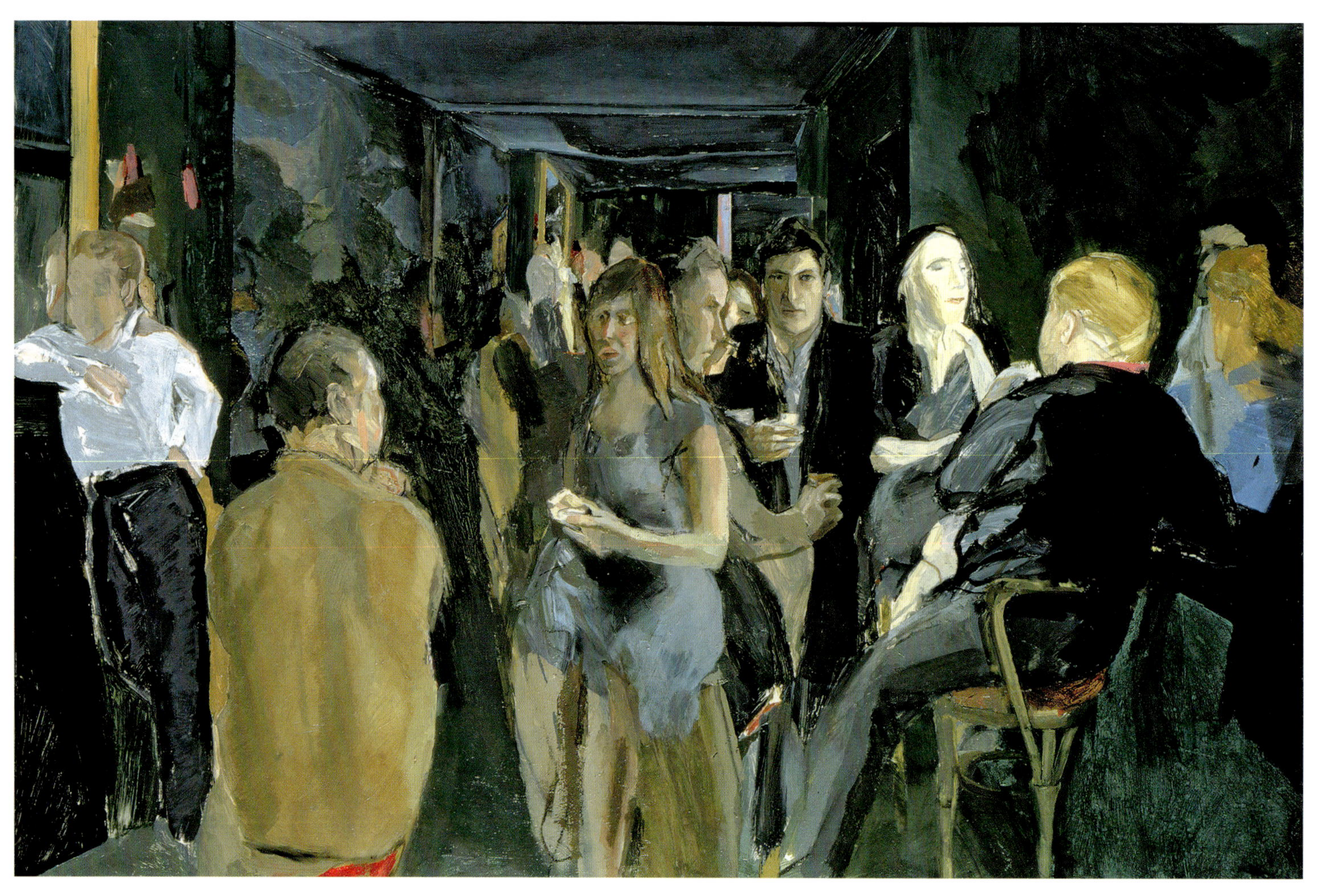

figure 2
Michael Andrews (English, 1928–1995). *Colony Room I*, 1962. Oil on board, 120 × 182.8 cm (47¼ × 72 in.). Chichester, Pallant House Gallery (Wilson Gift through the Art Fund 2006). The painting is based on Andrews's recollections of a typical evening at the drinking club and includes portraits of several people he knew: (from left) the journalist Jeffrey Bernard; the photographer John Deakin (his back to the viewer); Henrietta Moraes, who sat for Bacon and Freud; the picture editor and photographer Bruce Bernard (in profile); Lucian Freud (facing out); Muriel Belcher, owner of the Colony Room (turned toward the bar); Francis Bacon (seated); Ian Board, the barman; and Carmel, Belcher's girlfriend.

The Intensity of the Living Body

Although the human figure was and remained a major preoccupation of all the artists discussed, their approaches varied. In the case of Auerbach, Freud, and Kossoff, the painting emerges from a direct encounter with the subject, working through numerous sittings. In the case of Andrews, Kitaj, and notably Bacon, however, the subject was usually derived from reproduced images. Many of Bacon's subjects—including his screaming men and popes, figures of power and paternal authority—were based on reproductions of paintings, sculptures, photographs, and film stills taken from books, magazines, and newspapers.[5] They relate to an imaginary of angst that resonated with the artist as an individual as much as with historical circumstances.[6] From 1962 Bacon expanded the range of his photographic sources by commissioning particular shots of models to suit already developed ideas for his compositions. As the art historian Catherine Lampert has observed, working without a model did not lessen the power and poignancy of his figures; in fact it may have had the opposite effect, as the artist reanimated the mechanically reproduced image through the treatment of paint, stretching the expressive potential of the medium.[7]

Figure in a Landscape (1945; p. 33), one of the earliest examples in which Bacon took a reproduced image as his starting point, is based on a photograph of the painter's lover Eric Hall dozing on a seat in Hyde Park. A substantial section of the body was overpainted, suggesting a black void. An open, bloodied mouth can be discerned, possibly speaking into microphones, a detail that may have been derived from photographs of Nazi leaders giving speeches. The same apparatus has also been described as a machine gun.[8] Whatever the case, the blue sky and pastoral setting are contrasted with the intimation of organized political violence, making this an early example of Bacon's conflation of aggression and the everyday. This painting is also important in that it marks the early stages of the artist's efforts to synthesize powerful images of expressive physicality with personal and often autobiographical references.

Triptych August 1972 (1972; pp. 46–47) is one in a series that followed the suicide of Bacon's lover George Dyer. All the figures are set against a black background. Dyer appears on the left, and Bacon is on the right. The central group is derived from a photograph of wrestlers by Eadweard Muybridge from his book *The Human Figure in Motion* (1901) and is suggestive of a sexual encounter with violent connotations.[9] Bacon's application of paint in the representation of the human figures, dense and textured in contrast to the smooth uniformity of the surrounding space, renders the material quality of the body. If for the American critic Clement Greenberg even sculpture had become open, linear, and ultimately optical, paint for Bacon and, in different ways, for Auerbach and Kossoff was to embody a complex perceptual affair. It conveyed tactile sensations such as the texture and the physical properties of the subject.

There are relationships that could productively be established between Bacon and Freud's work and that of a painter from an older generation, Stanley Spencer.

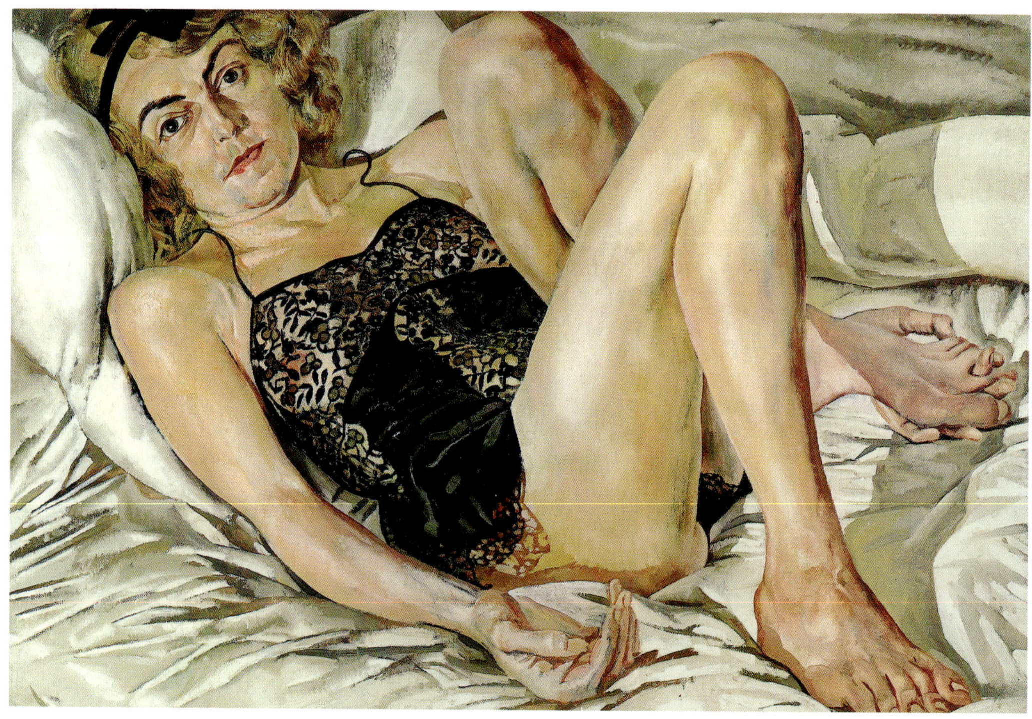

Writing in 1935, the artist and art critic D. S. MacColl described Spencer's work as that of a "Super Realist, a visionary who sees violently and strangely, transforming, swelling or deflating forms."[10] This approach is dominant in Spencer's early religious subjects and is still present in his portraits from the 1930s (fig. 3). They maintain an intensity of feeling that seems to bubble under the skin of the figures, offering a sense of tense and enlivened presentness. Bacon and Freud rejected Spencer's religious feelings in favor of an existentialist stance. Nonetheless, MacColl's description of a form of realism that detects, projects, and blows up certain truths about the relationship between external image and internal feelings can be extended to their work.

In Freud's paintings from the late 1940s and 1950s the subjects often look as if they are strapped into unnatural poses, exposed to and frozen by the painter's gaze and lost in the contemplation of their inner world and frailty. This is the case with Freud's various paintings of his first wife, Kitty Garman, the subject of *Girl with a White Dog* (1950–51; p. 55). This picture belongs to a period when Freud was tightly controlling every aspect of his paintings, creating psychologically charged images in which the details of his subjects' appearances and surroundings were meticulously recorded. The young woman's act of self-exposure seems to lack sensuality and complicity, as if she was responding to a request by the painter that she was unwilling to grant and yet unable to refuse. The loyalty of the sitter is amplified by the figure of the dog, a symbol of docility and submission to its master. We have grown accustomed to thinking of Freud's work from the second half of the 1940s on as having little relation to that painted before, one relying on an imaginative drift (fig. 4), the other rooted in observed reality. Yet the artist Lawrence Gowing

figure 3
Stanley Spencer (British, 1891–1959). *Nude (Portrait of Patricia Preece)* or *Girl Resting*, 1936. Oil on canvas, 61 × 91.5 cm (24 × 36 in.). Private collection

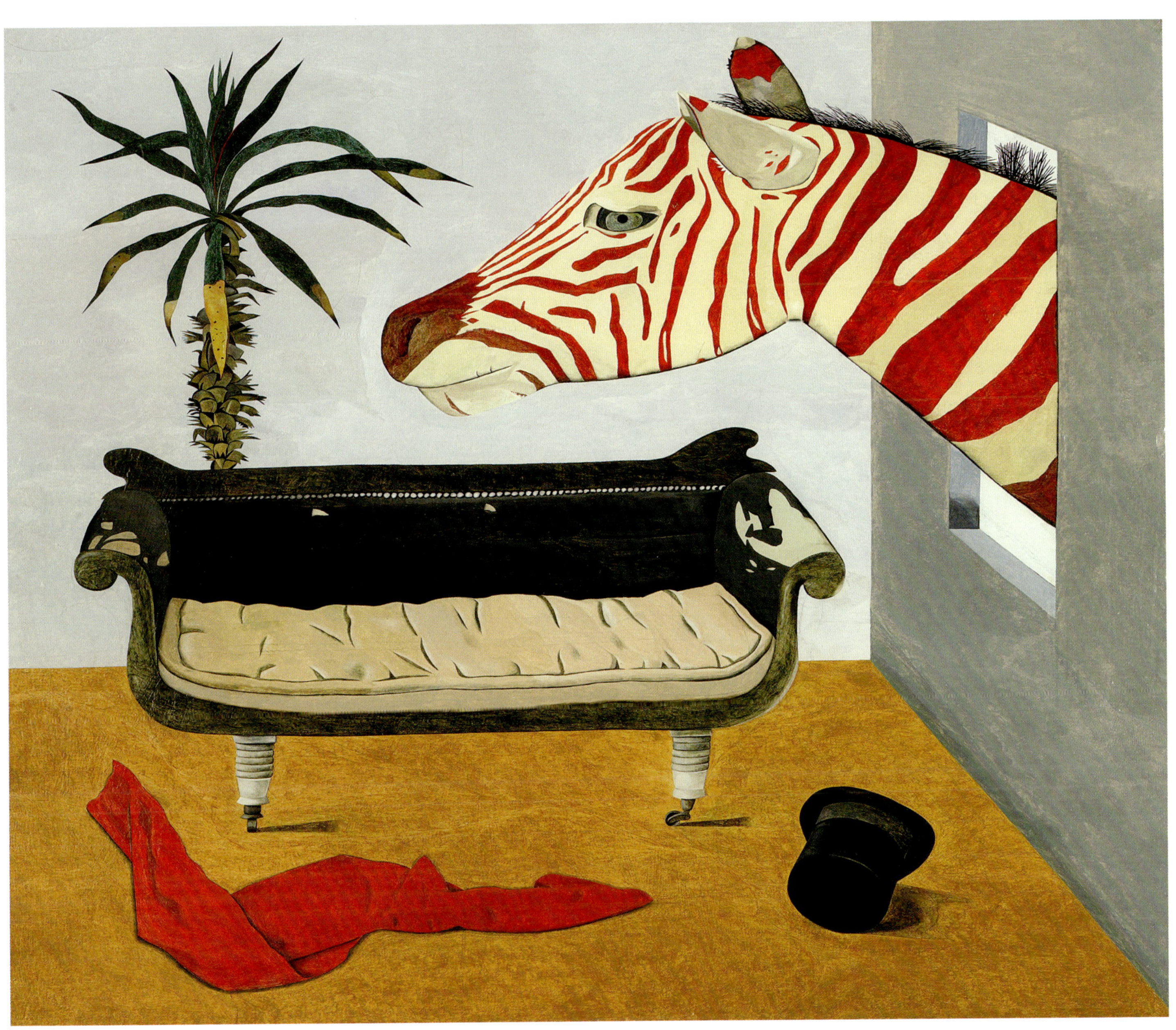

figure 4
Lucian Freud (British, born Germany, 1922–2011). *The Painter's Room*, 1944. Oil on canvas, 62.8 × 75.9 cm ($24\frac{3}{4}$ × $29\frac{7}{8}$ in.). Private collection

acknowledged the continuity: in his early work Freud "is teaching himself to dream a dream of the real, to dream from nature."[11]

In the 1960s Freud progressively moved from the linear approach of the 1940s and 1950s to a looser, more broadly worked painting style. The change was, as the art historian William Feaver has remarked, prompted by the painter's desire to exceed himself.[12] It certainly reflected changes in his life circumstances and, as is already apparent in works from the late 1950s, a more empathetic response to, rather than just intimacy with, his sitters. This is evident in the tender depiction of the subject of *Girl in a Striped Nightshirt* (1983–85; p. 61) and in the numerous paintings of his daughters and mother.

A Sense of Place

In addition to drawing and painting the figure, all the artists discussed here occasionally or consistently turned their gazes to their surroundings. Andrews described the process of translating life into art as that of representing the atmosphere of familiar places.[13] One thinks of the painter Walter Sickert and his ability to convey vividly a specific sense of place, particularly in his paintings of nudes in domestic interiors and the famous series of pictures relating to the Camden Town murder that he painted in the first decade of the twentieth century (fig. 5).[14]

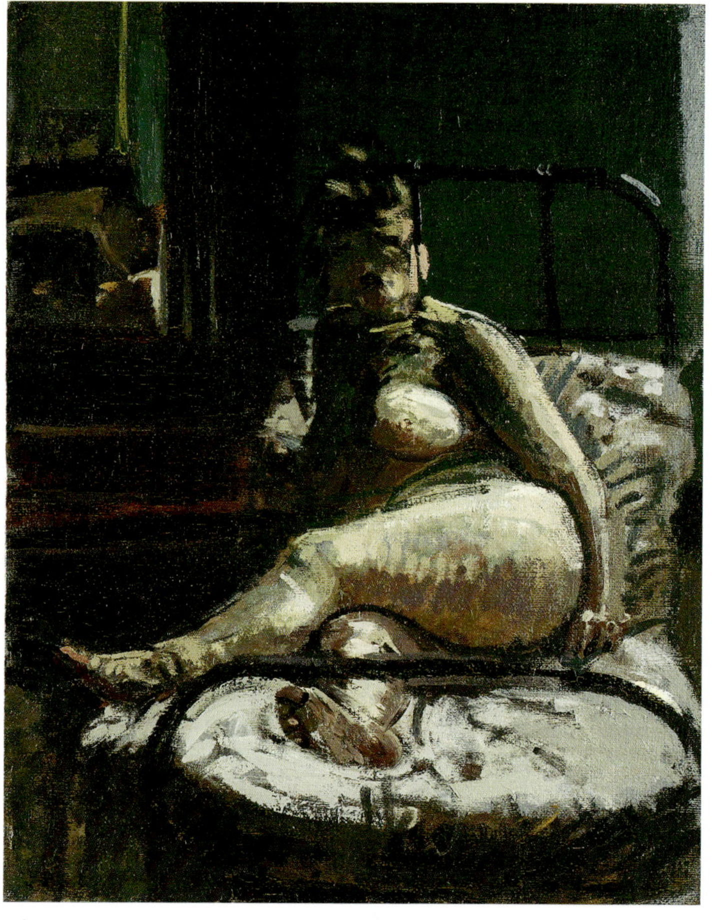

figure 5
Walter Richard Sickert (British, born Germany, 1860–1942). *La Hollandaise*, ca. 1906. Oil on canvas, 51.1 × 40.6 cm (20⅛ × 16 in.). London, Tate. Purchased 1983

A particular attachment to the London cityscape is characteristic of Auerbach and Kossoff. Fellow students at Saint Martin's School of Art in London, they also attended evening classes with the painter David Bomberg at Borough Polytechnic Institute between the late 1940s and 1954.[15] Having developed a highly personal style that bridged Cubism and Futurism, Bomberg progressively explored a New Realist approach (fig. 6). In his teaching, which emphasized drawing, he urged students to "define their experience of matter" not just through the eye but also through the impressions of other senses, especially touch.[16] His teaching proved influential in the development of Auerbach's and Kossoff's approaches to painting as a vehicle of haptic experience, unveiling sensations that are hidden behind appearance.

For around a decade, beginning with their student years in the early 1950s, Auerbach and Kossoff elected building sites around the bomb-scarred capital as one of their major subjects. For Auerbach, London after the war did not just speak of ruin but "was a marvellous landscape with precipice and mountain and crags, full of drama formally."[17] The preparatory drawings for his *Oxford Street Building Site I* (1959–60; p. 99) were made looking into a large construction site on Oxford Street, that of London's famous John Lewis department store, largely destroyed during the blitz in 1940. In the resulting painting, we are peering down into a building crater, its vertiginous depth framed by the scaffolding. As is always the case in his work

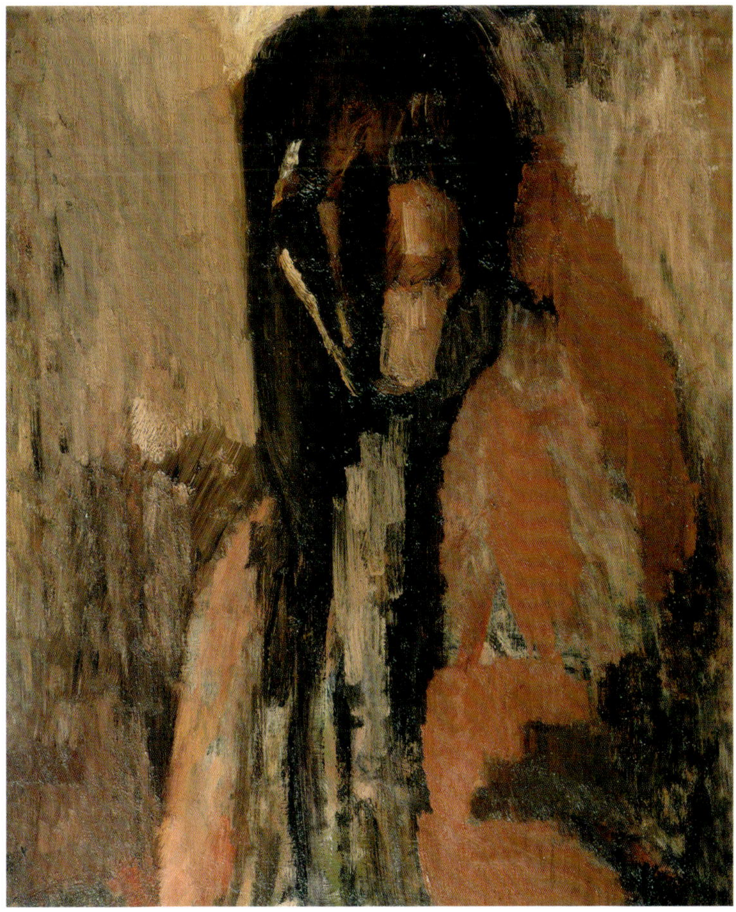

figure 6
David Bomberg (British, 1890–1957). *Vigilante*, 1955. Oil on board, 71.8 × 60 cm (28¼ × 23⅝ in.). London, Tate. Purchased 1968

from the period, Auerbach executed the picture by painting and repainting for months over the same still-wet surface, building up the image by progressive addition and obliteration. As observed by the art historian Barnaby Wright, Auerbach's process of making and the subject of building sites share a tension between a formless language of fragmentation—that of the bomb site—and a psychological and material need to reconstruct in the aftermath of the war, holding on to the sense of structure and space provided by the scaffoldings of the buildings being erected.[18]

Another recurring subject of Auerbach's work since the 1950s is Primrose Hill, adjacent to Regent's Park, in north London, not far from the artist's studio. By the time of the execution of *Primrose Hill* (1967–68; p. 106), Auerbach had begun scraping down the surfaces of his paintings before the next session, when he would start anew, the support becoming thinner and the brushstrokes more fluid.[19] As the eye wanders over the surface of *Primrose Hill*, exploring the changing relationships between shapes and colors, the brushstrokes offer a clear sense of movement and directionality. The coming together of these conflicting elements seems to reflect the experience of perceiving life, whereby a constantly changing set of relationships between viewer, object, and light means that what we are looking at is never static, never the same. The final image can nonetheless be grasped as a visual whole. As Freud wrote, "The mastery of these compositions is such that in spite of their often precarious balance, like a waiter pretending to slip while carrying a huge pile of plates, the structure never falters. It is the viewer who has to hold tight."[20]

While Auerbach's landscapes are populated mostly by simply rendered figures, anonymous inhabitants of the cityscape, in those of Kossoff and Kitaj men and women are often the protagonists of densely populated scenes set in the public spaces of the metropolis. Kossoff's intense and moving portrayal of the human presence developed alongside a continuous engagement with specific sites of London—the city where he was born and has lived all his adult life. He depicts locations that he knows intimately, and this intimacy is apparent in the way they are rendered, intensely and yet seemingly unhurriedly, a testament to the passing of time. Like Auerbach's compositions, Kossoff's paintings ultimately emerge through observations and drawings made in situ, with the artist often returning to the same sites over years if not decades, and the pictures are painted and scraped down over and over again, until finally something convincing and exciting appears.

Children's Swimming Pool, Autumn Afternoon (1971; p. 78) is one of five large paintings of swimming pools that Kossoff completed between 1969 and 1972. They represented an important transition in his work. The paint is relatively thinly applied and the scene rendered in a general atmosphere of movement, enhanced by the flickering reflections of the water in the crowded pool. While figures were little defined in his drawings, in his paintings each person became someone particular, known and often dear to the artist.[21] As a result these paintings are filled with a humanity that is never anonymous, the result of intimate observation and knowledge of others.

There are other London sites to which Kossoff has often returned. Christ Church is an imposing Anglican church built in the first half of the eighteenth century, one of many designed by the architect Nicholas Hawksmoor in a Baroque style. A prominent landmark in Kossoff's native district of Shoreditch, in the East End, the church has stood mostly unaltered through the area's many changes and recent gentrification. Kossoff first drew it in the 1950s, when it was semiderelict, and began painting it in the 1980s, returning to the subject in the 1990s (p. 85). In these paintings, as the art historian Andrea Rose has observed, "Kossoff orchestrates the intensity of his childhood feelings with the look of the building now," combining the unshakable quality of the building with the dreamy quality of the light that seems to emanate from within and envelop the entire scene.[22]

Painting Narratives

A number of these artists not only represented individuals in their paintings and drawings but also brought together groups of figures to tell a story, which could be drawn from the artist's imagination or a literary text or based on historical events with important ethical or political implications. Men and women are painted not only as individuals but also because of the narratives inscribed in their collective bodies. Although, as I have suggested, other artists discussed here implicitly or explicitly wove personal narratives into their paintings, Kitaj and Andrews were exceptional in actively pursuing the exploration of human behavior and storytelling in their work.

As the art historian Marco Livingstone has noted, Kitaj was a major exponent of a critical type of realism, not aligned with a specific political movement but motivated by a desire for social reform.[23] His reliance on poetry, history, and literature fed into visual narratives of events with broad social resonance. The critic Robert Storr has argued that Kitaj's approach allows us to define him as a "history painter" but one who created his own pantheon, populated by figures who mattered to him personally.[24] These narratives are often of past events, temporal distance allowing a certain degree of idealization.[25]

The Murder of Rosa Luxemburg (1960; p. 121) is one of the pictures in which Kitaj began to develop his preoccupations with the roots of socialism and political martyrdom. The title of the painting refers to the brutal killing in 1919 of the Marxist theorist and leader of the German Communist Party. Luxemburg was of Polish Jewish descent, and Kitaj has explained that the picture refers to the persecution of the Jewish people more generally, which affected two of his grandmothers—one of them also called Rosa—leading them to flee to the United States.[26] A battered corpse dominates the picture, and a collaged paper element at the top right provides a succinct if chilling verbal description of Luxemburg's killing. The painting also includes portraits of Kitaj's grandmothers and references to German nationalist monuments. Its fragmented nature is exemplary of his approach, bringing together and giving form and meaning to a constellation of disparate elements.

Following his introduction to screen printing in 1963, Kitaj adopted the medium as a way of bringing photographic materials, reproductions, and fragments of text into new configurations that could be made more widely available (pp. 123, 124).[27] Beginning in the mid-1960s his paintings lost some of their fragmented quality and acquired a stronger sense of overall structure and unity while continuing to communicate a sense of man's contradictory and at times disjointed condition in the modern world. This is the case with a picture dealing with refugees, a theme particularly dear to Kitaj: *Cecil Court, London W.C.2. (The Refugees)* (1983–84; p. 127). The painting's geographic setting—at the time a much-visited street in central London with many shops selling rare and secondhand books—merges with his experience as an American of Jewish origins living in the capital, where he encountered and was touched by individuals who came to the city as refugees. The characters depicted in the scene and their postures are inspired in part by people Kitaj knew and also reflect his passion for Yiddish theater, an expressive dramatic form that, at the turn of the twentieth century, brought together Jewish immigrants in London through a common vernacular. The distortions of the elongated bodies, their emphatic poses, and the freshness of the colors all contribute to a highly charged scene, while the characters remain poignantly isolated, apart from one another.

If we can speak of a critical type of realism in Kitaj's work, in the case of Andrews it seems more appropriate to refer to an existentialist type.[28] His exploration of the human condition was intensified and complicated by his imaginative engagement, which gave his pictures an odd quality—as if part of reality and yet out of sync with it. Gowing stated that Andrews's oeuvre is distinguished by "the numinous quality of the real," a quality already present in *A Man Who Suddenly Fell Over* (1952; p. 88), a painting that he made in response to an art school assignment.[29] The fallen man, of Andrews's father's generation, displays a pitiful and yet moving lack of physical prowess and self-assurance, a common feeling in the postwar years.

In *The Deer Park* (1962; p. 90), Andrews took as a starting point his personal experience of the vibrant nightlife in London's Soho district in order to create a portrait of a transhistorical mundane society, in which famous individuals—from the poet Arthur Rimbaud to Marilyn Monroe—project their genuine images. In his desire to render behavior as an expression of the unmediated self, Andrews took parties as a key subject, as he believed that personal traits that were ordinarily concealed could be revealed in such circumstances. The setting was the imaginary home of a dedicated partygoer, the protagonist of Norman Mailer's novel *The Deer Park* (1955). It provided a particular atmosphere in which specific encounters and interactions could be set, while the source for the background was Diego Velázquez's *Philip IV Hunting Wild Boar (La Tela Real)* (ca. 1632–37). Andrews's painting represented an important breakthrough in his development, in that he abandoned constraining assumptions regarding the fidelity and integrity of the final picture, composing a complex image in which disparate elements and treatments coexist.

If this discussion of specific works and approaches speaks of the sheer diversity and individuality of the painters brought together in this survey, it also confirms some of the common characteristics that have been noted in publications and exhibitions. All these artists seemed to share the view that painting is a daily activity anchored in a constantly renewed appraisal of the outside world as it is felt and shaped by one's personal sensibility and historical time. They created pictures enlivened by their subjects, which are convincing because they emerged from intimate knowledge and compelling because of their ability to incorporate disparate feelings and visual references into tightly structured and powerful images.

NOTES

1 The adoption of the expression School of London in this period relates to Kitaj's use of it in the catalogue of an exhibition he selected for the Arts Council of Great Britain, *The Human Clay* (1976). Among the exhibitions that limited the term to the six artists discussed in this text are two organized by the British Council, which traveled to various venues internationally: *A School of London: Six Figurative Painters* (1987–88) and *From London: Bacon, Freud, Kossoff, Andrews, Auerbach, Kitaj* (1995–96).

2 See Richard Morphet, "An Under-rated Art," in *The Hard-won Image*, exh. cat. (London: Tate Gallery, 1984), 4–16.

3 See Michael Peppiatt, "A School or Not a School," *Modern Painters* 8, no. 2 (1995): 64–66. Furthermore, other artists were as close in terms of relationships and idioms.

4 Andrews is here referring to his attitude and that of his fellow students at the Slade School of Art, where he studied between 1949 and 1953 and where Alberto Giacometti was a major reference. Freud was an important example and, as a teacher, offered him encouragement, and Bacon also visited to talk about his work, making a memorable impression on Andrews. See Michael Andrews and Victor Willing, "Morality and the Model," *Art and Literature*, no. 2 (1964), reprinted in Andrew Brighton and Lynda Morris, *Towards Another Picture: An Anthology of Writings by Artists Working in Britain, 1945–1977* (Nottingham, UK: Midland Group Nottingham, 1977), 9–10.

5 Bacon's use of images as sources was already discussed in the early 1950s, for example, in Sam Hunter, "Francis Bacon: The Anatomy of Horror," *Magazine of Art* 45 (January 1952): 11–15 (with a photograph, taken in Bacon's studio, of reproductions torn from books). For a detailed study of Bacon's work in relation to its photographic sources, see Martin Harrison, *In Camera: Francis Bacon; Photography, Film, and the Practice of Painting* (London: Thames & Hudson, 2005).

6 On Bacon's election of specific biographical events as key to the interpretation of his work, see Andrew Brighton, *Francis Bacon* (London: Tate, 2001), 13–18.

7 See Catherine Lampert, "Painting from Life: 'A Long Affair with Objects, Images, Appearances, Sensations . . . the Passions,'" in *Bare Life: Bacon, Freud, Hockney, and Others; London Artists Working from Life, 1950–80*, ed. Hermann Arnhold, exh. cat. (Münster: LWL-Museum für Kunst und Kultur; Munich: Hirmer, 2014), 175.

8 Harrison, *In Camera*, 44.

9 See Eadweard Muybridge, *The Human Figure in Motion: An Electro-Photographic Investigation of Consecutive Phases of Muscular Actions* (London: Chapman & Hall, 1901), 75 (fifth image in the second row).

10 Keith Bell, *Stanley Spencer: A Complete Catalogue of the Paintings* (London: Phaidon, 1992), 127.

11 Lawrence Gowing, *Lucian Freud* (London: Thames & Hudson, 1982), 19.

12 William Feaver, *Lucian Freud* (New York: Rizzoli, 2007), 20.

13 Michael Andrews, "Notes and Preoccupations," *X* 1, no. 1 (1960–61), reprinted in Brighton and Morris, *Towards Another Picture*, 95.

14 Sickert, who died in 1942, was recognized as a leading figure during the post–World War II period, and his work was presented in numerous retrospectives. On his legacy and the influence of his work, see James Hyman, *The Battle for Realism: Figurative Art in Britain during the Cold War* (New Haven, CT: Yale University Press, 2001), 56–63; Harrison, *In Camera*, 75–79; and William Feaver, *Frank Auerbach* (New York: Rizzoli, 2009), 14.

15 See Catherine Lampert, *Frank Auerbach: Speaking and Painting* (London: Thames & Hudson, 2015), 24–31.

16 Robert Hughes, *Frank Auerbach* (London: Thames & Hudson, 1990), 31.

17 Auerbach, quoted in Barnaby Wright, "Creative Destruction: Frank Auerbach and the Rebuilding of London," in *Frank Auerbach: London Building Sites, 1952–1962*, exh. cat. (London: Courtauld Gallery and Paul Holberton, 2009), 14.

18 Ibid., 22–32.

19 See a conversation between Frank Auerbach, Taco Dibbits, Pilar Ordovas, and Geoffrey Parton (2013), published in *Raw Truth: Auerbach—Rembrandt*, exh. cat. (London: Ordovas, 2013), 9, 15–16.

20 Lucian Freud, "Frank Auerbach's Paintings," in *Frank Auerbach and the National Gallery: Working after the Masters*, exh. cat. (London: National Gallery, 1995), 5.

21 Paul Moorhouse, "'The Eye Sees More than the Heart Knows': The Work of Leon Kossoff," in *Leon Kossoff* (London: Tate Gallery, 1996), 21–22.

22 Andrea Rose, introduction to *Leon Kossoff*, exh. cat. (London: British Council, 1995), 10.

23 Marco Livingstone, *Kitaj*, 3rd ed. (London: Phaidon, 1999), 15–17, 24.

24 Robert Storr, "A Draftsman's Painter," in *R. B. Kitaj: A Survey, 1958–2007*, exh. cat. (London: Marlborough Fine Art, 2015), n. p.

25 Livingstone, *Kitaj*, 16.

26 Kitaj, quoted in *The Tate Gallery, 1980–82: Illustrated Catalogue of Acquisitions* (London: Tate Gallery, 1984), 156–57.

27 Livingstone, *Kitaj*, 22.

28 Paul Moorhouse, "'Strange Consolation': The Art of Michael Andrews," in *Michael Andrews*, exh. cat. (London: Tate Publishing, 2001), 9.

29 Lawrence Gowing, introduction to *Michael Andrews*, exh. cat. (London: Arts Council of Great Britain, 1980), 6–7.

AN INTENSIFICATION OF REALITY

CATHERINE LAMPERT

> The later 1940s were no time for fantasy. Artists and writers alike felt compelled to dwell on the bitterness of actual existence.
>
> —Lawrence Gowing

> There was a curious feeling that the barriers had broken down and we were all naked, bare-forked animals together, people who had survived the war.
>
> —Frank Auerbach

The legacy of World War II was unavoidable in Britain. Those who experienced living in cities while they were being bombed and left in ruins were shocked by the destruction of Dresden, Hiroshima, and Nagasaki and unnerved by reports from the concentration camps and later the forced labor camps of the Soviet Union as well as by the mass displacement of people. And of course there was the bomb. The continuation of rationing, along with the determination to extend the sense of common effort among classes, left a deep mark on life in Britain in the postwar years. Yet despite this destruction and privation, the painters Michael Andrews, Frank Auerbach, Francis Bacon, Lucian Freud, and Leon Kossoff—five of the six artists whose work is the subject of this exhibition—were determined not to be subsumed in the rallying cries for collective national rebuilding. As soon as possible after the end of the war, they acted on a desire to reengage with French art and artists.

For Lucian Freud it was a life-transforming experience. Helped by his connections with the artist and writer Roland Penrose, the collector Peter Watson, and others, this charismatic, precocious artist, age twenty-three, was taken up by Princess Marie Bonaparte, a disciple of his grandfather Sigmund, and Marie-Laure de Noailles and her salon. In Paris Freud mingled with the Left Bank circle. As his friend and contemporary John Richardson wrote, their group revolved around the young poet Olivier Larronde, who had been drawn by Alberto Giacometti, and the artist and stage designer Christian Bérard.[1] Freud was invited to Pablo Picasso's studio and frequented those of Giacometti and Balthus, and their standards and work ethics became his own. Bacon associated France with staying in Chantilly and visiting the Musée Condé, where he found the anguished standing mother in

Nicolas Poussin's *Massacre of the Innocents* (ca. 1628–29) unforgettable, and also in 1927 encountering the biomorphic abstractions that Picasso had begun that summer. Years later Bacon responded to their bestial, metamorphic nature in works such as *Three Studies for Figures at the Base of a Crucifixion* (ca. 1944).[2] After the war he began to divide his time between London, Monte Carlo, Tangier, and later Paris.

During these years London was well served by exhibitions. *Picasso—Matisse* opened at the Victoria and Albert Museum in December 1945. The star loan of the Institute of Contemporary Arts' *40,000 Years of Modern Art* in 1948 was Picasso's *Demoiselles d'Avignon* (1907). American Abstract Expressionism was a part of this exposure to new art, both in the group exhibitions at the Tate in 1956 and 1959 and in the solo shows of Jackson Pollock, Mark Rothko, and Philip Guston at the Whitechapel Gallery, all initiated by the International Council of the Museum of Modern Art, New York.

The work of the so-called School of London has often been seen as an essentially reactionary art grounded in the figure and thus out of touch with what was happening elsewhere, not least the art of contemporary European and American painters. It is true that the artists pursued strategies that began with observation, facts, images, and ideas, but from the outset their way of handling paint was risky. Many subjects were imbued with a considerable degree of invention, impatience, and anxiety, until the artist started to inhabit the motif to such an extreme that, as Auerbach described it, "the will is surrendered."[3] Even a very brief account of this history must acknowledge the role of superb critics, especially John Berger, Lawrence Gowing, and David Sylvester, who supported these artists and shaped the interpretation and reception of their work.

Radical Precedents in British Art

The longest text by Freud to appear in print, "Some Thoughts on Painting," was published in *Encounter* magazine in July 1954. It begins with a sentence that applies to all the artists represented in this exhibition, though it was certainly not meant to be prescriptive: "My object in painting pictures is to try and move the senses by giving an intensification of reality." When a painter is very familiar with what is being painted, detachment is necessary: he "needs to put himself at a certain emotional distance from the subject in order to allow it to speak. He may smother it if he lets his passion for it overwhelm him while he is in the act of painting." Freud was already determined to portray the subject, as an actor does, through constricted settings and meticulous detail: the thistle, garment, and cigarette as well as the person's unblinking eye: "the aura given out by a person or object is as much a part of them as their flesh, the painter must be as concerned with the air surrounding his subject as with that subject itself."[4]

In a curious way William Coldstream, who became professor of fine art at the Slade School of Fine Art in 1949, had a relationship to Freud, Michael Andrews, and the painter Euan Uglow that is as revealing as the better-known, physically and verbally electric one between Bacon, Freud, Auerbach, and Andrews. Coldstream was born in 1908, and his formative years coincided with the deepening of the Great Depression in Europe, which brought with it poverty and the rise of fascism. He came to believe that communication with the public had broken down and should be built up again, which implied returning to realism, yet this direction was difficult, as his generation "had been taught to regard all movements except those away from realism as artistically reactionary."[5] Film seemed a more relevant medium, and at the invitation of John Grierson, Coldstream joined the GPO Film Unit, then charged with recording day-to-day life. He was also one of three painters who in 1937 established the short-lived Euston Road School, an "atelier" studio where artists could work from life models. Coldstream's personality was impressive, nervous, and intelligent, his sparing point-blank confessions laced with attendant doubt. In order to calm himself and regain conviction, he would paint in front of the subject, concentrating on objective tasks like measuring the distance between elements in the field of vision, which to outsiders, especially as a method, has seemed rigid and perhaps pointless. Realistic painting could be nothing like reality: "But I believe that my own reactions to facts are much freer, more unexpected and more genuine, when my attention is occupied with the manifest problem of more or less accurate representation."[6] In Coldstream's best works, such as *Reclining Nude* (1974–76; fig. 7), the result seems miraculously alive and impossible to imagine with any more, fewer, or different marks.

As a young man Coldstream was an admirer of both Henri Matisse and Walter Sickert. In the 1920s the latter had turned away from his "Camden Town nudes," paintings of working-class people in very bare interiors, shocking for their depic-

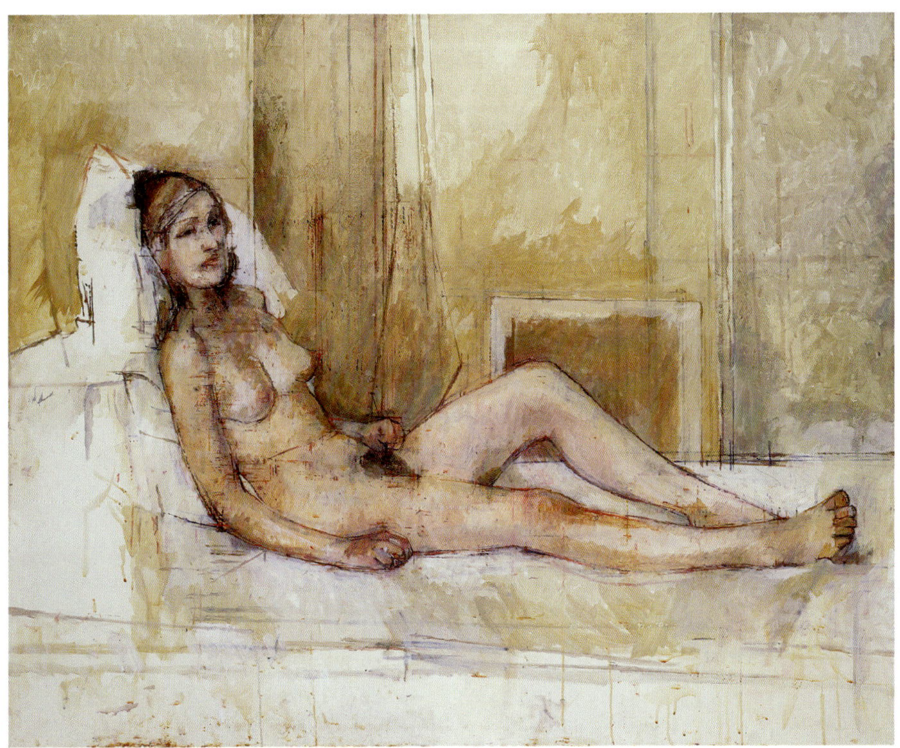

figure 7
William Coldstream (British, 1908–1987). *Reclining Nude*, 1974–76. Oil on canvas, 101.6 × 127 cm (40 × 50 in.). London, Tate. Purchased 1976

tion of genuine, sweaty bodies. Sickert's late paintings began with press photographs, cropped, squared up, enlarged, and transferred to canvas and finally made into paintings that ingested this material and brought out an indefinable quality that belonged to the times. The subjects were usually easy to recognize: Amelia Earhart at the aerodrome outside London in 1937, Winston Churchill, and various public figures whom we would now call celebrities.

Such works served as a precedent for post–World War II British artists who used material gleaned from the print media and news footage. The American critic Sam Hunter took photographs of Bacon's "working documents" during a studio visit in 1950. Later others described how they were piled on the floor, most likely randomly, the debris routinely culled and even burned.[7] Bacon was loath to offer backstories, but the particulars were gradually acknowledged in interviews, initially those with David Sylvester, first broadcast in 1962 and published in 1975.

British artists associated with Pop Art—among them Richard Hamilton and Eduardo Paolozzi, who were frequently around the Slade during Coldstream's early years of teaching there, and David Hockney and the American-born R. B. Kitaj, who were part of a later generation linked to the Royal College of Art in the early 1960s—also found ways of infusing documents from contemporary culture with personal issues. Andrews used newspaper photographs as early as 1952, and his decision to experiment with spray paint was linked to his reaction to Bacon's choice of unprimed canvas, in which, because of the visible weave, there is "an atmospheric illusion as an optical illusion of depth" and the image "becomes anthropomorphic or takes on the object's corporeality. Things not only look real but feel to be there, near close to."[8] Andrews eventually discovered how to paint "the actuality of the image," as is evident in his depiction of the veneer on the staircase in *The Deer Park* (1962; p. 90).[9] A report of a hot-air balloon flying over a green landscape supplied the first image for the Lights series (1970–75). These seven paintings explored the concept of enlightenment, which he understood as a state of being that can't be achieved by will. Andrews's ideas developed from his extensive reading, in particular works by Confucius and Kierkegaard as well as Eugen Herrigel's *Zen and the Art of Archery*. He made annotated collage studies using cuttings, photographs of aerial views, postcards of seaside resorts, and much more as part of his working process, and he began to use spray paint. Each of the Lights and Ayers Rock landscapes went through protracted compositional modifications. For example, Andrews decided to remove the figures from *Lights IV: The Pier and the Road* (1973; p. 91), after realizing that "it looks less empty having it deserted than it does with a few people in it."[10]

David Bomberg attended Sickert's life-drawing classes, engaged with Cubism, and made seminal works in the Vorticist style between 1913 and 1915, before deciding after the war to turn away from a hard-edged, invented structure and work directly in front of the motif. As a teacher at the Borough Polytechnic Institute, he had a deep influence on Leon Kossoff and Frank Auerbach, who took in Bomberg's assertion that "visual art is made with resistant matter and comes up against awkward rebarbative obstacles" and his advice that painters should enter every work from the inside, guided by their own sensations.[11] This outlook meant that the young Auerbach was excited by the conviction and scale of paintings by Americans like Franz Kline and Jackson Pollock but that what they were doing was in "no sense news."[12] Auerbach added to this memory the qualification that Bomberg rarely allowed himself to become profoundly involved in a subject, something that contrasts from the beginning with his own intense early pictures of his lover E.O.W. (p. 97) and similarly with Kossoff's engagement with those he knew intimately, like his parents, in *Two Seated Figures No. 2* (1980; p. 83), and the artist John Lessore, in *Man in a Wheelchair* (1959–62; p. 76).

While still at the Royal College of Art in the early 1950s, Auerbach and Kossoff began frequenting building sites, making drawings there and then returning to their very basic spaces to paint. Auerbach recalled, "It was sexy in a way, this semi-destroyed London. There was a scavenging feeling of living in a ruined town."[13] The earth, girders, and laboring figures are subsumed into sweeping fields and long brushstrokes, the results as much about touch, deep space, freedom, flux, and the materiality of paint as they are both topographically true and abstract. The urban landscapes that these artists are making today—for example, scenes around Arnold Circus, in Shoreditch, where Kossoff grew up, and Mornington Crescent, where Auerbach has worked since 1954—document the messy, construction- and traffic-riddled metropolis. Here, as with the other artists, the continuity, as well as the immediacy, is inseparable from autobiography.

The Artists, Their Exemplars, and a Few of Their Critics

On the eve of Kossoff's retrospective at the Tate in 1996, he and John Berger exchanged letters. Kossoff asked, "Do you remember when we first saw the revealing, and moving photographs of [Constantin] Brancusi's and [Alberto] Giacometti's studios in the 1950s? It was a special time."[14] Auerbach reflected that in the 1950s "an artist like Giacometti offered hope, to continue to give everything for a truthful art without any compromises. . . . The image of Giacometti who created a rich oeuvre, inventive and refined, with modest means in a small room, was very attractive."[15] Giacometti (fig. 8) drew and painted in ways that responded to the impermanence of visual readings, to changing internal sensations, and the proximity of his models, most often his brother and wife, creating work that Jean-Paul Sartre claimed was there "to give perceptible expression to pure presence."[16] His art, shown in Arts Council exhibitions in 1955 and 1965, resonated with what was happening in London and the general skepticism about movements and discoveries. Characteristically Bacon resisted the veneration of Giacometti and praised only his drawings, asking in 1979, "Did he isolate man in his absurdity any more than any other artist? I don't feel that. I know that people used to always talk about that, but it always was to me nonsense."[17]

Giacometti's art was deemed to fit into the category of *modernist realism*, about and for individuals and thus solipsistic or existential if need be, while the

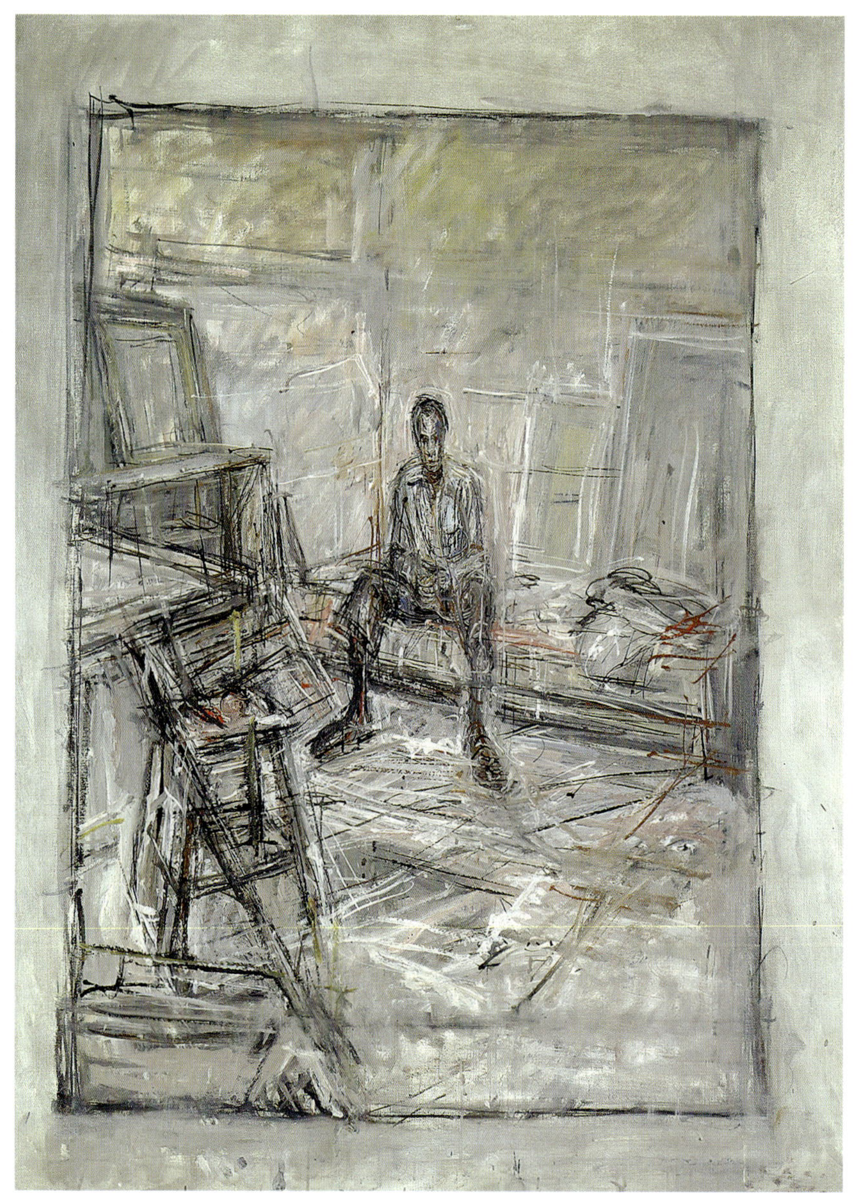

contrasting term, *social realism*, implied an obligation for contemporary culture to embrace a public beyond an educated elite, even to encourage people to claim their social rights. The difficulty was that appealing to a wider public required a degree of illustration and narrative, objectives that the artists represented in *London Calling* hated.

The opposing terms have also been used to sum up the contrast between those artists whose work was championed by Sylvester, on the one hand, and by Berger, on the other. In 1966 Berger, a Marxist, wrote that Giacometti's work "reflects the social fragmentation and manic individualism of late bourgeois intelligentsia," yet he also noted that the works "are unforgettable."[18] As the art historian Brendan Prendeville has pointed out, the difference lay more in their approaches: "Berger is provocative, but in a productive way, since he gives the grounds for his

figure 8
Alberto Giacometti (Swiss, 1901–1966). *Diego*, 1950. Oil on canvas, 80 × 58.4 cm (31½ × 23 in.). Norwich, Sainsbury Centre for Visual Arts, University of East Anglia, Robert and Lisa Sainsbury Collection

judgement and thereby a means of engaging with it—we know where he stands," whereas Sylvester followed his intuition, and his best judgments came from "a close identification with the artist's endeavour, efforts and failures, an exceptional ability to get inside a particular creative practice, and a corresponding commitment to it and concern for it."[19] Sylvester both praised and disparaged work from particular periods in an artist's career; Berger connects experiences and images, in his latest book tracing a linear development from the Chauvet Cave and the fifteenth-century Italian mathematician and artist Piero della Francesca to a Palestinian sculptor born in 1983.

In the 1950s the ideas of these and other critics reflected to some degree the thinking of Maurice Merleau-Ponty, whose presentation of phenomenology—based on the idea that we perceive the world through our bodies—struck a chord.[20] Kossoff spoke of "the shuddering feel of the sprawling city," which lingered in his mind like a memory, perhaps of a never-experienced childhood, "which, if rediscovered and illuminated, would ameliorate the pain of the present."[21] Looking back in 1981, Auerbach described Coldstream's contribution as "a moral lesson in behaviour," and in his own case the tension leading to the moment "where the painting, not as an object on the wall or as a canvas but as the set of forces evoked in the mind, is absolutely steadfast; it doesn't wilt, doesn't in its tiniest segment become repetitive or predictable; doesn't for one second grow tediously descriptive, but is a totally sheer, locked, living, organic engine without a gap in it."[22] The artist didn't attempt to feed the work with his own emotions; if there were attachments and feelings for the subject, the painting would absorb and transmit these, and by necessity brushstrokes and passages that might be described as abstract would be key.

One can see why there seemed to be a schism between these artists and the performative aspect, or "accident," as Bacon called it, and those who were aligned with a reductive modernism: for example, Ben Nicholson, whose work seemed to "our" painters refined and bland, or Henry Moore, whose archetypal images deliberately embodied a honed-down, life-affirming reference to maternity and nature. The poet and critic Herbert Read recognized the originality of Bacon and Freud early on. By the time he wrote *A Concise History of Modern Painting*, in 1959, however, Read's central thesis had narrowed to the assertion that modern art flows from Fauvism and Expressionism. In his review of the book, Lawrence Gowing observed, "For Herbert Read the essential test, which all subsequent non-German painting must pass or be failed utterly, is that once the perceptual image is broken down, it should be combined again only in 'a non-representational (rational or conceptual) structure.'"[23]

When Sylvester, at the age of twenty-six, came across works by Arshile Gorky, Jackson Pollock, and Willem de Kooning in the American pavilion at the Venice Biennale in 1950, he was wary of a parallel danger: "American painting has fallen prey to a Germanic overestimation of the importance of self-expression."[24] After a deeper look at the work of the American Abstract Expressionists in January 1956, however,

Sylvester underwent what he called a "Damascene" conversion, which led to an invitation from the State Department to visit the United States in 1960, resulting in the outstanding interviews broadcast by the BBC with Willem de Kooning, David Smith, Franz Kline, Philip Guston, and others.[25] Meanwhile in England the psychoanalytic route was anathema, and Bacon was ignored or dismissed by nearly all the American critics, particularly Clement Greenberg and Harold Rosenberg, who, as Gary Tinterow put it, found his art "too figurative, too narrative, too concerned with Christian imagery yet dangerously unpious in its view of religion."[26] At the same time declarations like the one made by Barnett Newman in 1948—"We are freeing ourselves of the impediments of memory, association, nostalgia, legend, myth, or what have you that have been the devices of Western European painting"—seemed hubristic to the British artists.[27]

Auerbach remembers seeing black-and-white reproductions of American painting long before the pictures came to the Tate and bought Thomas B. Hess's book

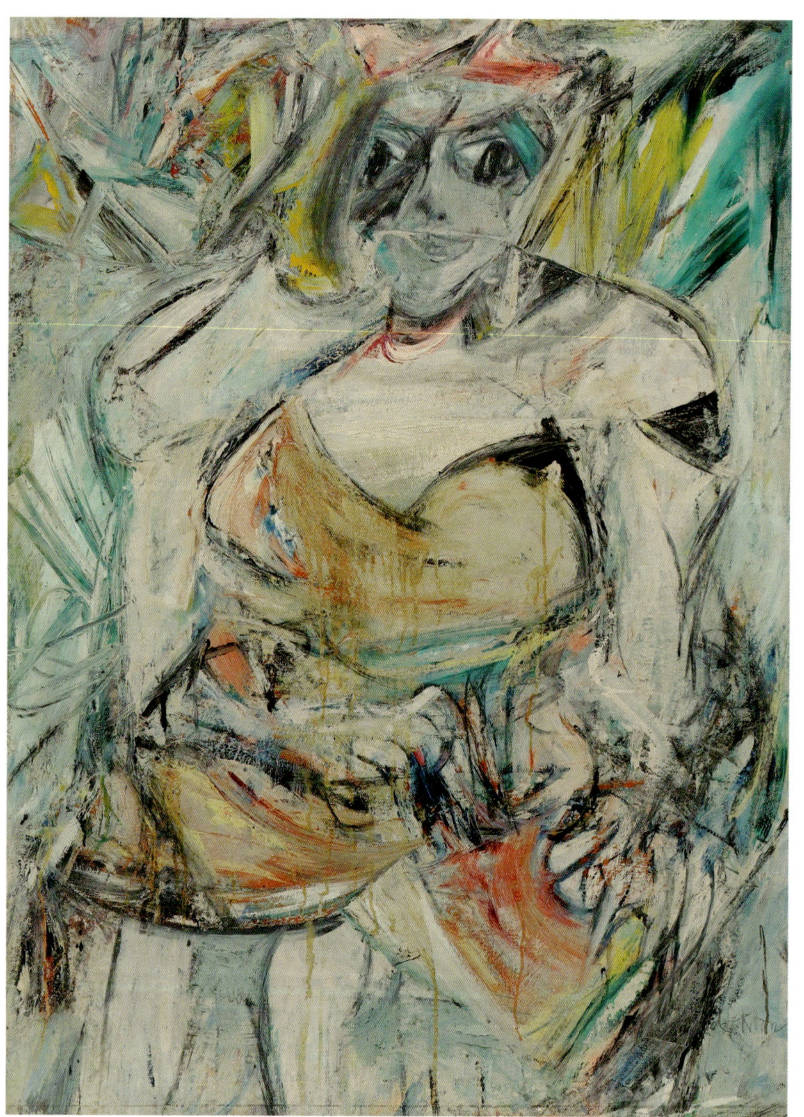

figure 9
Willem de Kooning (American, born the Netherlands, 1904–1997). *Woman II*, 1952. Oil on canvas, 149.9 × 109.3 cm (59 × 43 in.). New York, The Museum of Modern Art, Gift of Blanchette Hooker Rockefeller

on de Kooning when it came out. He regards "every work from that period [as] stimulating, each work a fresh undertaking."[28] De Kooning's Woman series (fig. 9) compares to the half-length female figures that Auerbach began making in 1958 (see *J.Y.M. Seated No. 1*, 1981; p. 114), while the words Dore Ashton used in 1957 to describe the Dutch-born artist's trees, clouds, roads, and vistas could be applied to landscapes by Andrews, Kossoff, and Auerbach from the same years: "It is the response of a sensory, vital man to a complex of experiences—to the luxurious sensation of space, the magic of light in space and his own motor negotiation of space."[29] Or as Kossoff found when he occupied a builder's shed in Willesden Junction in 1962, every time he looked at a subject, he saw something different. All the differences amounted to a sort of presence, and out of desperation the scene was suddenly reconstructed in a way that seemed genuine. By 1960 Freud, like Kossoff, was building up his granular paint, intending the brush marks to *work* on the viewer's nervous system as flesh does, and for his "naked portraits" not to be *like* their subjects but to *be* or indeed replace the person.

Masters: Old and New, at Home and Abroad

On the walls of Bacon's first show at the Hanover Gallery in 1949 were strangulated heads, one identified as a portrait of a pope. The critics remarked on the sooty paint, the strange curtains, and the elephant-hide textures. Gowing picked up on something that was the opposite of postwar trauma; he remembered this exhibition as "an outrage, a disloyalty to the existential principle, a mimic capitulation to tradition," and, moreover, "a surrender also to tonal painting which earnestly progressive painters have never forgiven."[30] *Study after Velásquez's Portrait of Pope Innocent* (1953) made the connection to seventeenth-century portraiture obvious, as did *Figure with Meat* (1954; p. 35), with its association with Rembrandt's carcasses of beef as well as the impasto-laden versions by Chaïm Soutine. The stillness and smooth surfaces of Freud's paintings from this period were compared with the facture and shallow space of Northern Renaissance painting—for example, Hans Memling's—yet differed in the lack of costume, dignity, or a moral position. Indeed *Girl with a Kitten* (1947; p. 52) and *Boy Smoking* (1950–51; p. 54)—which portrayed Freud's young wife, Kitty Garman, and Charlie Lumley, a neighborhood lad, respectively—seemed both disturbing and radiant.

Berger also noticed references to historical painting. In 1959 he wrote an article on Kossoff titled "The Weight," in which he observed: "His brooding, hunched-up figures fit into their panels as tensely, as properly, as medieval figures into their niches. His heads are as solid as their stone ones and the clotted disfigurations of the pigment are as superficial as disfigurations caused by time and weather." Berger went on to compare the receding plane of a turned head to the work of the Renaissance painters Masaccio and Andrea Mantegna, asserting that despite "the primacy of matter," the artist "is overwhelmed by the powerlessness of man in face of the material world—hence his profound pessimism. He is too honest to resort to religion, and yet can find no explanation for the crushing weight of suffering."[31]

Kossoff vividly remembers his first encounter with Rembrandt's *A Woman Bathing in a Stream* (1654), on a visit to the National Gallery at around the age of ten, when he felt that he could draw from this intimate painting of a woman raising her dress. Reproductions of a handful of works, among them Paul Cézanne's seated figure in shallow space, *Portrait of Achille Emperaire* (1867–68; fig. 10), and Rembrandt's *Bathsheba at Her Bath* (1654), have been forever pinned to his wall. However, the existential and real suffering that Berger mentioned was countered by Kossoff's landscapes from 1976, which were developed through drawing people in crowded public situations, for example, in the forecourts of Underground stations, at Kilburn and later the Embankment and King's Cross (*Booking Hall, Kilburn Underground*, 1987; p. 84). These landscapes also borrowed pictorial drama from the artist's continuing practice of drawing directly from populated works by Poussin,

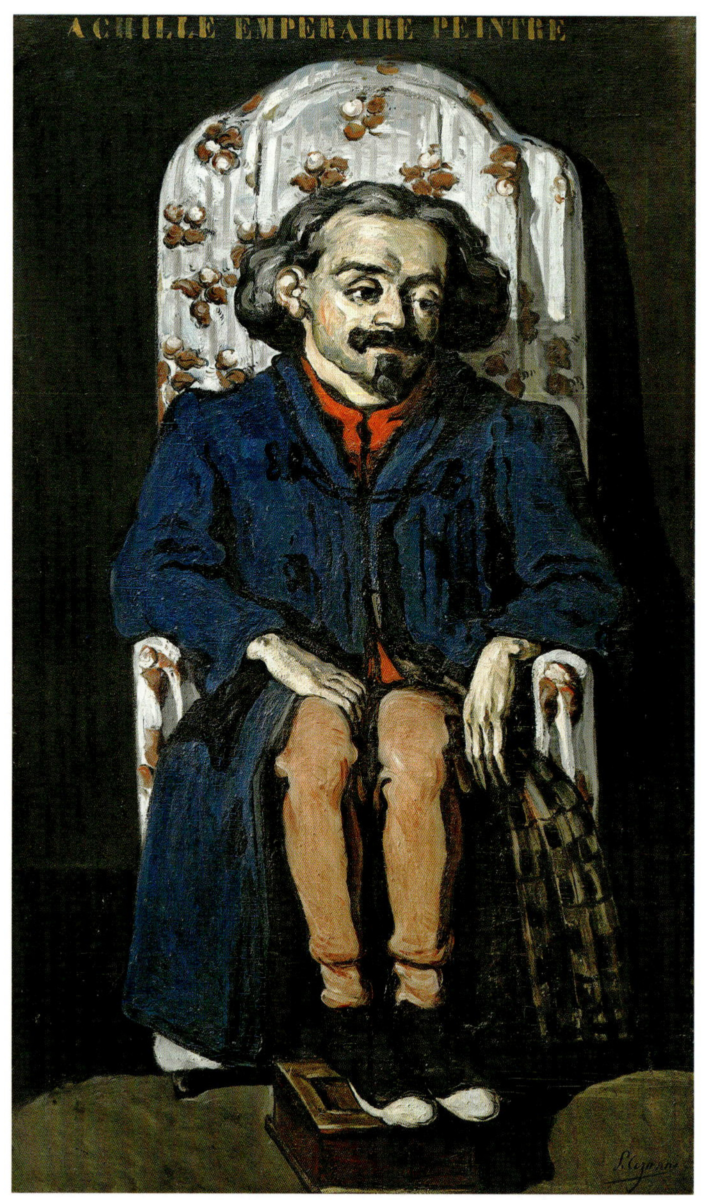

figure 10
Paul Cézanne (French, 1839–1906). *Portrait of Achille Emperaire*, 1867–68. Oil on canvas, 200 × 120 cm (78½ × 47¼ in.). Paris, Museé d'Orsay, Gift of MM René Lecomte and Mme Louis de Chaisemartin

Francisco de Goya, and others. Kitaj spoke of arriving in London in 1955 or 1956 "still in the US Army of Occupation in Germany" and being drawn to the early Italian Renaissance paintings in the National Gallery, especially the panels from Duccio's *Maestà* (1307/8–11).[32] Kitaj continued his deep engagement with the collection until the end of his life, when Cézanne's late bathers became his obsession. Auerbach spoke of doing "portraits" of paintings in the National Gallery, such as Titian's *Bacchus and Ariadne* (1520–23), the bright colors in his version partly a reaction to the painting's restoration.

Such experiences are formative, and these affinities surface when the National Gallery invites living artists to select works from the collection for an exhibition, most notably in the series the Artist's Eye. Thus Bacon juxtaposed Michelangelo's *Entombment* (ca. 1500–1501) and Vincent van Gogh's *Van Gogh's Chair* (1888). On the cover of the catalogue for Freud's selection, he placed his own drawing of a gelatinous detail from J. M. W. Turner's *Sun Rising through Vapour: Fishermen Cleaning and Selling Fish* (before 1807), explaining in a brief statement, "One quality these paintings share is that they all make me want to go back to work."[33]

At the end of his life, suffering from cancer, Andrews embarked on a series of works about the river Thames. For *Thames Painting, the Estuary* (1994–95; p. 93), he mixed real sediment into the paint, and while working he kept a reproduction of John Constable's *Chain Pier, Brighton* (1826–77) by his side. Clearly an analogy to mortality was intended: a scrawled note read, "Accept the flow and flux of things through the mind, the continual change, disappearance and reappearance."[34]

One worries, however, that this or any summary account of the abandoned, strange, extreme work in *London Calling* can be construed as indicating a conservative attachment to the old masters. In fact, the artists represented in the exhibition were inspired by a diverse group of twentieth-century predecessors and contemporaries, including Fernand Léger, Nicolas de Staël, Hans Hofmann, Antonin Artaud, Soutine, and more, never mind the direct stimulus of primitive art, literature, and poetry in particular. Iconoclasm underpins Bacon's remarks: for example, when asked about his relationship to Surrealism, he asked what could be more surreal than Shakespeare and Aeschylus. The occasional designation of these artists as not really British, by implication outsiders or émigrés, hardly applies. Freud and Auerbach were brought to England as children; Bacon's parents were English. Only Kitaj, who was American and Jewish, always felt essentially foreign and later identified with the diasporic condition and a historical sense of alienation.

Alfred Barr's famous hand-drawn chart from around 1936 plotted the principal modern movements, a constellation of isms joined with arrows and bordered by a time line.[35] In many ways the normative, didactic idea of art history as a progressive discipline continued at least through the 1970s, and even today the institutional account of art in the second half of the twentieth century routinely bypasses the artists represented in *London Calling*.[36] A shift in opinion, however, is evident when one considers the comments of younger artists, for example, Damien Hirst and Tracey Emin on Bacon, Peter Doig on Andrews and Auerbach, and Glenn Brown appropriating Auerbach (*The Day the World Turned Auerbach*, 1991).[37] This attention goes beyond Britain: for example, the American artist Ellen Altfest has cited Freud as an inspiration.[38] Jasper Johns was struck by John Deakin's photograph of Lucian Freud sitting on a bed shielding his head from the camera (fig. 11). A source for Bacon's *Study for Self-Portrait* (1964), it was reproduced in a Christie's sales catalogue that Johns received in the mail in 2012. He made a tracing of the battered image and joined it to an inverted version as he embarked on the series of drawings, prints, and paintings titled Regrets (fig. 12). The doubling created space for a skull form at the top. The melancholy and fragmentation suggest, to me, the waning of youthful passion and rapport, in Johns's case with Robert Rauschenberg and here between Freud and Bacon, as well as of a sense of commonality.[39]

The German painter Georg Baselitz answered two questions I posed after hearing about his new half-length portraits that referenced Frank Auerbach and Egon Schiele, which were being shown for the first time in Hong Kong in November 2015. For many years Baselitz has regretted a linear view of art history and national groupings: "*Avant-garde* is always a fashionable term that defines the trend of the time as progressive. Nowadays I believe that it is often better to look back in time, and I have done so quite often lately. This might be considered a sentimental approach—but why not? I wanted to clarify for myself what mainstream art and the artists who work outside it are all about. I have always felt close to the British artists of the School of London. In the last few years I have paid my respects to these

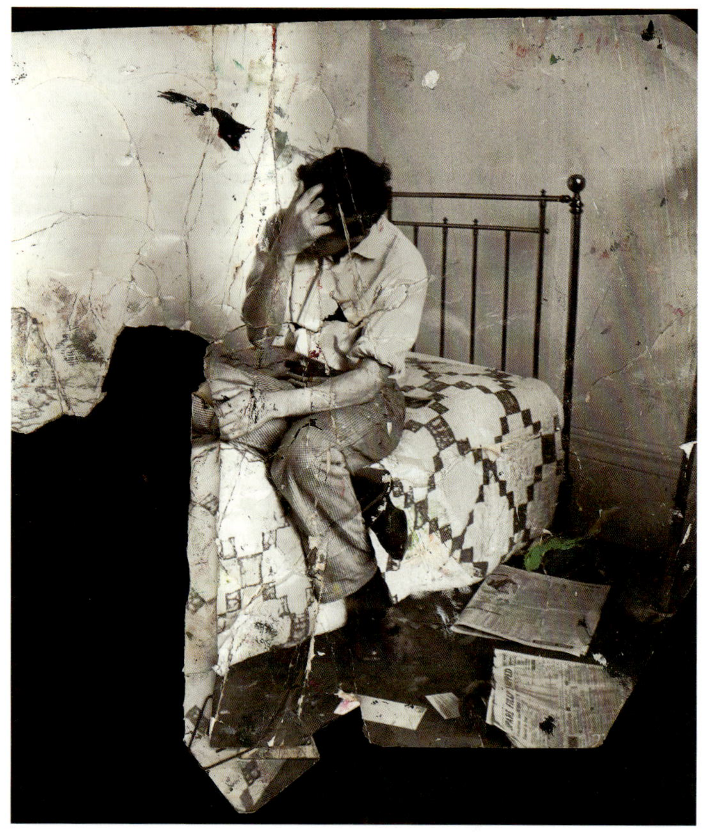

figure 11
John Deakin (British, 1912–1972). *Black-and-White Photograph of Lucian Freud Sitting on a Bed Taken by John Deakin*, ca. 1963. Gelatin silver print with paper clips, 32.3 × 32.3 × 1.5 cm (12¼ × 12¼ × 9⁄16 in.). Dublin City Gallery The Hugh Lane

great artists by including numerous references to them in my work." Baselitz continued with a statement that echoes the autobiographical foundation of the work in this exhibition: "During the seventies I started working with Polaroid portraits of my wife and myself. Later I took new photographs, and now I am working with those as well. For me, the question of model and motif is always an intimate and restrained one. Indeed, I can only use the very few things that are in direct relation to my life—i.e., figures, portraits, landscape."[40]

As the artists discussed in this essay aged, their motifs tended to be literally and metaphorically close to home: Kitaj's homages to those creative types he identified with, Kossoff's cherry tree dying limb by limb, Auerbach's red pillar box. In 2003 Freud moved his easel to a London stable to paint a gray gelding; in words that echo what he wrote in 1954, he insisted, "If you look at Chardin's animals, they're *absolute* portraits. It's to do with the feeling of individuality and the intensity of the regard and the focus on the specific."[41] Bacon returned to the photographs of George Dyer sitting in his underpants taken twenty years earlier, inserting them into a 1988 triptych; he stressed that trapping appearances wasn't enough, with people the artist has to get near to "the way they have affected you, because every shape has an implication."[42] De Kooning, speaking about Soutine and by proxy his own work around 1977, responded to the "lush" surface quality of the Russian painter's work, which allowed for "a kind of transfiguration, a certain fleshiness," to emanate from each landscape or portrait.[43] To nourish these long, independent careers, the studio became somewhere to entertain oneself, allowing pictures to have unruly passages and areas that look like the motif is washed ashore only temporarily. In the end it is not the idiom that counts. The artists featured in *London Calling* have been consistently celebrated for the quality of their work and their ability to transcend historical movements, to begin with something organic and personal and end by touching the nerve of individual viewers wherever and whenever.

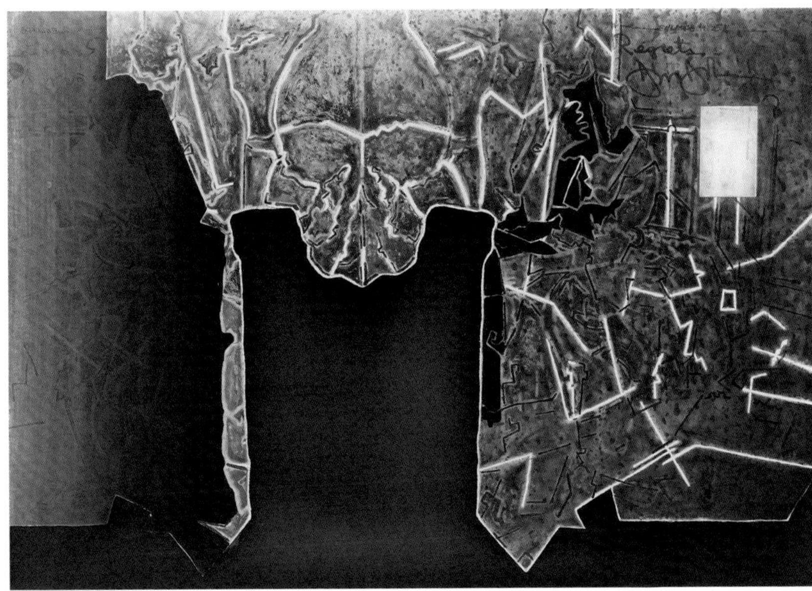

figure 12
Jasper Johns (American, born 1930). *Regrets*, 2014. Aquatint on chine-collé, 66.7 × 86.7 cm (26¼ × 34⅛ in.). New York, The Museum of Modern Art. Acquired through the generosity of Mary M. and Sash A. Spencer

NOTES

Epigraphs: Lawrence Gowing, "Francis Bacon: The Human Presence," in *Selected Writings on Art*, ed. Sarah Whitfield (London: Ridinghouse, 2015), 422; Frank Auerbach, in Nicholas Wroe, "Frank Auerbach: Painting Is the Most Marvellous Activity Humans Have Invented," *Guardian*, May 16, 2015.

1 John Richardson, "Remembering Lucian Freud," in *Lucian Freud Portraits*, exh. cat. (London: National Portrait Gallery, 2012), 10–11.

2 Martin Harrison, *In Camera: Francis Bacon; Photography, Film, and the Practice of Painting* (London: Thames & Hudson, 2005), 17–19. Harrison points out that despite the oft-quoted memory, the "Dinard" works that Bacon revered were not in Picasso's exhibition at Galerie Paul Rosenberg.

3 Frank Auerbach, quoted in Lawrence Gowing, *Eight Figurative Painters: Michael Andrews, Frank Auerbach, Francis Bacon, William Coldstream, Lucian Freud, Patrick George, Leon Kossoff, Euan Uglow*, exh. cat. (New Haven, CT: Yale Center for British Art, 1981), 24. He presented the artists' different maneuvers as simply ways of getting to the point where painting starts. The exhibition included works by Patrick George and Euan Uglow, a radical and magnificent painter whose work could well be in *London Calling*.

4 Lucian Freud, "Some Thoughts on Painting," *Encounter* 3 (July 1954): 23–24, reprinted in *Lucian Freud: Naked Portraits*, exh. cat. (Ostfildern, Germany: Hatje Cantz; Frankfurt: MMK Museum für Moderne Kunst, 2001), 281, 283.

5 William Coldstream, "How I Paint," *Listener*, September 15, 1937, 510.

6 Ibid., 512.

7 Harrison, *In Camera*, 83, referring to Sam Hunter, "Francis Bacon: The Anatomy of Horror," *Magazine of Art* 45 (January 1952): 11–15.

8 Michael Andrews, unpublished text on Francis Bacon (ca. 1995); courtesy of Virginia Verran.

9 Michael Andrews, interview with the author, 1980.

10 Ibid. Sylvester's claims for modernist realism were sometimes mocked as being more about a trend and were attacked by a variety of critics. Lawrence Alloway and the Independent Group vigorously promoted a synthesis of realism and abstraction that gave equal status to high and low culture.

11 Auerbach, in Judith Bumpus, "Frank Auerbach" (interview), *Art and Artists*, no. 237 (June 1986): 24.

12 Catherine Lampert, *Frank Auerbach: Speaking and Painting* (London: Thames & Hudson, 2015), 30.

13 Martin Gayford, "Auerbach's London," *Apollo* 170 (October 2009): 59.

14 John Berger and Leon Kossoff, "A Marathon Swim through Thick and Thin," *Guardian*, June 1, 1996. They refer to a review by John Berger, "The Weight," *New Statesman*, September 19, 1959, reprinted in "Leon Kossoff (1926–)," in *Portraits: John Berger on Artists* (London: Verso, 2015), 410–12.

15 Lampert, *Frank Auerbach*, 92. David Sylvester brought Giacometti to the Slade to meet Coldstream in June 1955, and the artists later exchanged works. The similarities in their approaches have been discussed by James Hyman and Bruce Laughton. Bruce Laughton, "Coldstream and Giacometti in London," *British Art Journal* 9 (Spring 2009): 79–85; James Hyman, *The Battle for Realism* (New Haven, CT: Yale University Press, 2001).

16 Jean-Paul Sartre, "The Quest for the Absolute," quoted in Paul Moorhouse, *Giacometti: Pure Presence*, exh. cat. (London: National Portrait Gallery, 2015), 36.

17 Francis Bacon, quoted in David Sylvester, *Looking Back at Francis Bacon* (London: Thames & Hudson, 2000), 244. Bacon praised Marcel Duchamp but described Rothko's paintings in 1961 as "dismal," with dull colors, and Jackson Pollock's canvases as looking like "old lace." These comments do not, however, rule out an influence, and as Martin Harrison has discovered, Bacon was familiar with Pollock's chronology, and his own *Painting* (1950) may have been a response to Rothko. See "Martin Harrison in Conversation with Richard Calvocoressi," in *Francis Bacon: Late Paintings*, exh. cat. (New York: Gagosian Gallery, 2015), 133–34.

18 Berger, "Alberto Giacometti" (1966), in *Portraits*, 327.

19 Brendan Prendeville, "That Uncertain Object: David Sylvester's Conception of Criticism as a Personal Affair," *Tate Papers*, no. 21 (Spring 2014), www.tate.org.uk/research/publications/tate-papers/21/that-uncertain-object-david-sylvesters-conception-of-criticism-as-a-personal-affair.

20 Andrew Wilson, "Lucian Freud," in *The Simon Sainsbury Bequest to Tate and the National Gallery*, exh. cat. (London: Tate Publishing, 2008), 110, referring to David Mellor's writing on this subject.

21 Leon Kossoff, *Recent Paintings and Drawings*, exh. cat. (London: Fischer Fine Art, 1973), 5.

22 John Russell, reviewing this show, wrote, "It still looks as if every figurative painter in England still uses Coldstream as a buoy by which to steer his course." "The Pervasive Presence of William Coldstream," *New York Times*, November 8, 1981.

23 Gowing, "History and Faith," in *Selected Writings*, 44. See Richard Calvocoressi, "Moore and Bacon: Affinities," in *Francis Bacon, Henry Moore: Flesh and Bone*, exh. cat. (Oxford: Ashmolean Museum, 2013), 15–29.

24 David Sylvester, "The Venice Biennale," *Nation*, September 9, 1950, 232. He pitted himself against Clement Greenberg, citing as alternatives Hans Hartung and Eugène de Kermadec and the European sensibility of André Masson, Pierre Tal-Coat, and Francis Gruber.

25 David Sylvester, "Curriculum Vitae," in *About Modern Art: Critical Essays, 1948–96* (London: Chatto & Windus, 1996), 29. Sylvester remained a critic and curator, whereas Berger left Britain in 1962 and over the next decades channeled his outlook into storytelling and rural life, reconsidering earlier opinions, as he continues to do today.

26 Gary Tinterow, assisted by Ian Alteveer, "Bacon and His Critics," in *Francis Bacon*, exh. cat. (London: Tate Publishing, 2008), 28.

27 Barnett Newman, "The Sublime Is Now," in *Barnett Newman: Selected Writings and Interviews*, ed. John P. O'Neill (New York: Knopf, 1990), 173.

28 Frank Auerbach to Catherine Lampert, October 2015. For the Hess book, see Thomas B. Hess, *Willem de Kooning* (New York: Museum of Modern Art, 1969).

29 Dore Ashton, "Art," *Arts and Architecture* 74 (June 1957): 74. De Kooning said in 1960, following the mixed reception of the 1959 group exhibition, "It is a certain burden this American-ness, a sense of . . . I know if you come from a small nation, you don't have this." David Sylvester, "Willem de Kooning (1960)," in *Interviews with American Artists* (New Haven, CT: Yale University Press, 2001), 48. Andrews cited de Kooning as a mentor when painting *Late Evening on a Summer Day* (1957).

30 Gowing, "Human Presence," 423. Robert Melville also made this point; see Tinterow and Alteveer, "Bacon and His Critics," 31.

31 Berger, "Leon Kossoff (1926–)," in *Portraits*, 411–12.

32 R. B. Kitaj, in Anthony Rudolf and Colin Wiggins, *Kitaj: In the Aura of Cézanne and Other Masters*, exh. cat. (London: National Gallery, 2001), 10.

33 *The Artist's Eye: Lucian Freud*, exh. cat. (London: National Gallery, 1987), 12.

34 William Feaver, "An Actual Present Atmosphere," in *Michael Andrews*, exh. cat. (London: Tate Publishing, 2001), 60.

35 Barr's chart is preserved in the archives at the Museum of Modern Art, New York; see www.moma.org/learn/resources/archives/archives_highlights_02_1936.

36 Auerbach answered a questionnaire sent by *London Magazine* in 1961 asking how he saw his work in relation to an international style, explaining that although the artist was affected by his circumstances and the events of his time, "he seems to me to be the sole coherent unit. . . . I cannot think of British painting as an entity, I do not understand the phrase 'international style.' These concepts seem to me irrelevant to an activity which postulates the persistence of a unique and individual experience." In an important article from 1970 William Feaver referred to these painters as "Stranded Dinosaurs" (*London Magazine*). U.S. museums have rarely presented monographic exhibitions devoted to Auerbach, Kossoff, and Andrews or made major acquisitions of their work.

37 See Sean O'Hagan, "Damien Hirst on Francis Bacon: 'He's One of the Greatest Painters of All Time,'" *Guardian*, August 9, 2008; Tracey Emin and Simon Grant, "Perfect Bedfellows: Tracey Emin and Francis Bacon," *Tate Etc.*, no. 34 (Summer 2015), www.tate.org.uk/context-comment/articles/perfect-bedfellows; Peter Doig, in "Francis Bacon (1909–1992)," *Tate Etc.*, no. 14 (August 2008), www.tate.org.uk/context-comment/articles/francis-bacon-1909-1992.

38 See Ridley Howard, "Nudes in Venice: Interview with Ellen Altfest," in *Ellen Altfest: Painting Close-up*, ed. Anthony Spira, exh. cat. (London: Occasional Papers, 2015), 89–90.

39 Johns owns a 1988 painting by Freud.

40 Georg Baselitz, interview with the author, with questions kindly posed via Andrea Schlieker, November 5, 2015, and conversation with the author in the artist's studio, January 2016.

41 Sebastian Smee, *Lucian Freud 1996–2005* (London: Jonathan Cape, 2005), 8.

42 Hugh M. Davies and Sally Yard, *Francis Bacon* (New York: Abbeville, 1986), 88.

43 De Kooning, quoted in Margaret Staats and Lucas Matthiessen, "The Genetics of Art: Interviews with de Kooning, Motherwell, and Nevelson," *Quest* 1 (March–April 1977): 70.

ARTISTS

BIOGRAPHIES BY SARAH OLIVEY

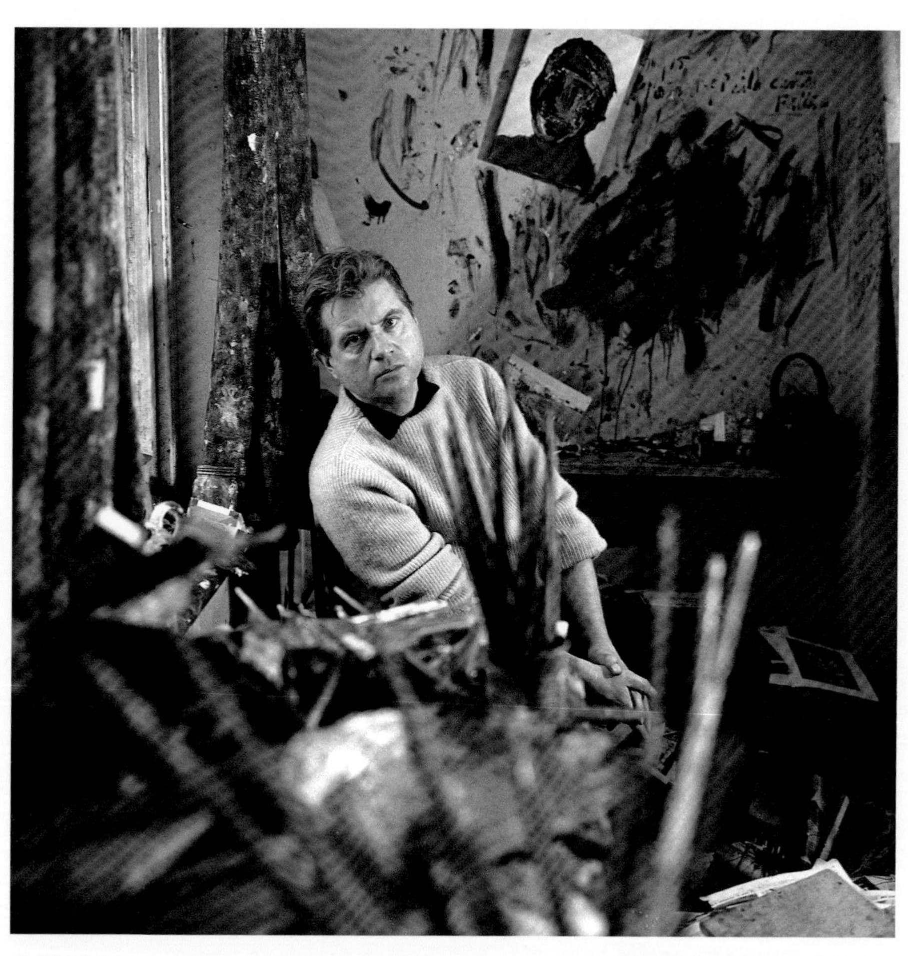

Francis Bacon, 1960.
Photo: Cecil Beaton

FRANCIS BACON

Francis Bacon was born in Dublin to English parents on October 28, 1909. His mother, Christina Firth, was a steel heiress and his father, Edward Bacon, a racehorse trainer and former army officer. The second of five children, Bacon spent his childhood in a small town in County Kildare, Ireland. At the outbreak of war in 1914, his father joined the Ministry of War and the family moved to London, where they remained until 1919.

Bacon left the family home in Ireland in 1926 and spent the next few years traveling between London, France, and Germany. He was impressed by an exhibition of Pablo Picasso's work at Galerie Paul Rosenberg in Paris, which inspired him to begin to make his own drawings and paintings. On returning to London the following year, he worked briefly as a furniture and interior designer, with designs featured in the *Studio* in 1930. He continued to paint and, while largely self-taught, became close to the Australian artist Roy de Maistre, who provided technical advice. Some works survive from this early period, including *Crucifixion* (1933; London, Murderme Collection), a motif that Bacon would return to throughout his career. Around this time he met the businessman Eric Hall, who would became his patron and lover. In 1937 Bacon and de Maistre helped Hall organize *Young British Painters* at Thomas Agnew and Sons, London, which included works by Graham Sutherland, Victor Pasmore, and others.

At the outbreak of World War II in 1939, Bacon was exempted from military service because of his chronic asthma. He remained in London, where he met Lucian Freud. In 1945 he established his critical reputation with the first showing of his breakthrough painting *Three Studies for Figures at the Base of a Crucifixion* (1944; London, Tate), displayed for the first time alongside *Figure in a Landscape* (1945; p. 33) at the Lefevre Gallery, at a point when the war was just ending and the true horrors of the conflict were being revealed.

Following the war Bacon became central to an artistic milieu in Soho, along with Freud, Michael Andrews, various poets, and other drinking companions. From the late 1940s he began making works with reference to Diego Velázquez's *Portrait of Pope Innocent X* (1650; Rome, Galleria Doria Pamphilj), though he famously claimed never to have seen the painting in the flesh. He produced many variations on the subject with characteristic screaming mouths, based on a photographic still of the Screaming Nurse in Sergei Eisenstein's film *Battleship Potemkin* (1925). He also incorporated veils of vertical brushstrokes, as in *Head VI* (1949; London, Arts Council Collection), as well as confining and enclosing frameworks that demonstrated a new complexity in his handling of pictorial space. Around this time Bacon also began to reference Eadweard Muybridge's photographs of humans and animals in motion, resulting in homoerotic and almost animalistic images of wrestlers, such as *Two Figures in the Grass* (1954; private collection). Other pictorial and photographic sources included medical textbooks, film stills, physique magazines, and art historical reproductions. The pope paintings were included in Bacon's solo exhibition at Hanover Gallery, London, in 1952. Two years later he shared the British Pavilion at the 1954 Venice Biennale with Ben Nicholson and Lucian Freud.

From the early 1960s Bacon moved from largely monochromatic works toward heightened color and a shallower picture plane, emphasizing the surface of the painting. In 1962 he completed *Three Studies for a Crucifixion*, the first of many subsequent triptychs of identical size and format. A major retrospective was organized at the Tate Gallery in 1962, which was followed by another at the Solomon R. Guggenheim Museum, New York, in 1963. Throughout this time Bacon's subject matter consisted largely of portraits of his intimates, especially his friend Henrietta Moraes and his longtime lover George Dyer, mostly based on photographs he commissioned John Deakin to take for him as source material. On the eve of Bacon's large retrospective at the Grand Palais in Paris in 1971, Dyer committed suicide. Over the next four years Bacon painted three "memorial" triptychs, including *Triptych August 1972* (1972; pp. 46–47), as well as depicting Dyer in several other paintings.

Throughout the 1970s Bacon traveled regularly to New York and Paris and had international exhibitions in Mexico and Venezuela (1977–78) and in Spain, at Fundación Juan March, Madrid, and Fundació Joan Miró, Barcelona (both 1978). His works from this period continued to be dominated by the triptych, with figures set against flat expanses of color, including small-format "portrait" triptychs such as *Three Studies for a Self-Portrait* (1979–80; New York, Metropolitan Museum of Art). He also began to include references to myth and literature. The 1980s saw a second Tate retrospective (1985) and a further retrospective at the Hirshhorn Museum and Sculpture Garden, Washington, DC, touring to the Los Angeles County Museum of Art and the Museum of Modern Art, New York (1989).

Bacon continued to paint throughout his later years. In 1988, at the age of seventy-eight, he made a second version of *Three Studies for Figures at the Base of a Crucifixion*. In this painting, *Second Version of Triptych 1944* (1988; London, Tate), he changed the background color from orange to vivid red, allowed more space around the figures, and enlarged the canvases to the format that he had been using since the early 1960s.

On a visit to Madrid in 1992, Bacon was hospitalized with pneumonia exacerbated by asthma. He died on April 28.

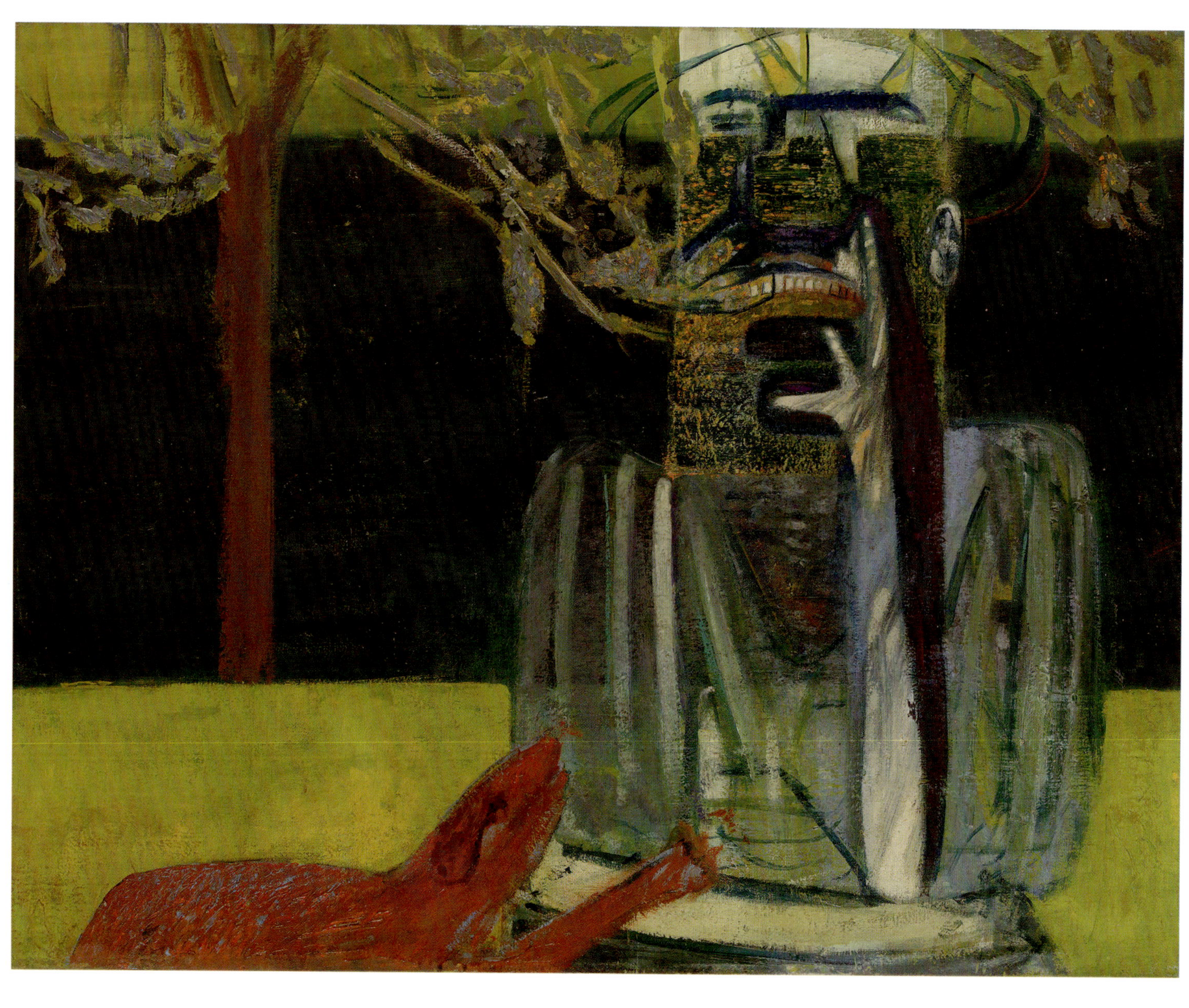

Francis Bacon
Figures in a Garden, ca. 1935

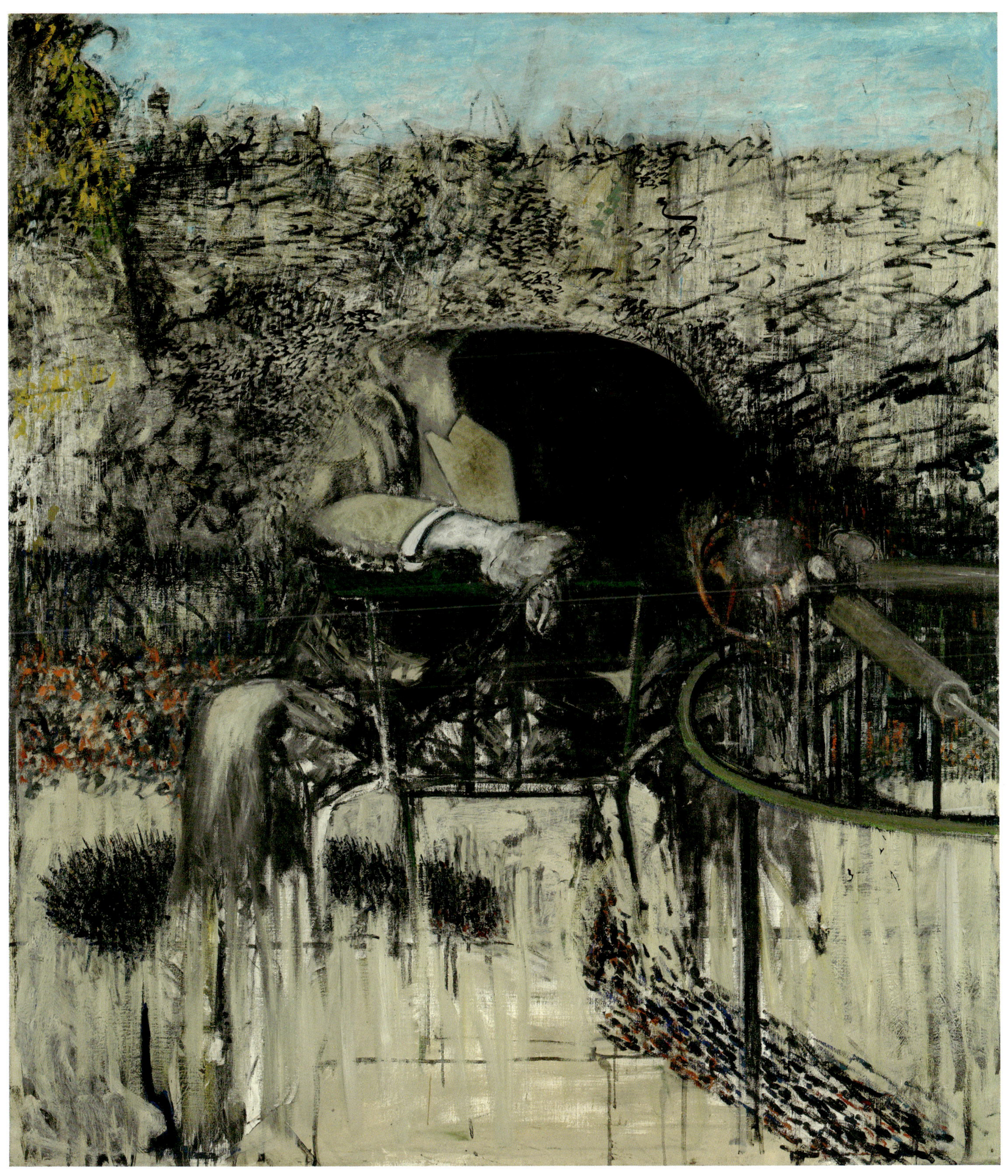

Francis Bacon
Figure in a Landscape, 1945

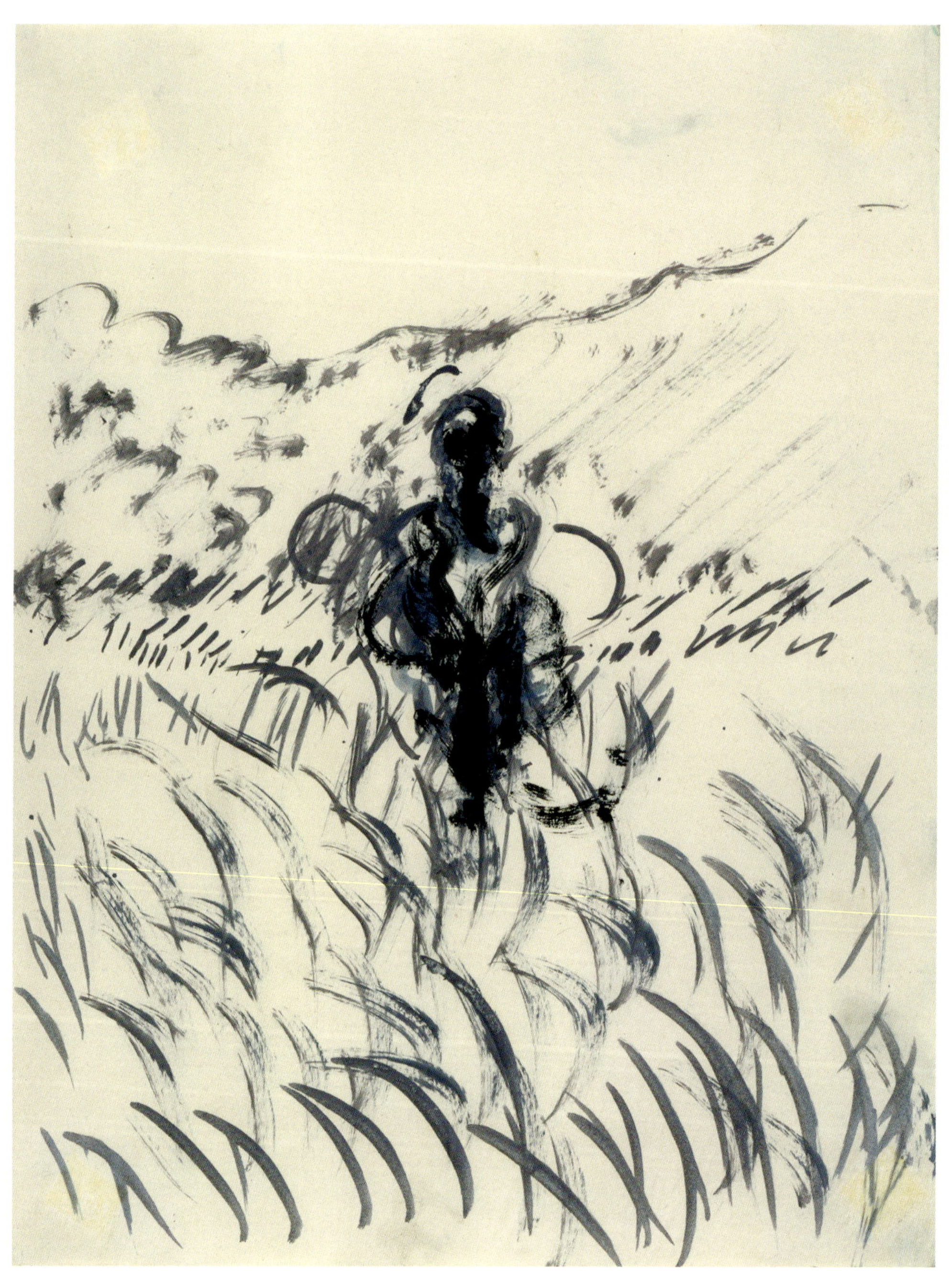

Francis Bacon
Figure in a Landscape, ca. 1952

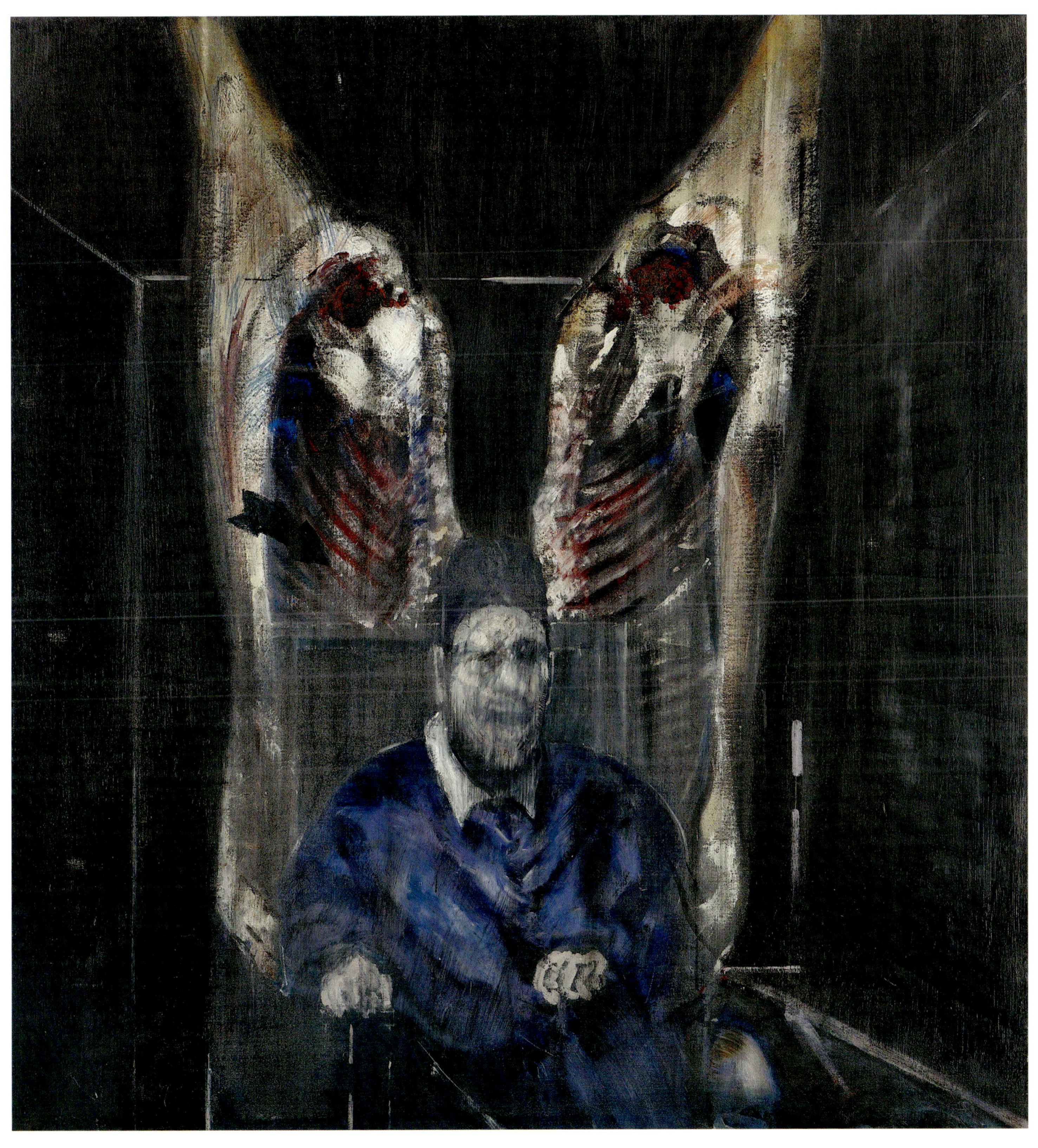

Francis Bacon
Figure with Meat, 1954

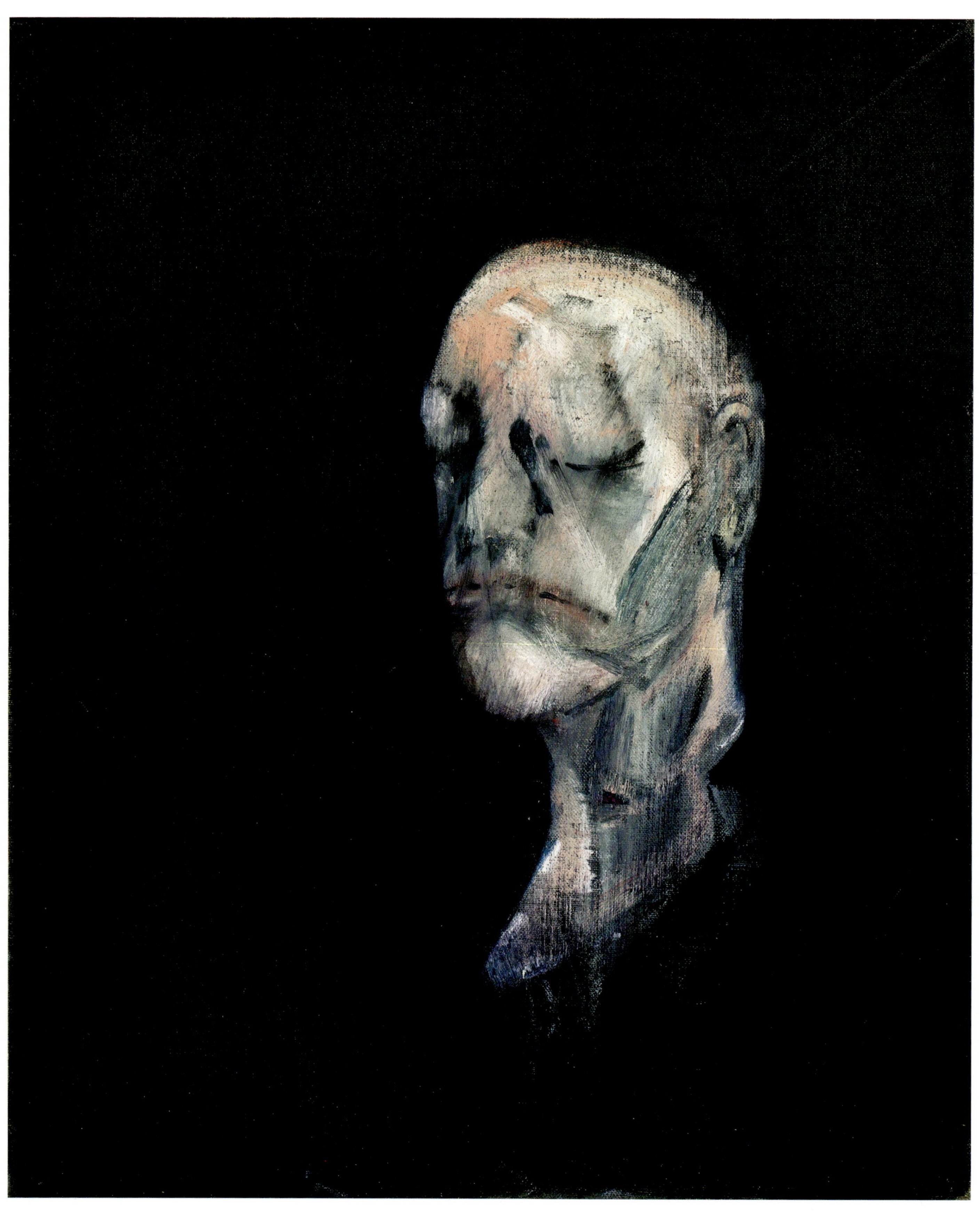

Francis Bacon
Study for Portrait II (after the Life Mask of William Blake), 1955

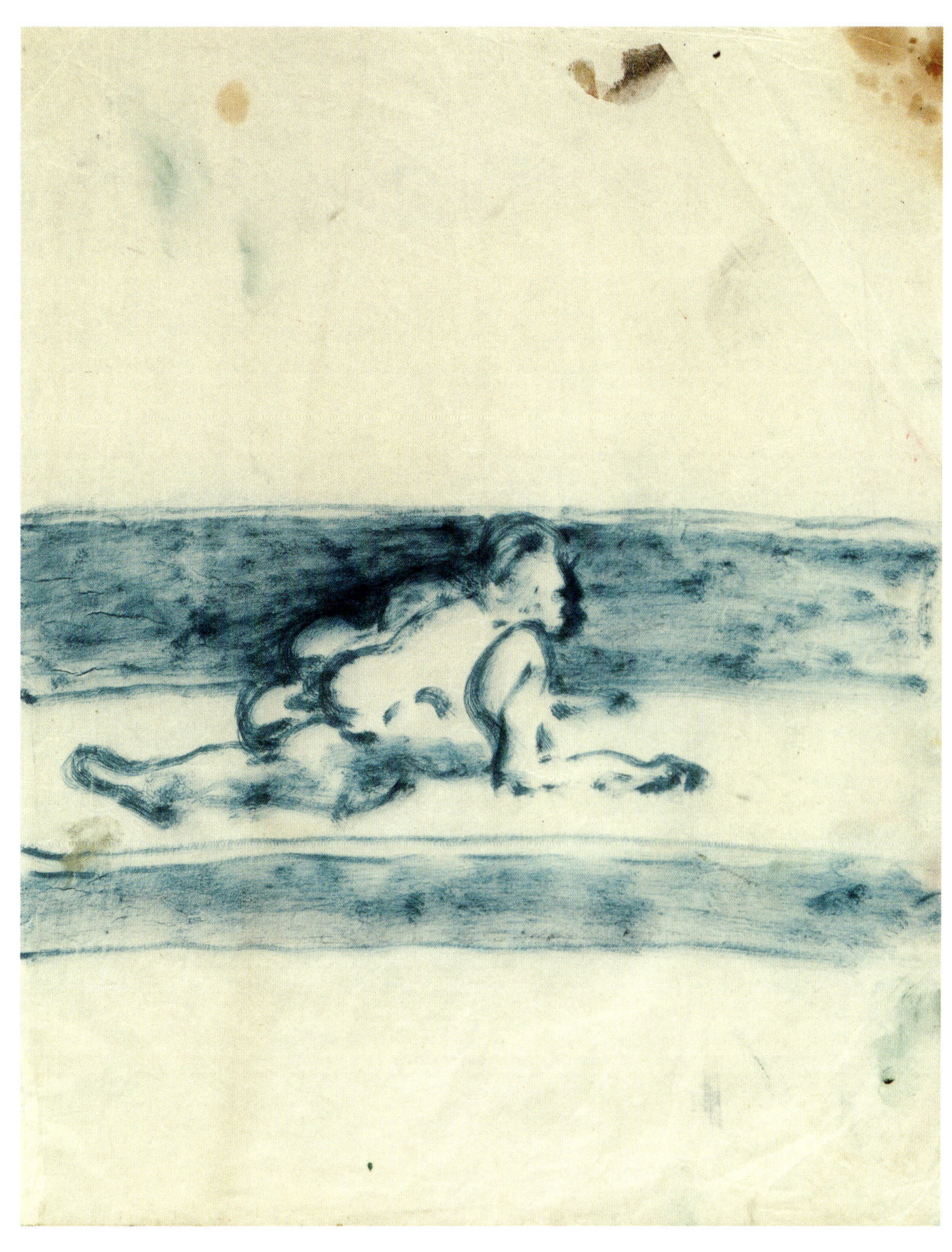

Francis Bacon
Blue Crawling Figure, No. 1, ca. 1957–61

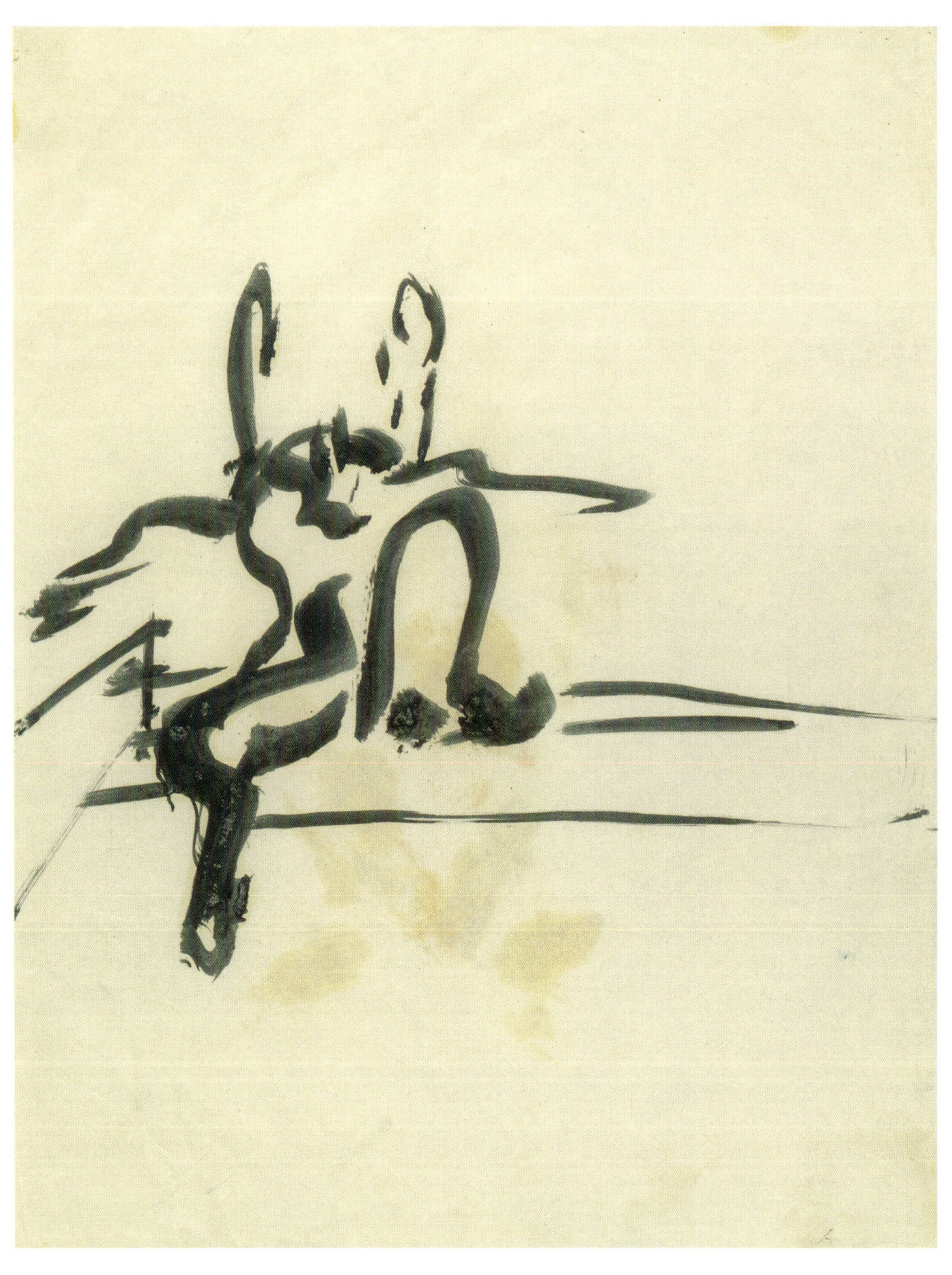

Francis Bacon
Collapsed Figure, ca. 1957–61

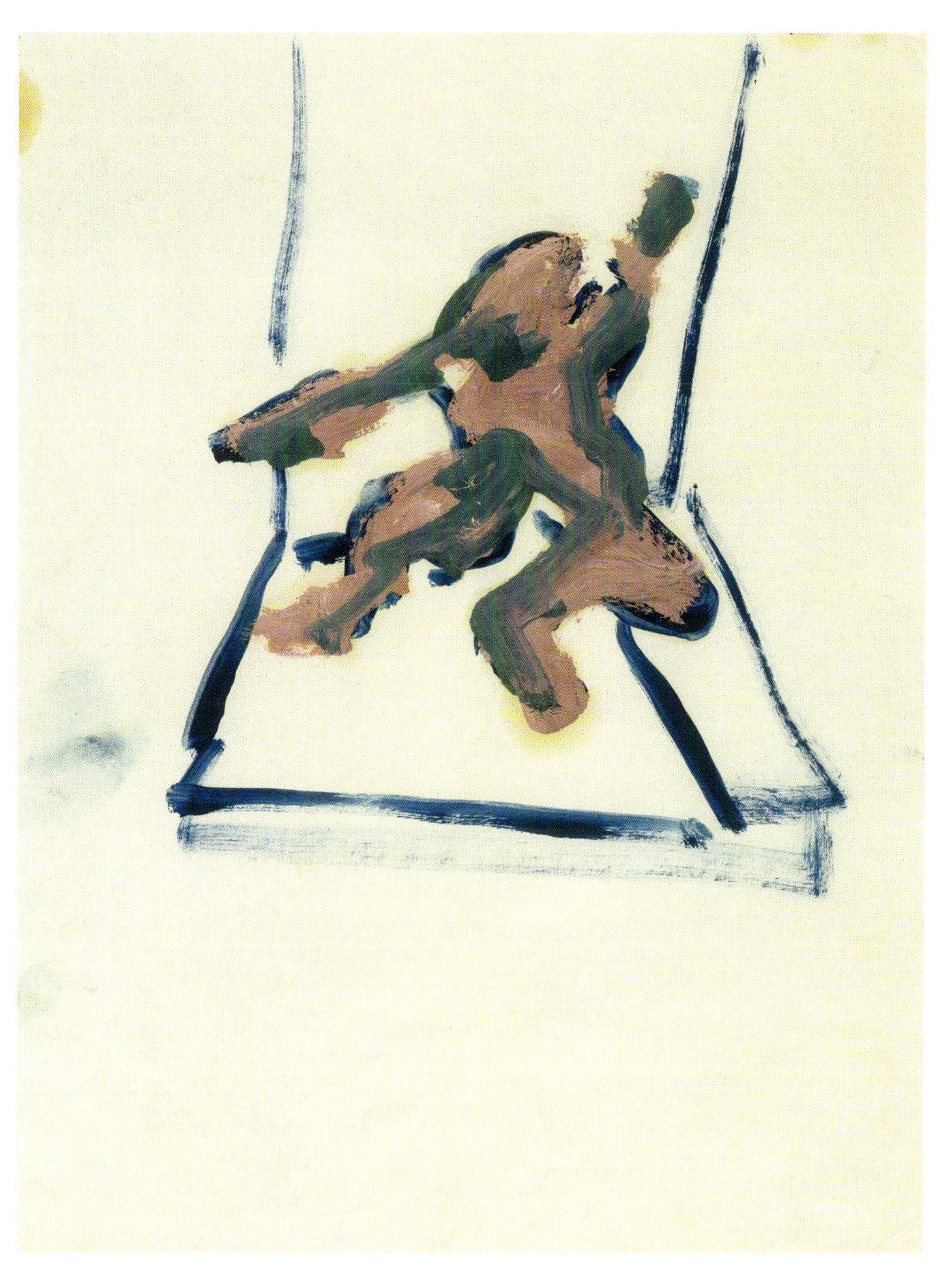

Francis Bacon
Figure with Left Arm Raised, No. 2, ca. 1957–61

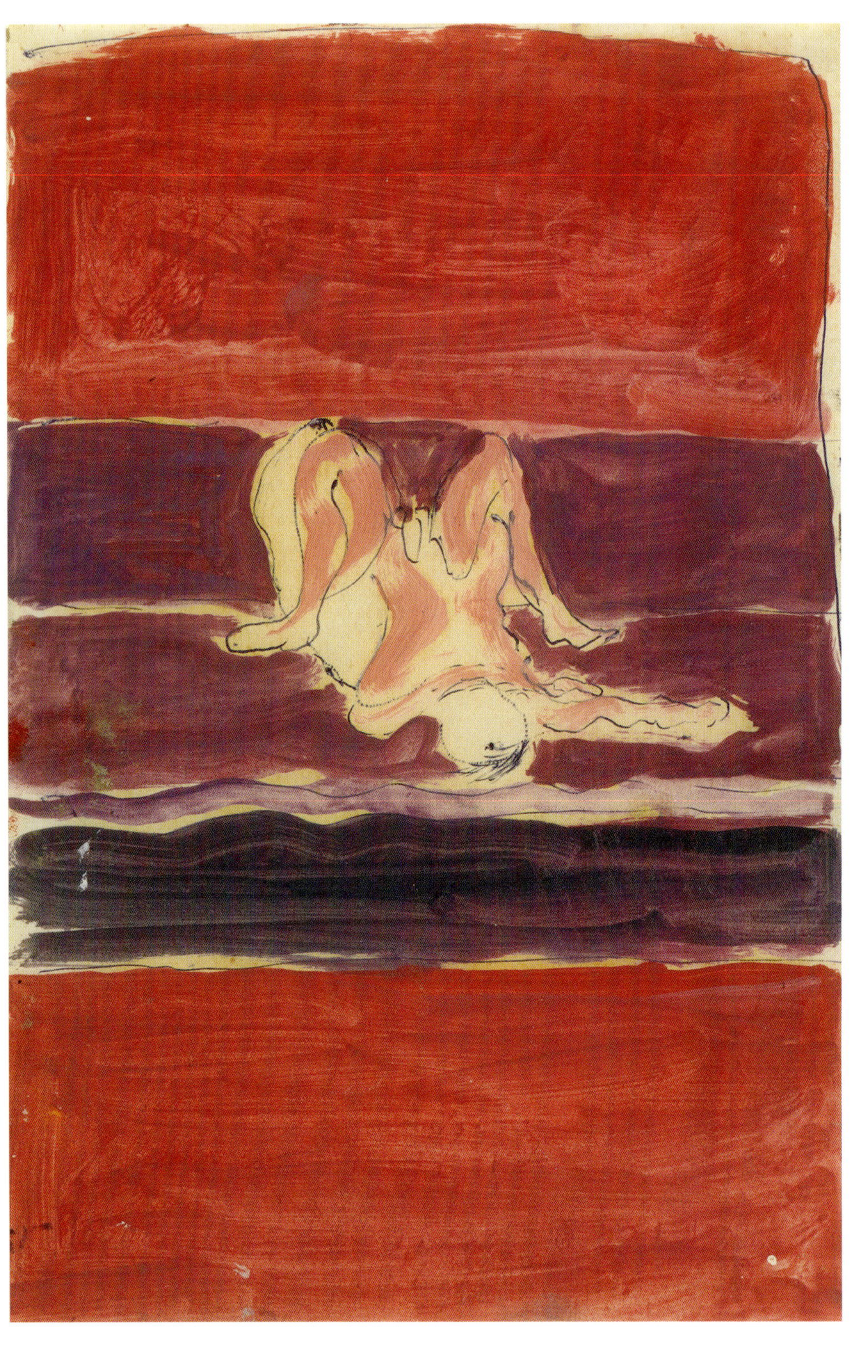

Francis Bacon
Reclining Figure, No. 1, ca. 1961

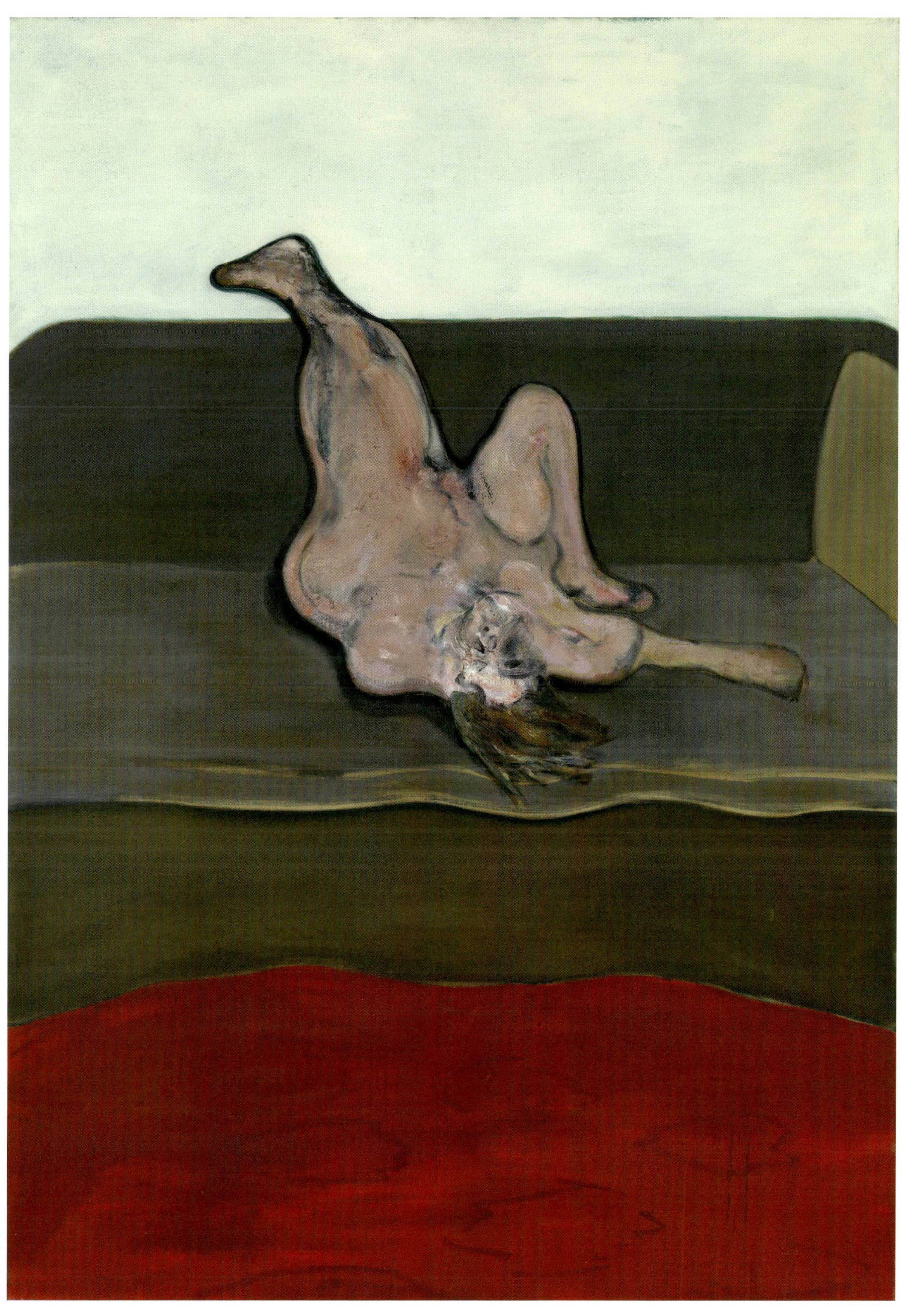

Francis Bacon
Reclining Woman, 1961

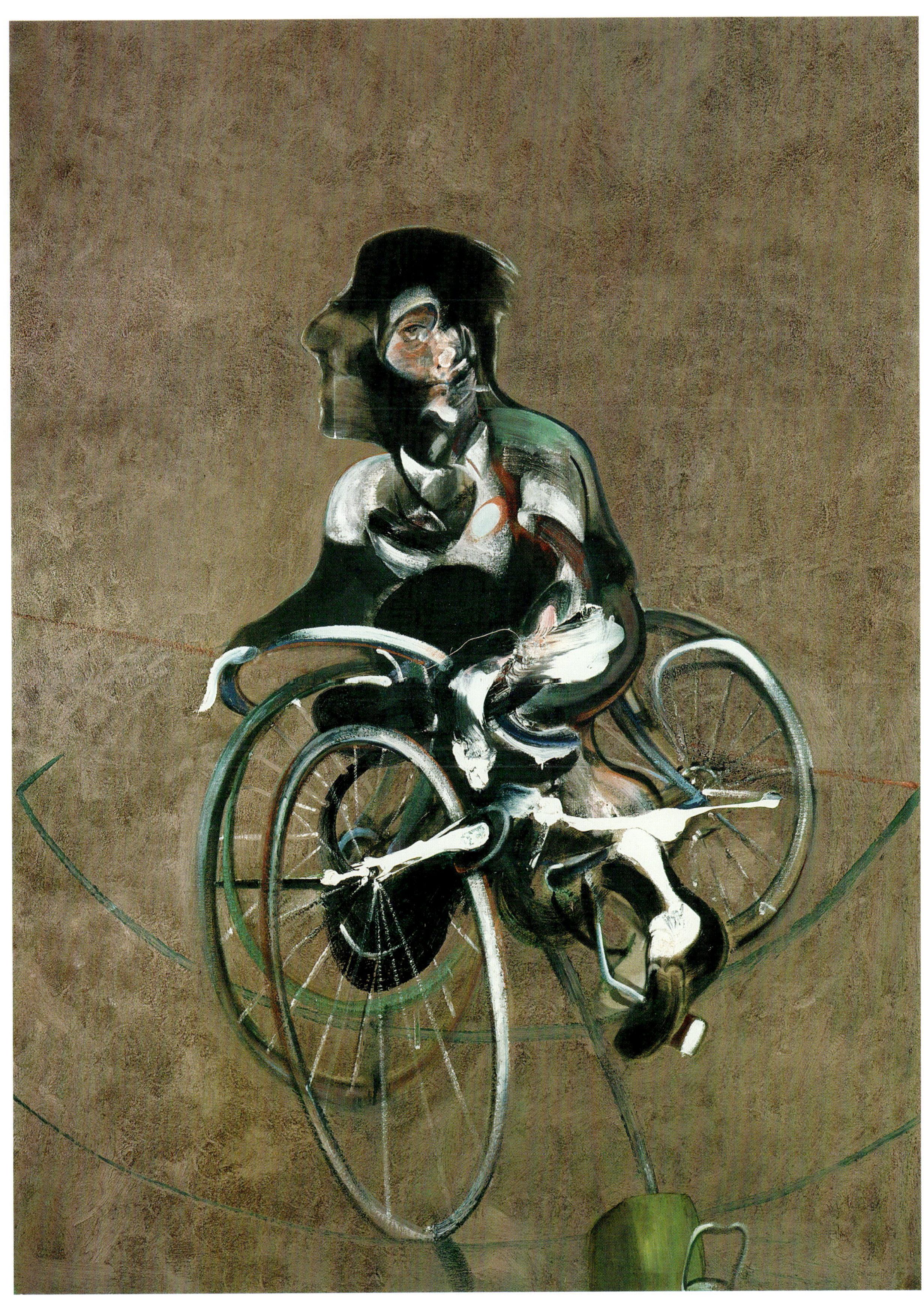

Francis Bacon
Portrait of George Dyer Riding a Bicycle, 1966

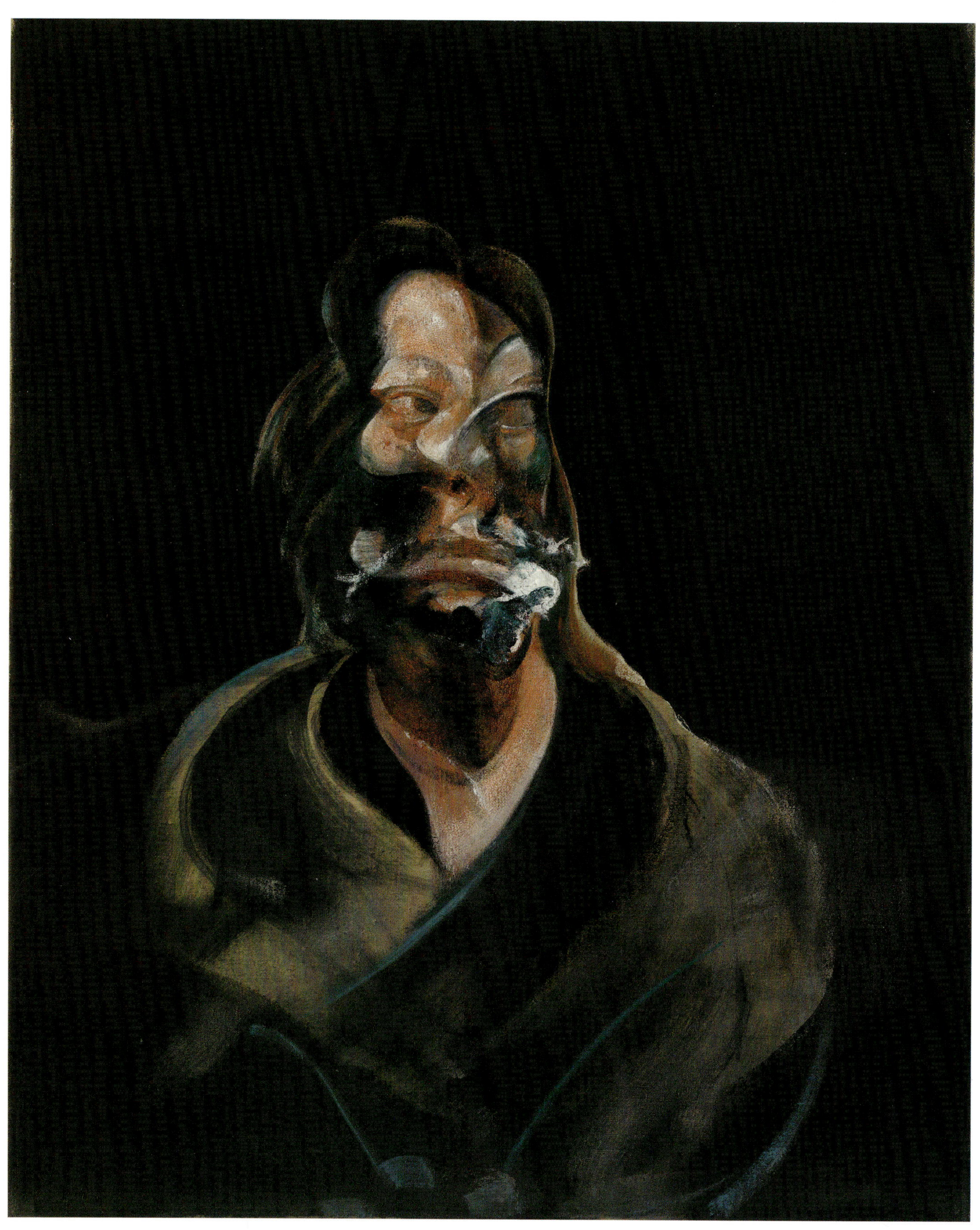

Francis Bacon
Portrait of Isabel Rawsthorne, 1966

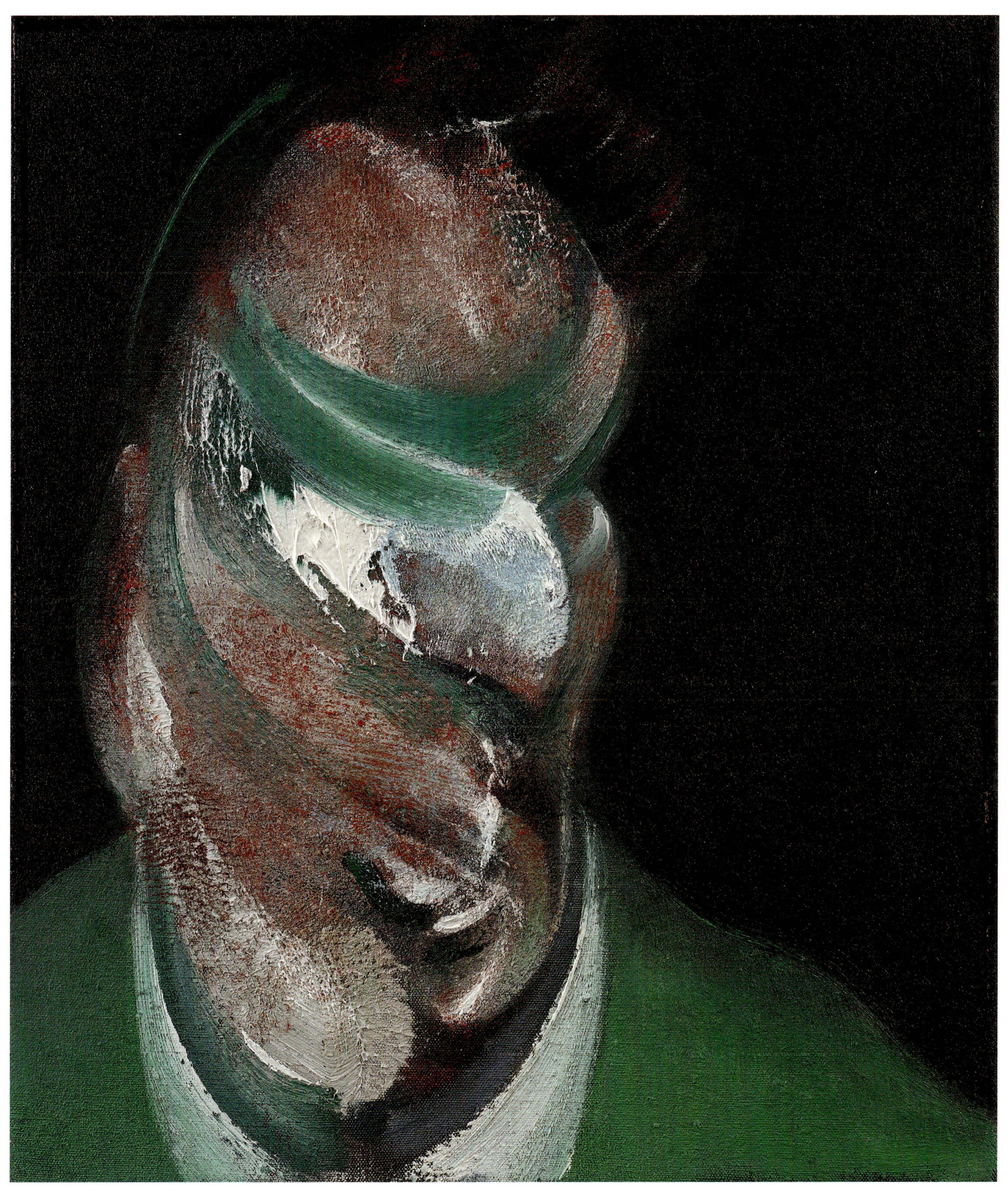

Francis Bacon
Study for Head of Lucian Freud, 1967

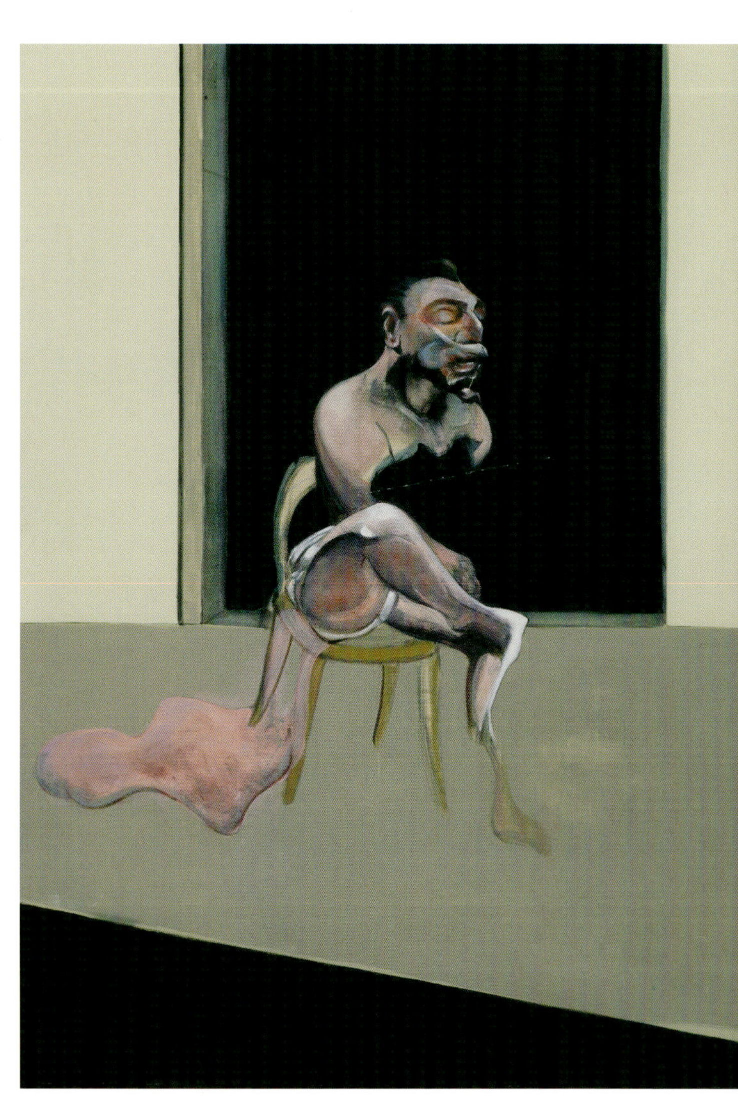

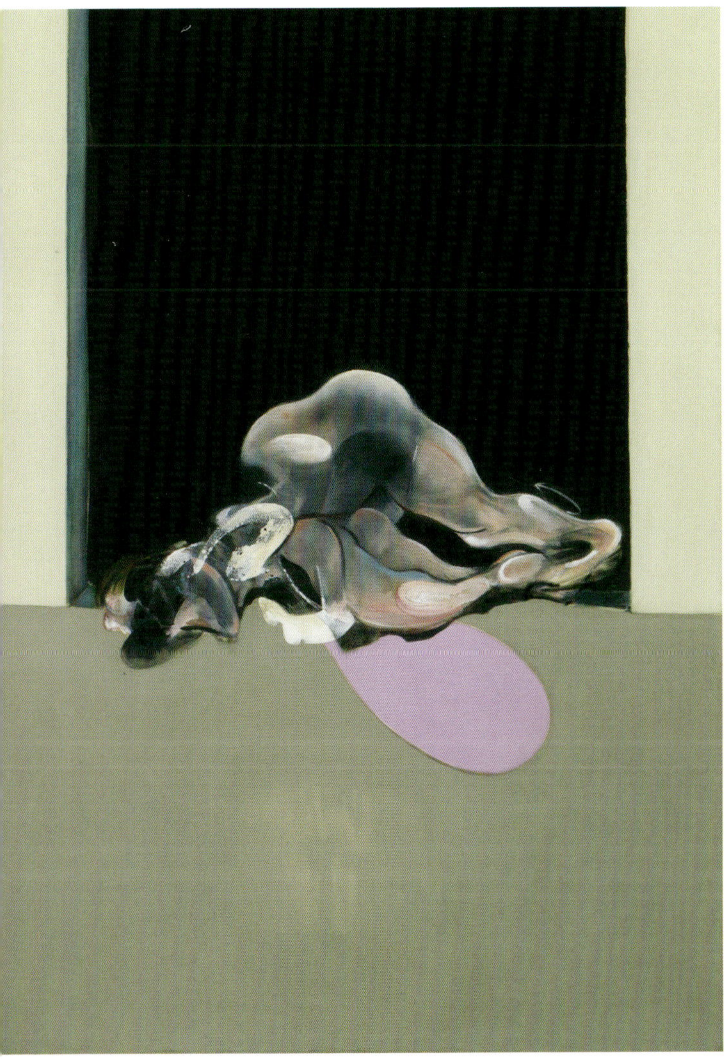
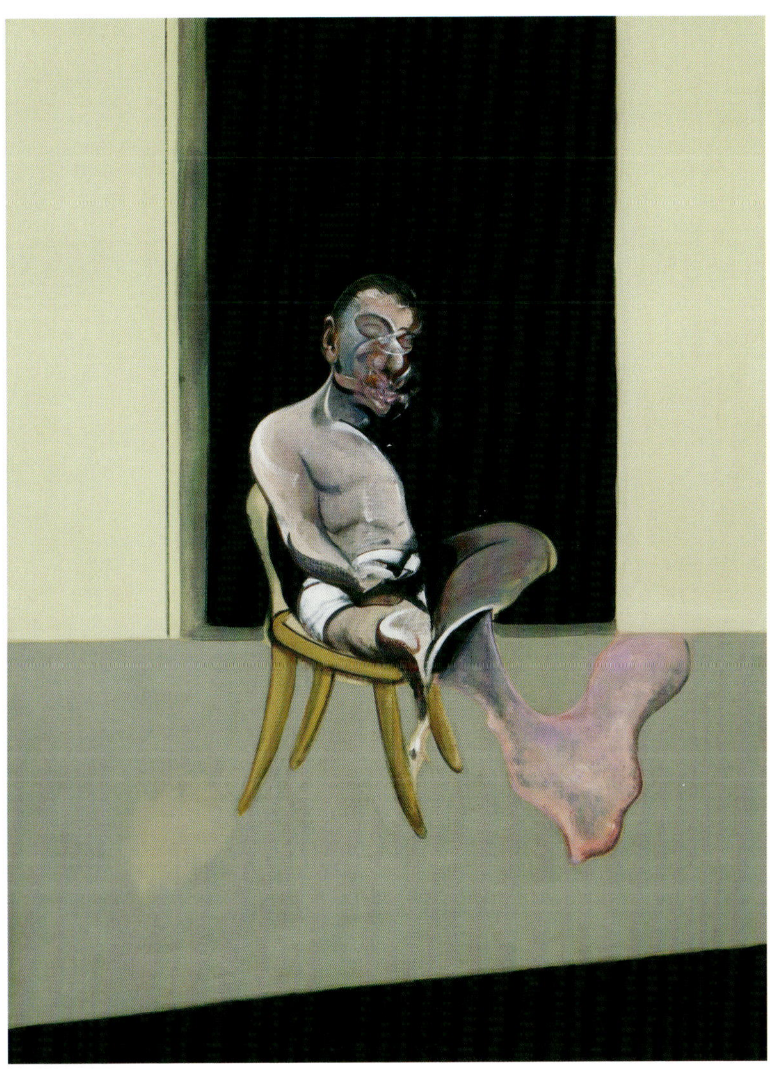

Francis Bacon
Triptych August 1972, 1972

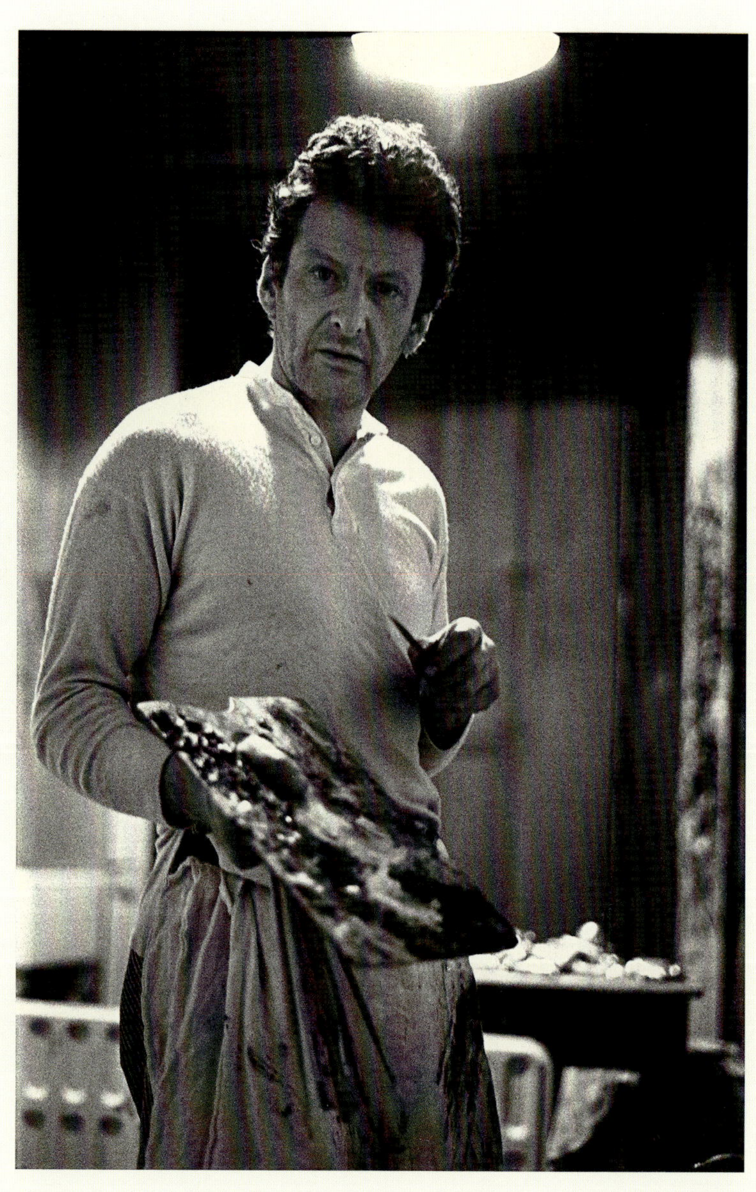

Lucian Freud, 1969.
Photo: Harry Diamond

LUCIAN FREUD

Lucian Freud was born in Berlin on December 8, 1922. His mother, Lucie, was the daughter of a grain merchant, and his father, Ernest, an architect, was the youngest son of the psychoanalyst Sigmund Freud. The family moved to Britain in 1933 to escape Nazism, and Freud attended school in Devon and Dorset, visiting the Tate and the National Gallery during school holidays.

Freud studied briefly at the Central School of Arts and Crafts in London (1938) and then at the East Anglian School of Painting and Drawing (1939) under Cedric Morris. In 1941 he enlisted as an ordinary seaman in the merchant navy, sailing to Nova Scotia on the North Atlantic convoy. On his return to London he continued to study with Morris (the school had relocated to Hadleigh, Suffolk) and attended life-drawing classes at Goldsmiths College, London, on the recommendation of Graham Sutherland.

In 1943 Freud moved to Delamere Terrace on the Grand Union canal in Paddington, an inner-city area of London where he would spend the next thirty years. The area was severely bomb damaged, and the building was condemned. He began to work on *The Painter's Room* (1944; p. 5), and his first solo exhibition was held at Lefevre Gallery in London in 1944. In that year he met Francis Bacon through their mutual friend Sutherland. Freud's early muse, Lorna Wishart, appeared as the subject of several portraits, among them *Woman with a Tulip* (private collection) and *Woman with a Daffodil* (New York, Museum of Modern Art), both 1945. Throughout this period he concentrated on drawing, particularly portraits, and also introduced uncanny juxtapositions that recall Surrealism.

During 1946 Freud spent two months in Paris, where he met Pablo Picasso and Alberto Giacometti. This was followed by five months on the Greek island of Poros with the painter John Craxton, a fellow former student at the East Anglian School. In 1947 Freud met Kitty Garman, daughter of the sculptor Jacob Epstein, who became the subject of one of his first major paintings, *Girl in a Dark Jacket* (1947; private collection). A series of meticulously executed, emotionally charged portraits of Kitty followed, including *Girl with a Kitten* (1947; p. 52). The pair married in 1948, and their first daughter, Annie, was born shortly afterward. Freud began teaching intermittently at the Slade School of Fine Art, London, where his students included Michael Andrews.

In 1951 Freud completed *Girl with a White Dog* (1950–51; p. 55) and *Interior in Paddington* (1951; Liverpool, Walker Art Gallery), which won the Arts Council of Great Britain prize at the Festival of Britain. These paintings established concerns that would preoccupy him throughout his career, situating the human figure in a stark interior with an overriding sense of alienation and intense psychological character.

Freud married his second wife, Caroline Blackwood, in 1953. She appeared as a subject of several paintings, including *Hotel Bedroom* (1954; Fredericton, Canada, Beaverbrook Art Gallery), a double portrait with the artist. In 1954 he represented Britain at the Venice Biennale, along with Ben Nicholson and Francis Bacon, exhibiting twenty-two paintings, including *Hotel Bedroom* and a portrait of Bacon.

During the late 1950s Freud became increasingly frustrated with the minute detail he sought to capture and the tight way of working he had developed. He switched to coarser brushes and began to paint standing up, with a more vigorous approach. *Woman Smiling* (1958–59; private collection) marks this departure, with loose brushstrokes mapping out the landscape of the skin and suggesting the structure of bones beneath the flesh. The subject, Suzy Boyt, became the mother of four of his children. Throughout the next decade Freud developed the use of spatial brush marks to suggest shape and form, particularly in female nudes, with a muted palette of blotchy flesh tones. In the late 1960s he began to concentrate on whole figures painted from a high viewpoint, producing a slightly distorted perspective. His style remained forensically observed yet decidedly impassive.

Freud's father died in 1970. Two years later he completed *The Artist's Mother* (1972; private collection), the first in a series of paintings and drawings of his mother, who continued to sit for him almost daily until 1984 (she died in 1989). Several of his children also posed for him during this time. In 1977 he moved to a large top-floor studio in Holland Park and began painting on a larger scale. He completed *Large Interior W11 (after Watteau)* (1981–83; private collection), a complex composition of five figures in which several of those closest to him appear. This marked the beginning of a series of increasingly ambitious compositions throughout the 1980s and early 1990s. In 1987–88 his first major retrospective, organized by the British Council, traveled to the Hirshhorn Museum and Sculpture Garden, Washington, DC; the Musée National d'Art Moderne, Paris; the Hayward Gallery, London; and the Neue Nationalgalerie, Berlin.

During the 1990s Freud became interested in "extreme" body types and the depiction of flesh without muscle. He met the performance artist Leigh Bowery, who was able to maintain awkward poses, as in *Nude with Leg Up* (1992; Hirshhorn Museum and Sculpture Garden), and became his principal model from 1990 to 1994. Bowery also introduced him to Sue Tilley, who appeared in *Benefits Supervisor Sleeping* (1995; private collection).

The 1990s and 2000s were marked by several major exhibitions, including *Recent Work* at the Whitechapel Gallery, which toured to the Metropolitan Museum of Art, New York, and the Museo Nacional Centro de Arte Reina Sofía, Madrid (1993–94); a retrospective at Tate Britain, touring to Barcelona and Los Angeles (2002); and a retrospective at the Centre Pompidou, Paris (2011).

In his later years Freud continued to concentrate on portraits, particularly large-scale paintings of his assistant David Dawson. He died in London on July 20, 2011.

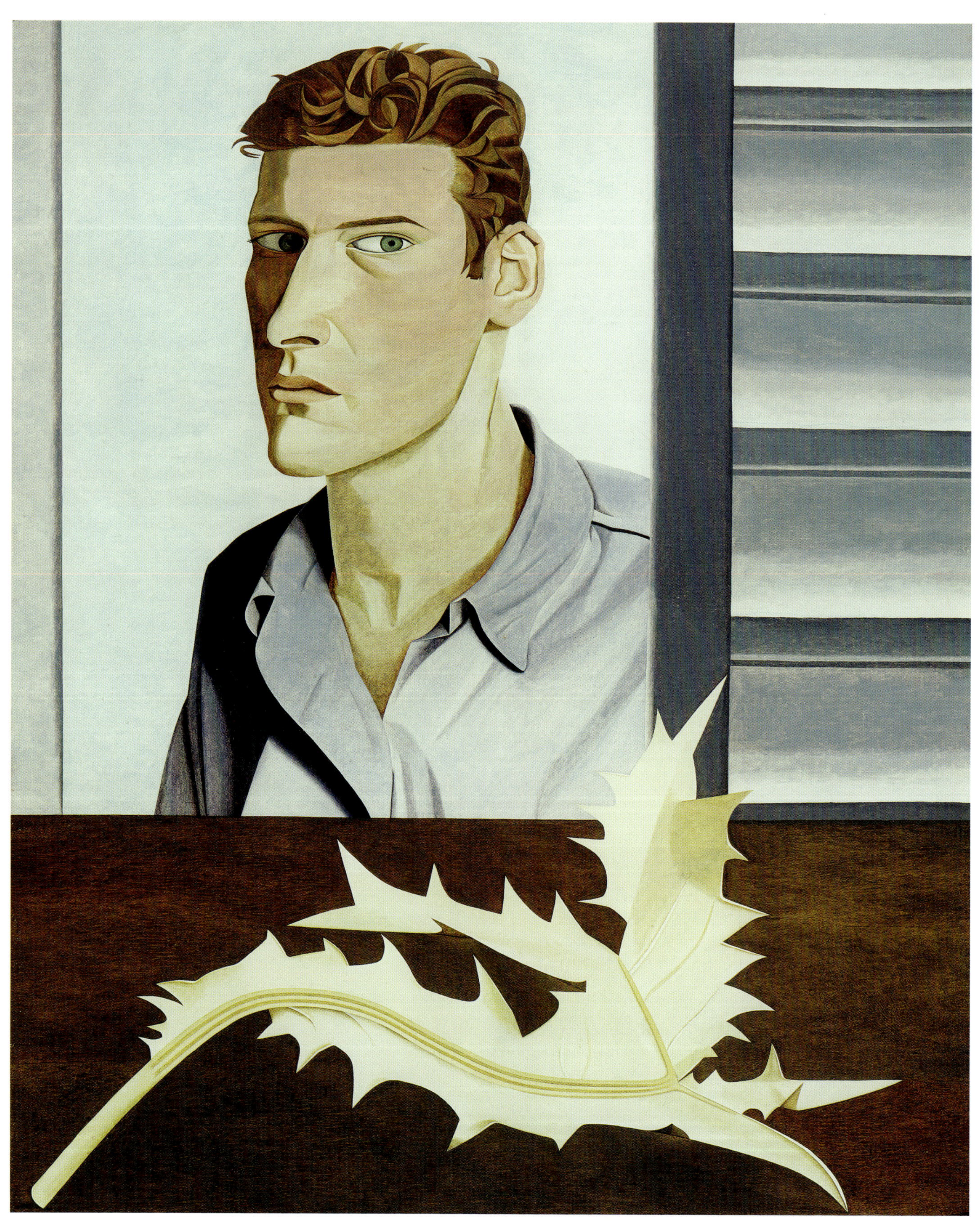

Lucian Freud
Man with a Thistle (Self-Portrait), 1946

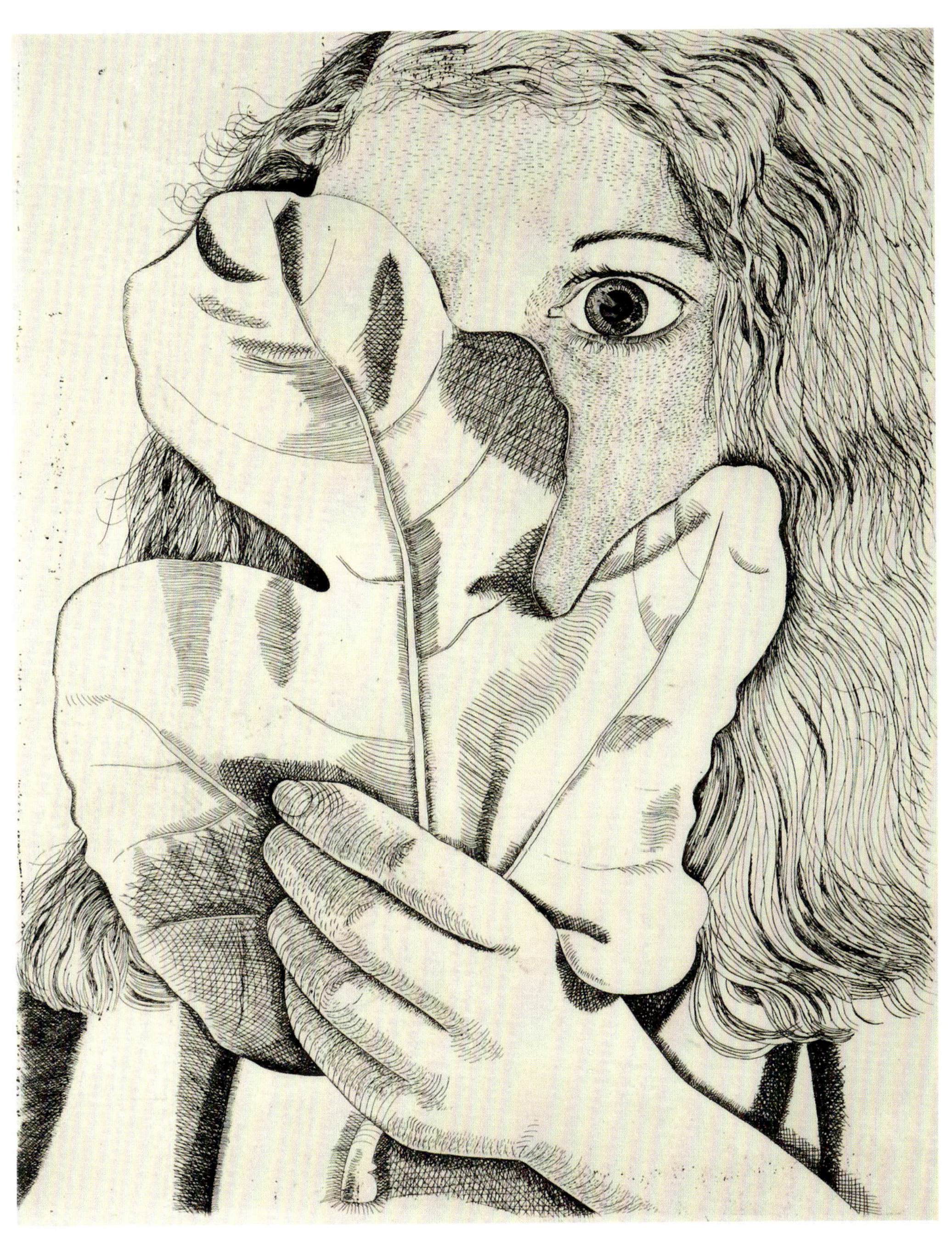

Lucian Freud
Girl with a Fig Leaf, 1947

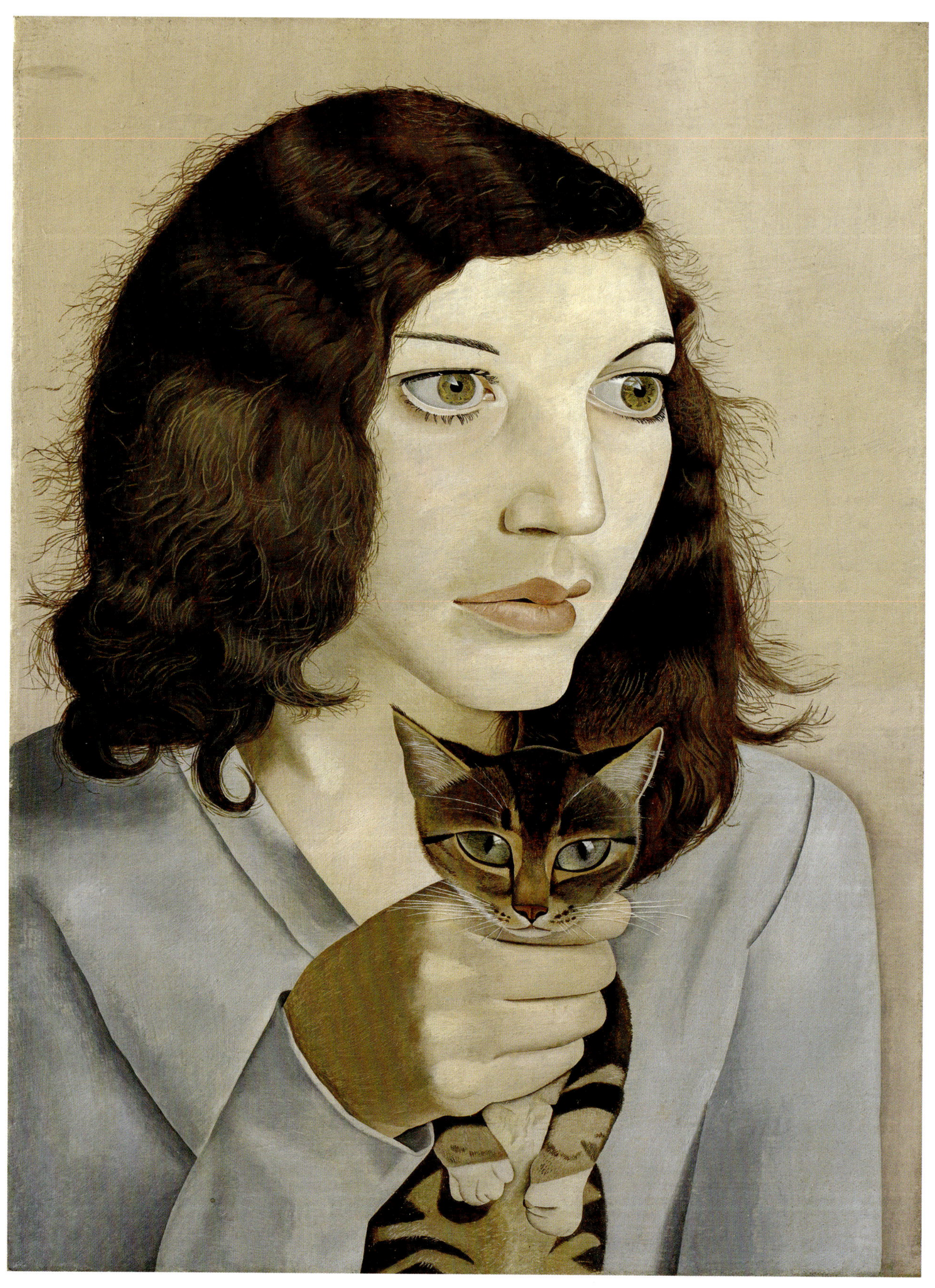

Lucian Freud
Girl with a Kitten, 1947

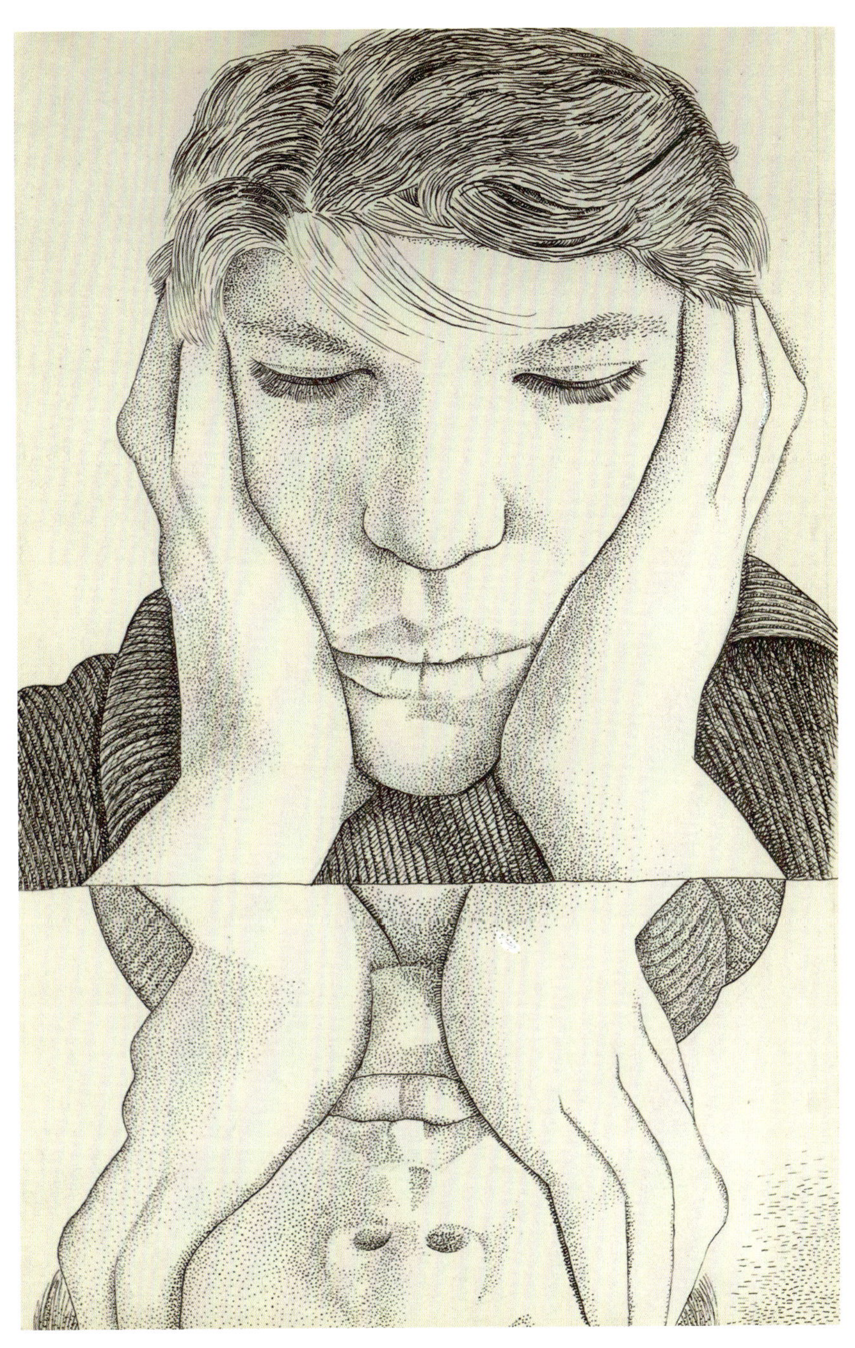

Lucian Freud
Narcissus, 1948

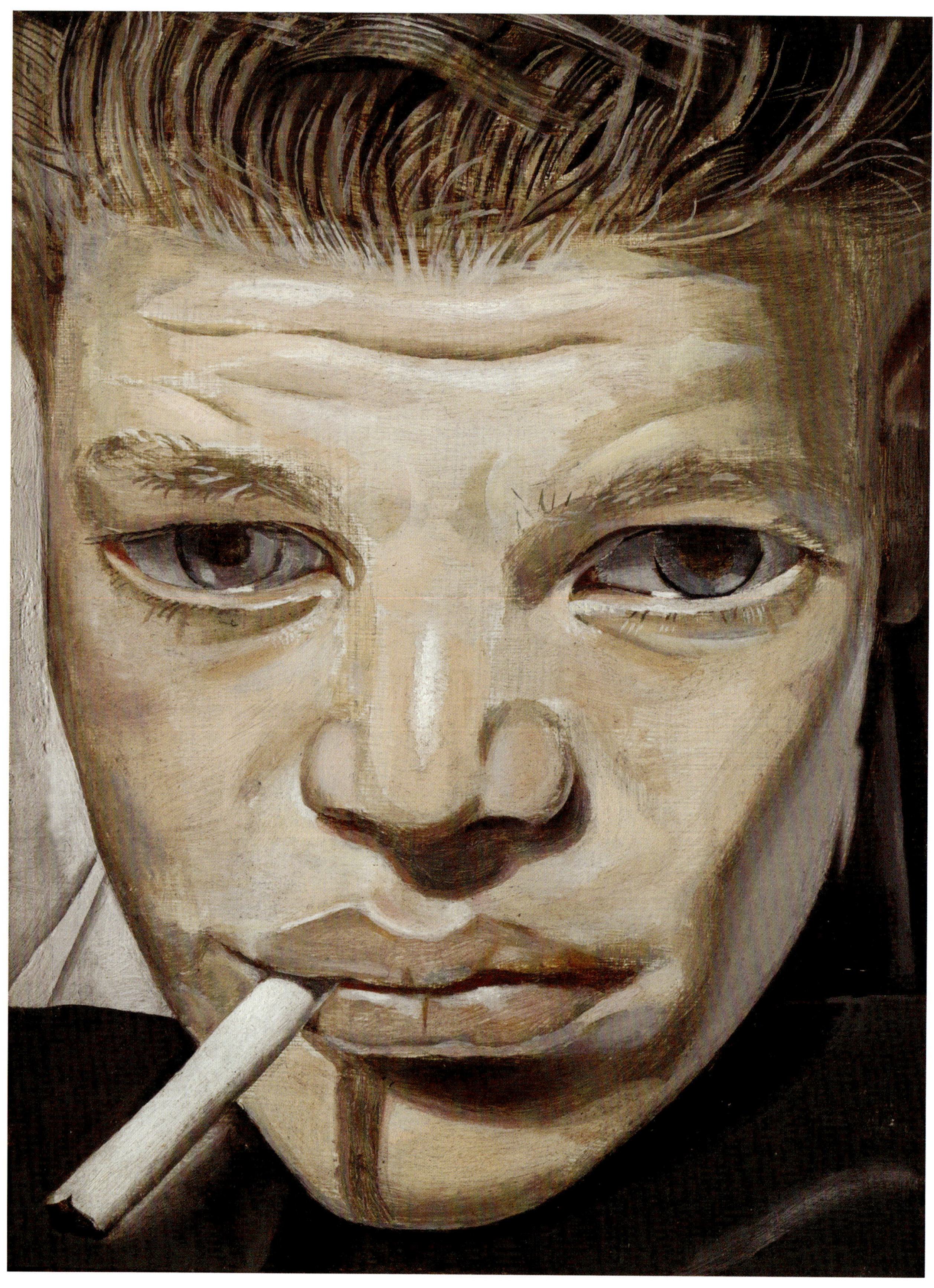

Lucian Freud
Boy Smoking, 1950–51

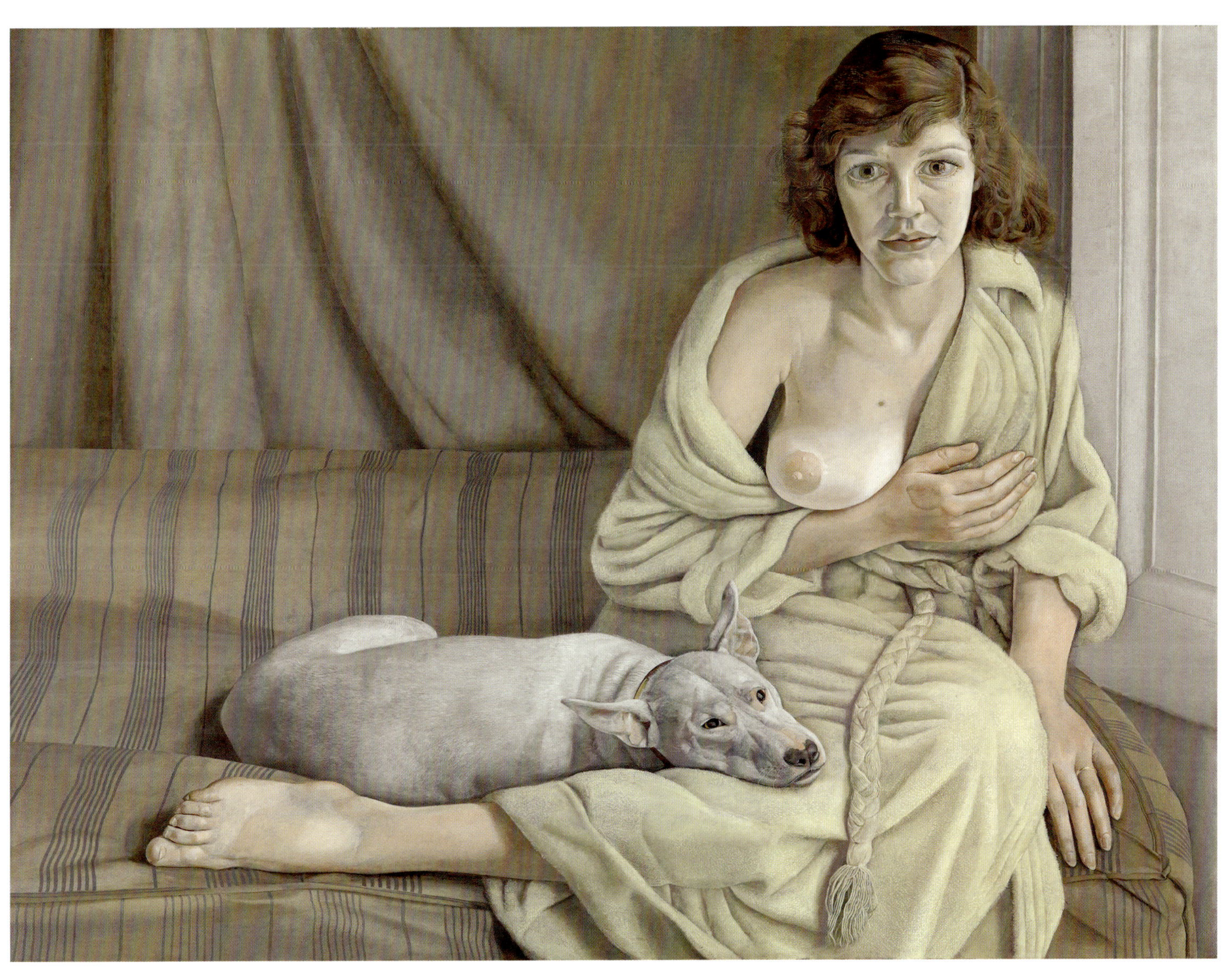

Lucian Freud

Girl with a White Dog, 1950–51

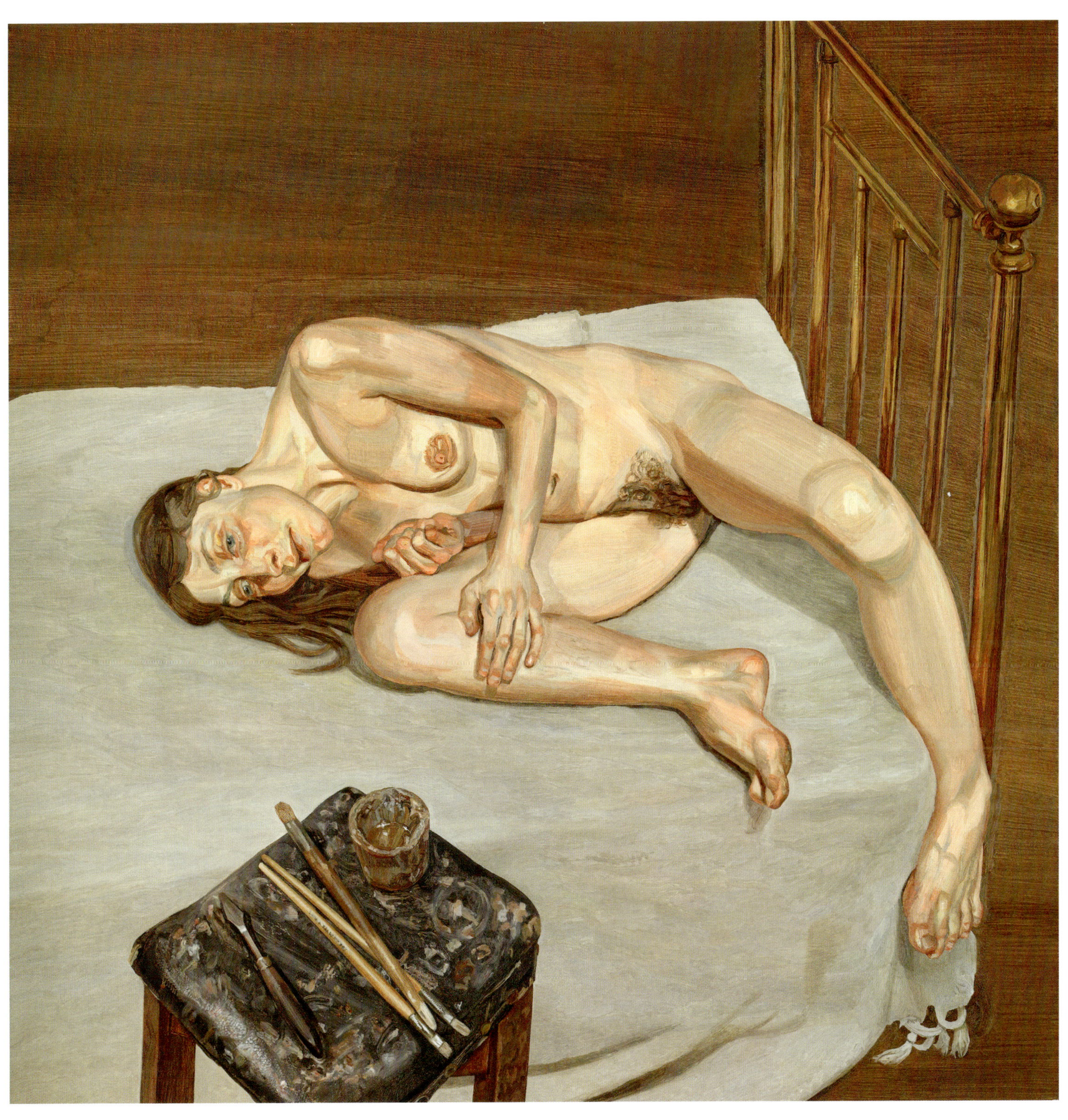

Lucian Freud
Naked Portrait, 1972–73

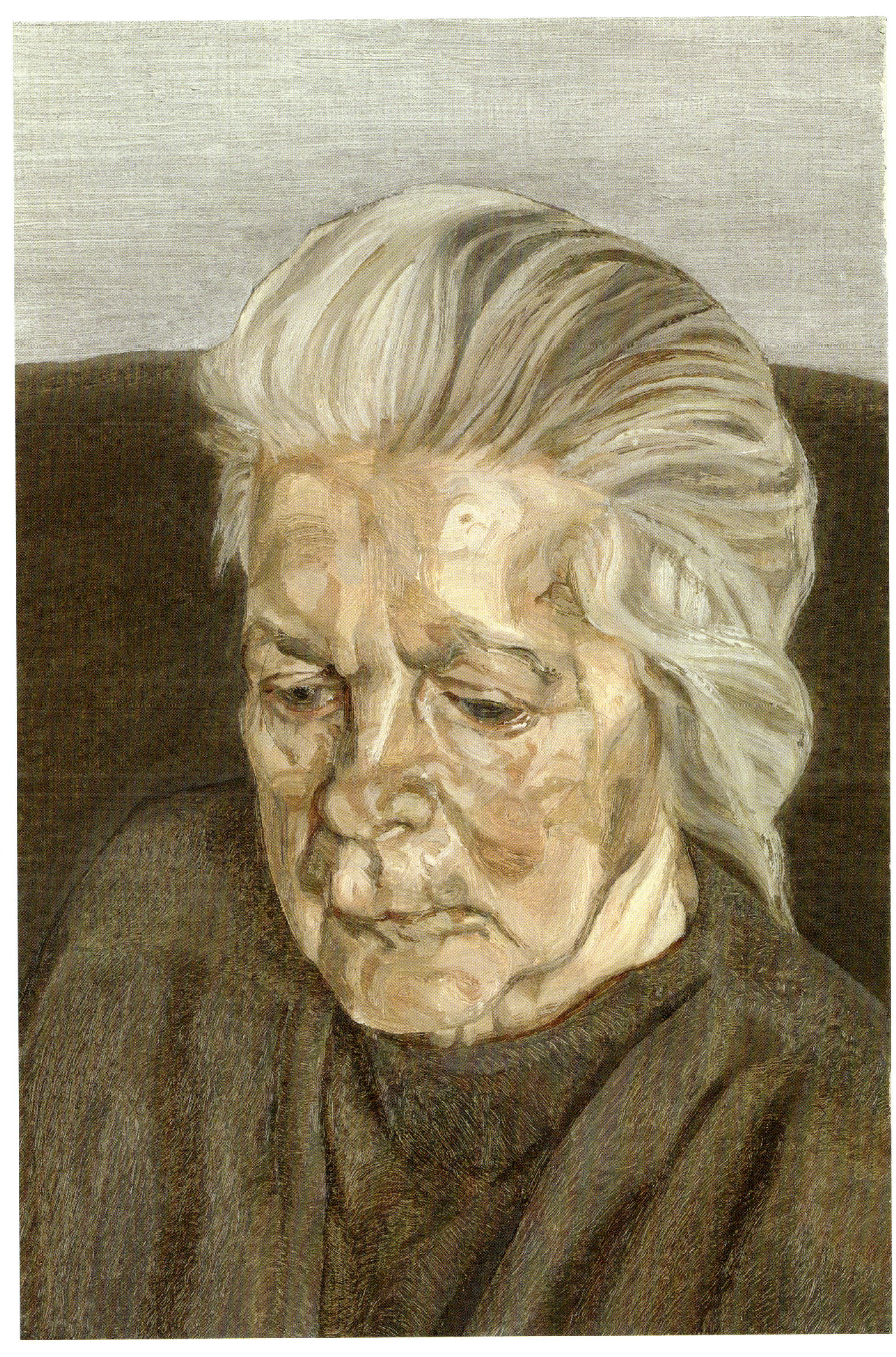

Lucian Freud
The Painter's Mother IV, 1973

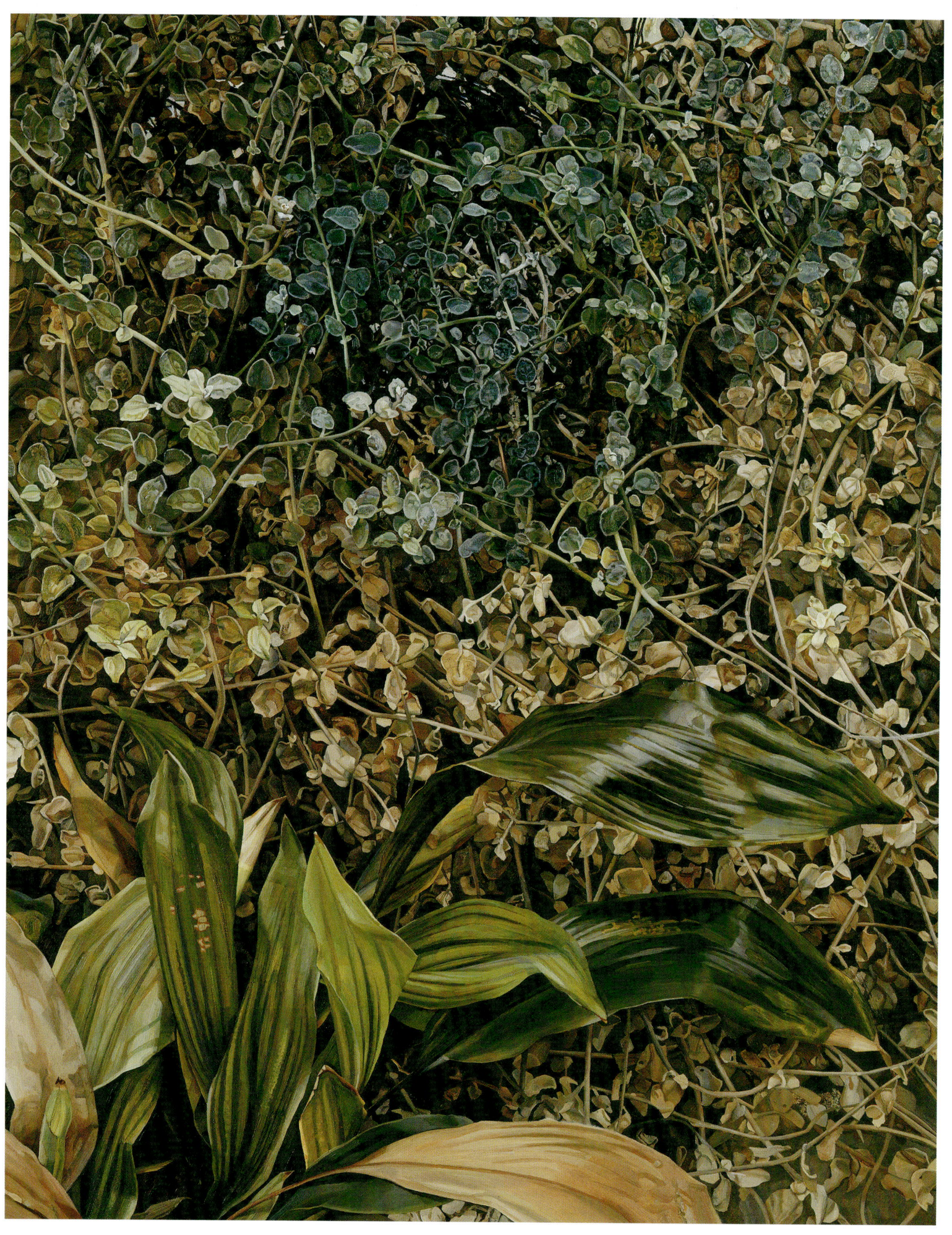

Lucian Freud
Two Plants, 1977–80

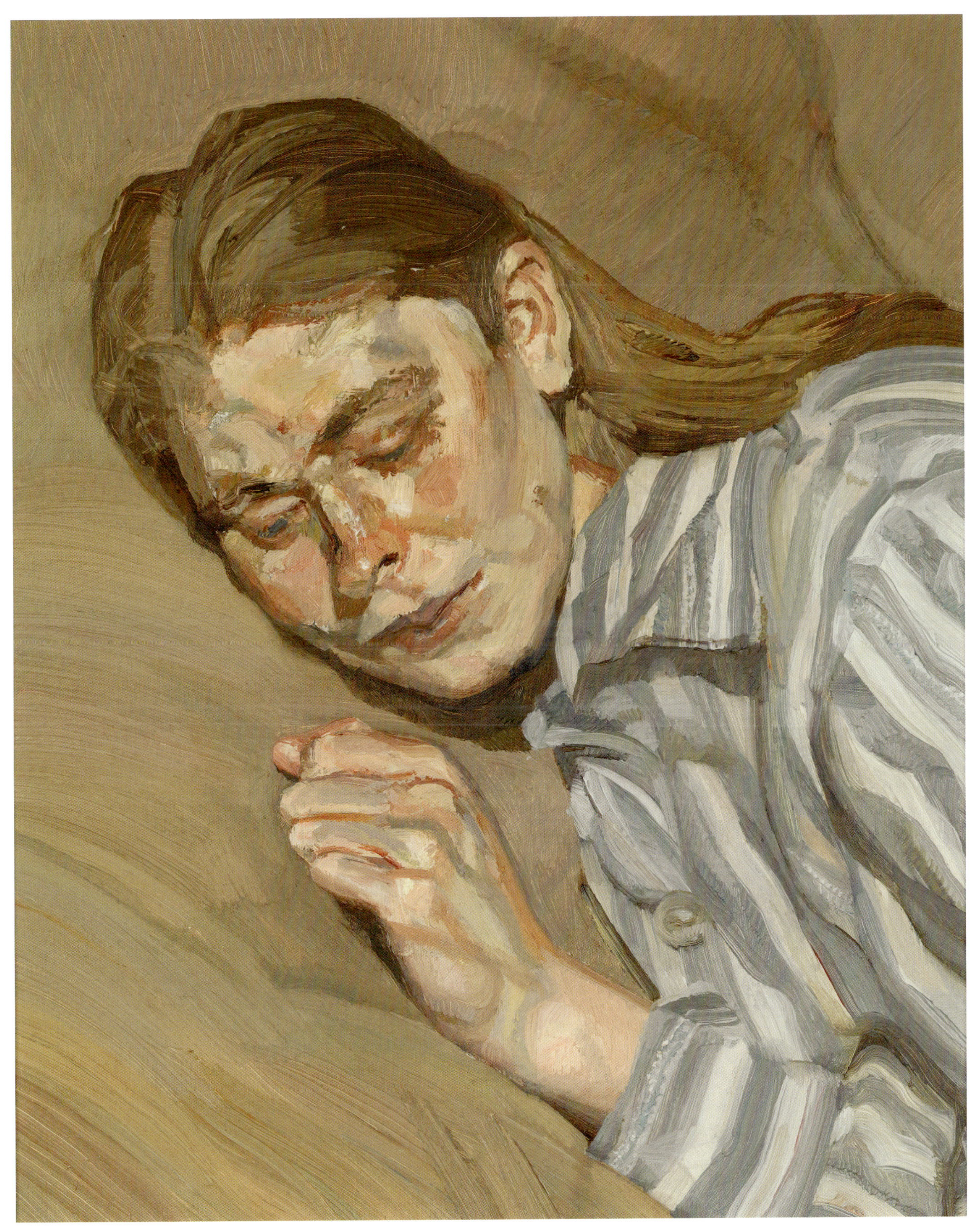

Lucian Freud
Girl in a Striped Nightshirt, 1983–85

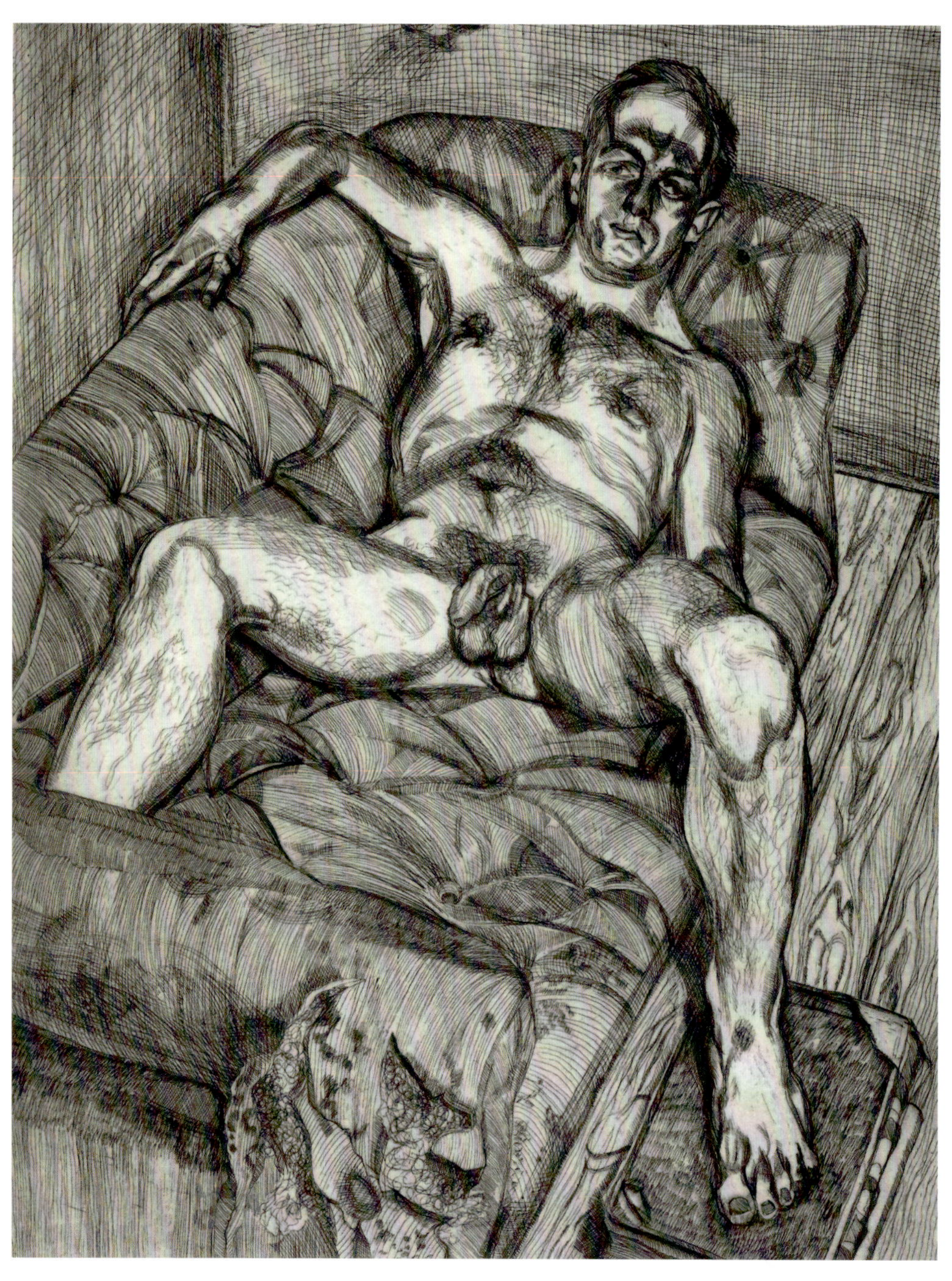

Lucian Freud
Man Posing, 1985

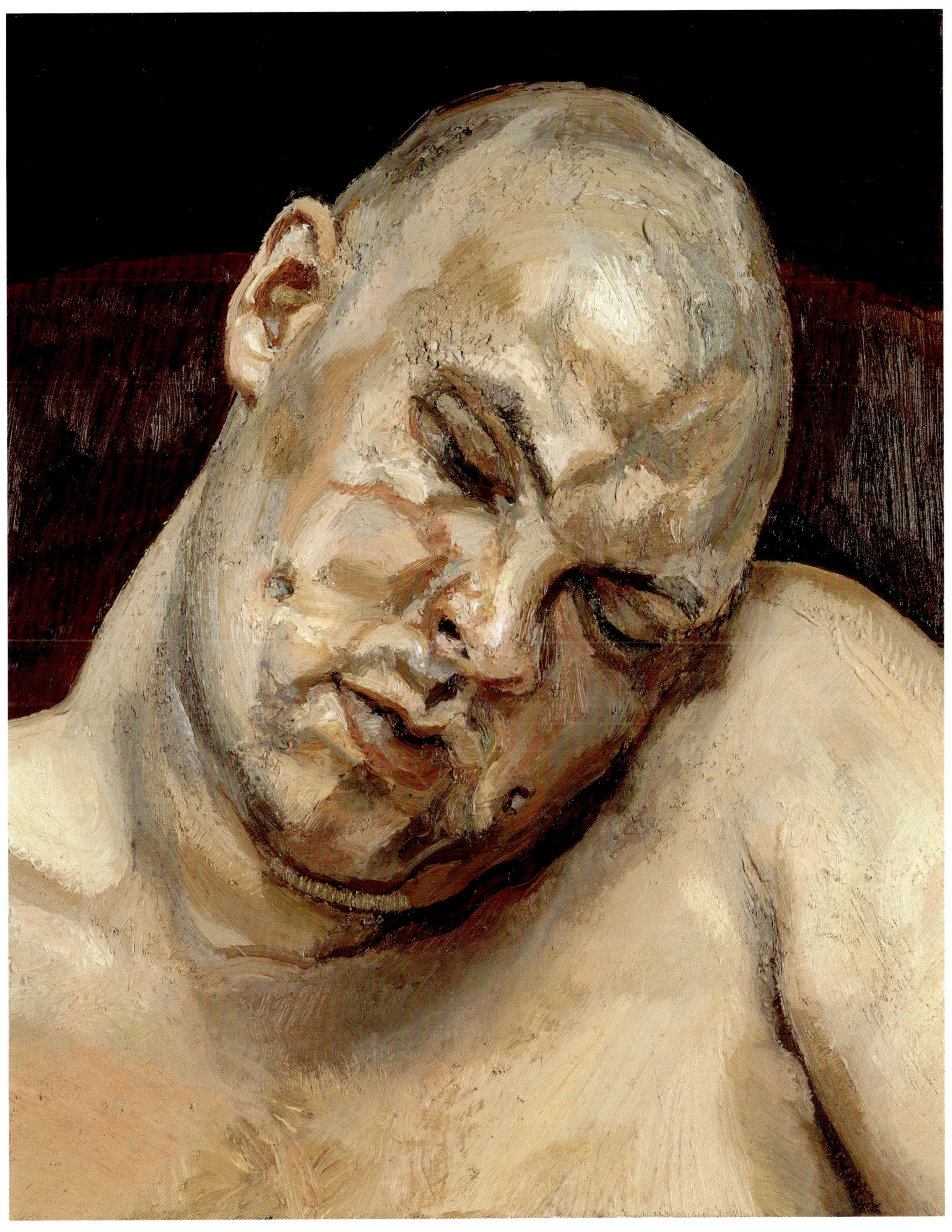

Lucian Freud
Leigh Bowery, 1991

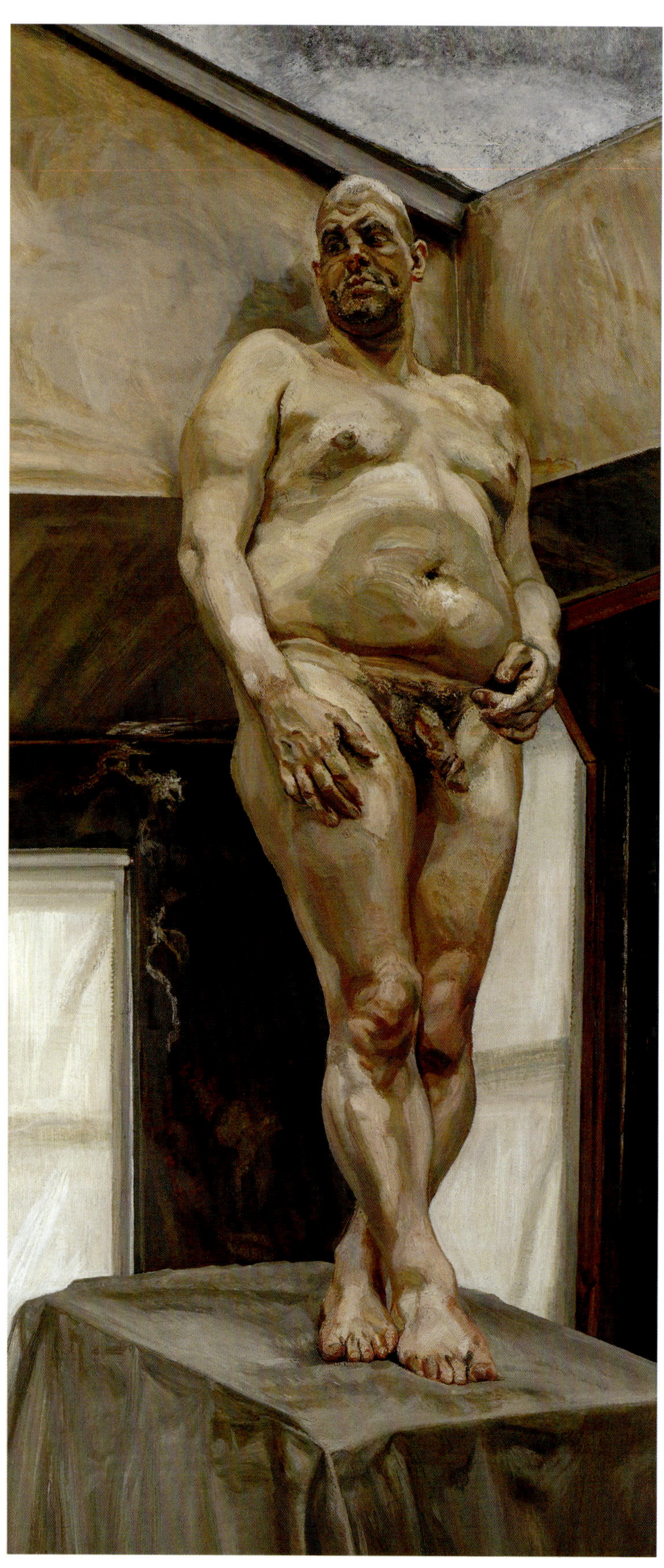

Lucian Freud
Leigh under the Skylight, 1994

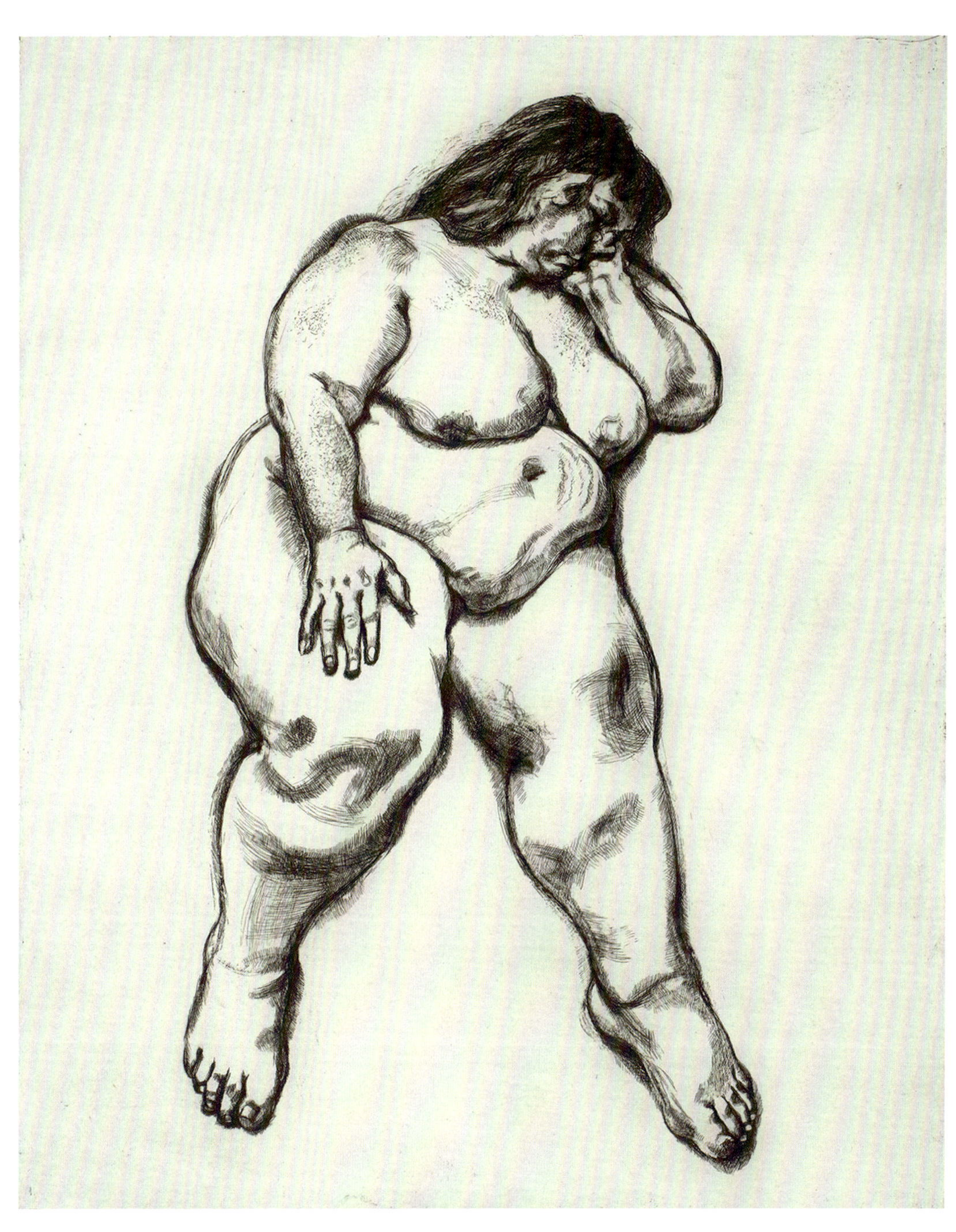

Lucian Freud
Woman Sleeping, 1995

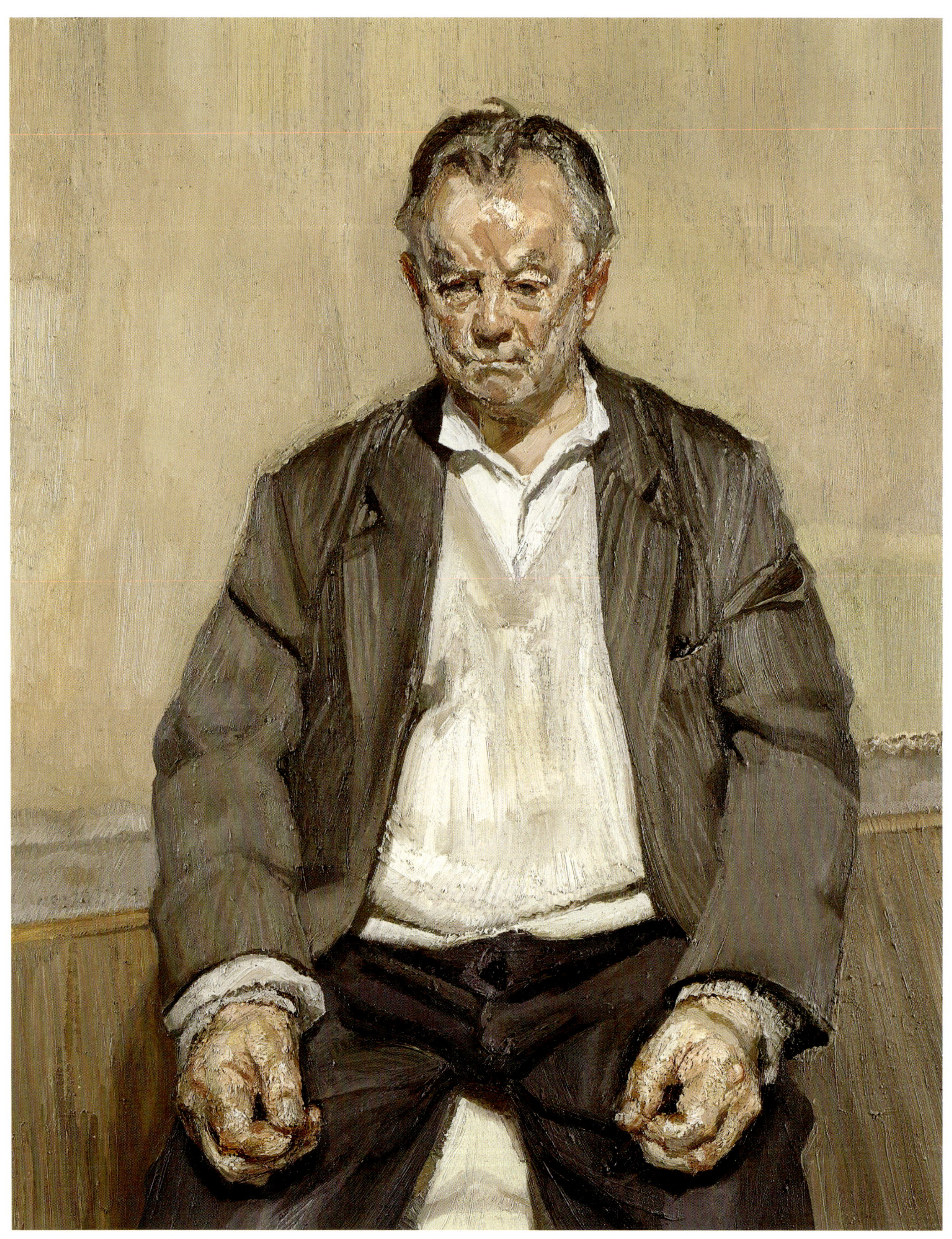

Lucian Freud
Bruce Bernard (Seated), 1996

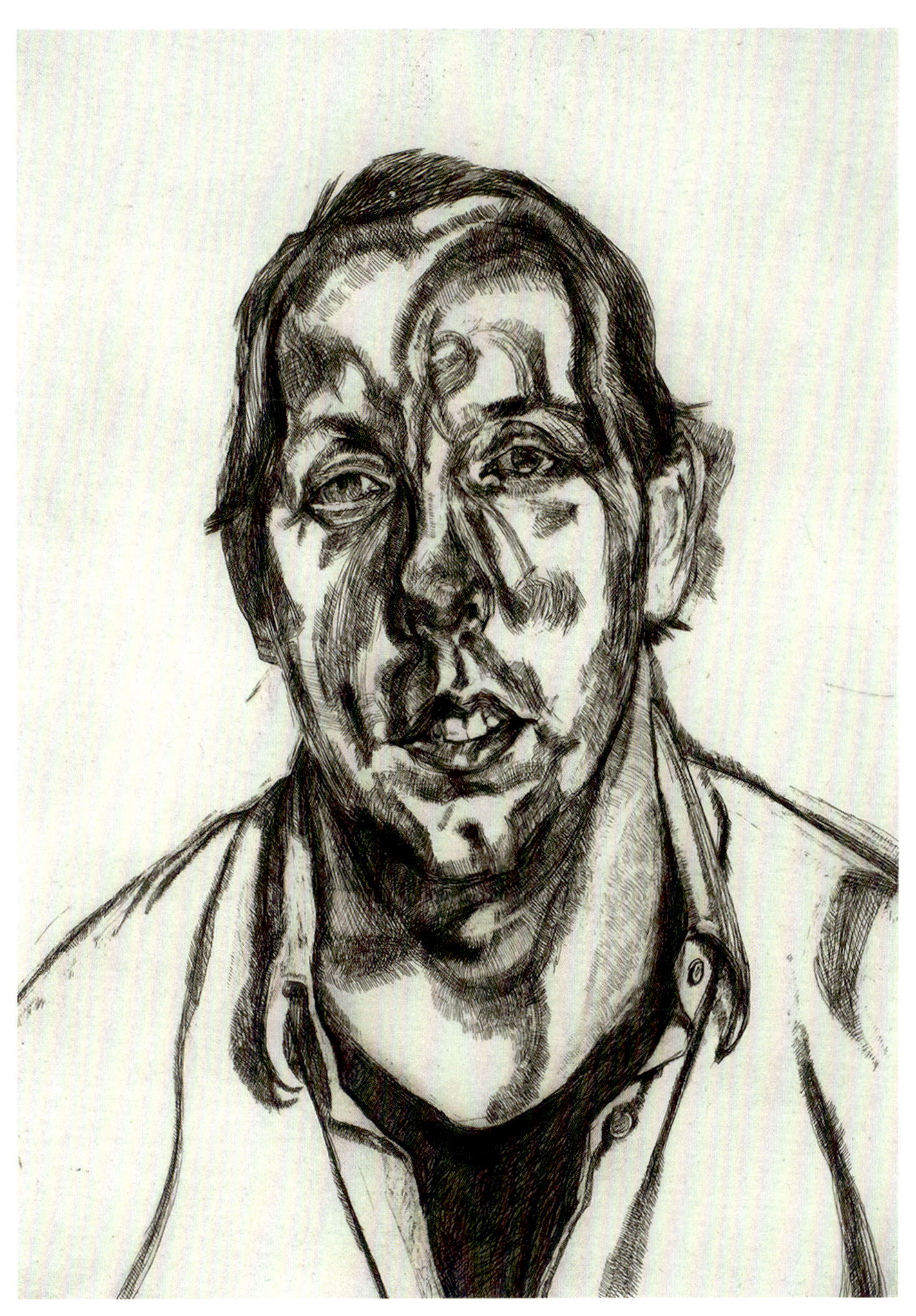

Lucian Freud
David Dawson, 1998

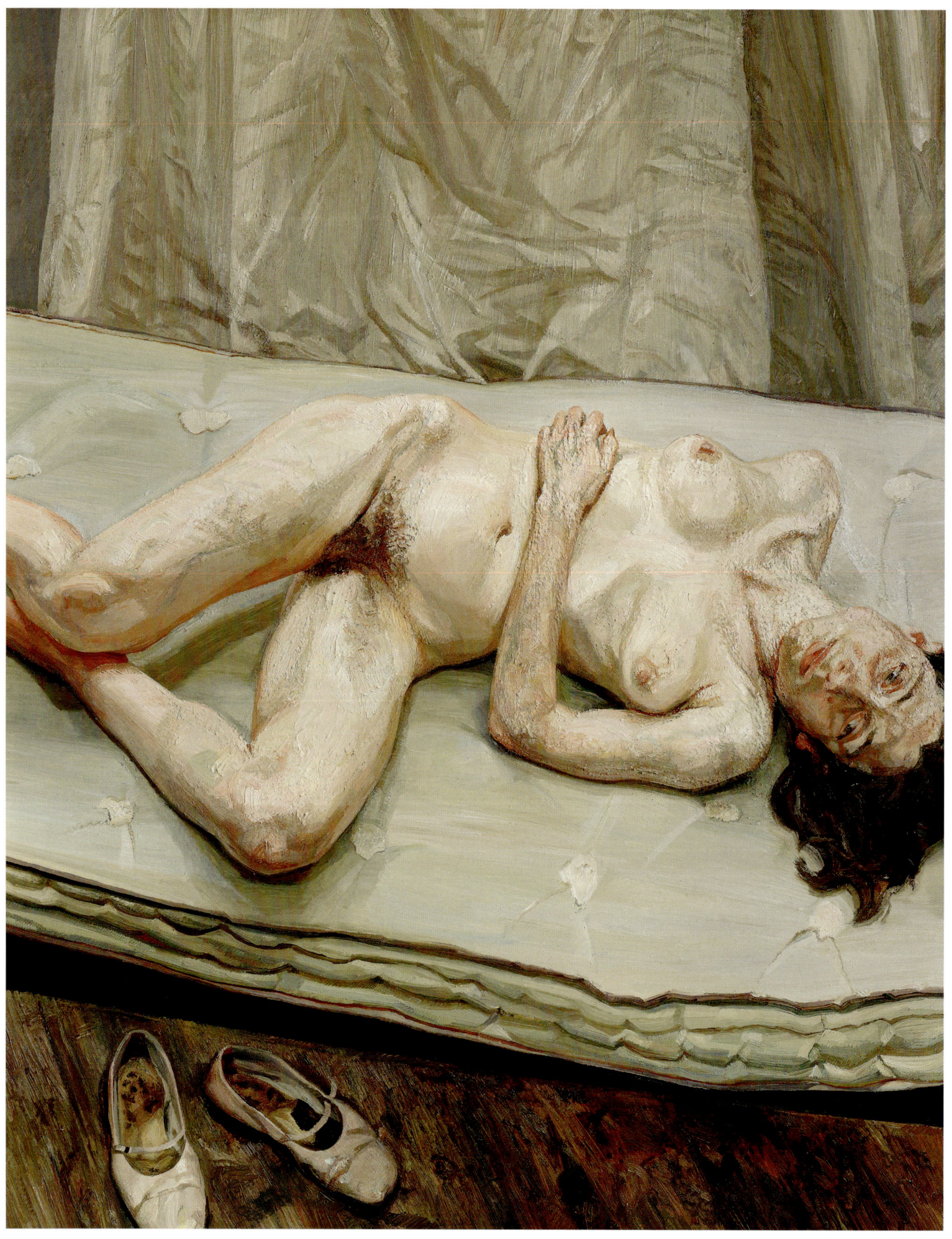

Lucian Freud
Naked Portrait, 2001

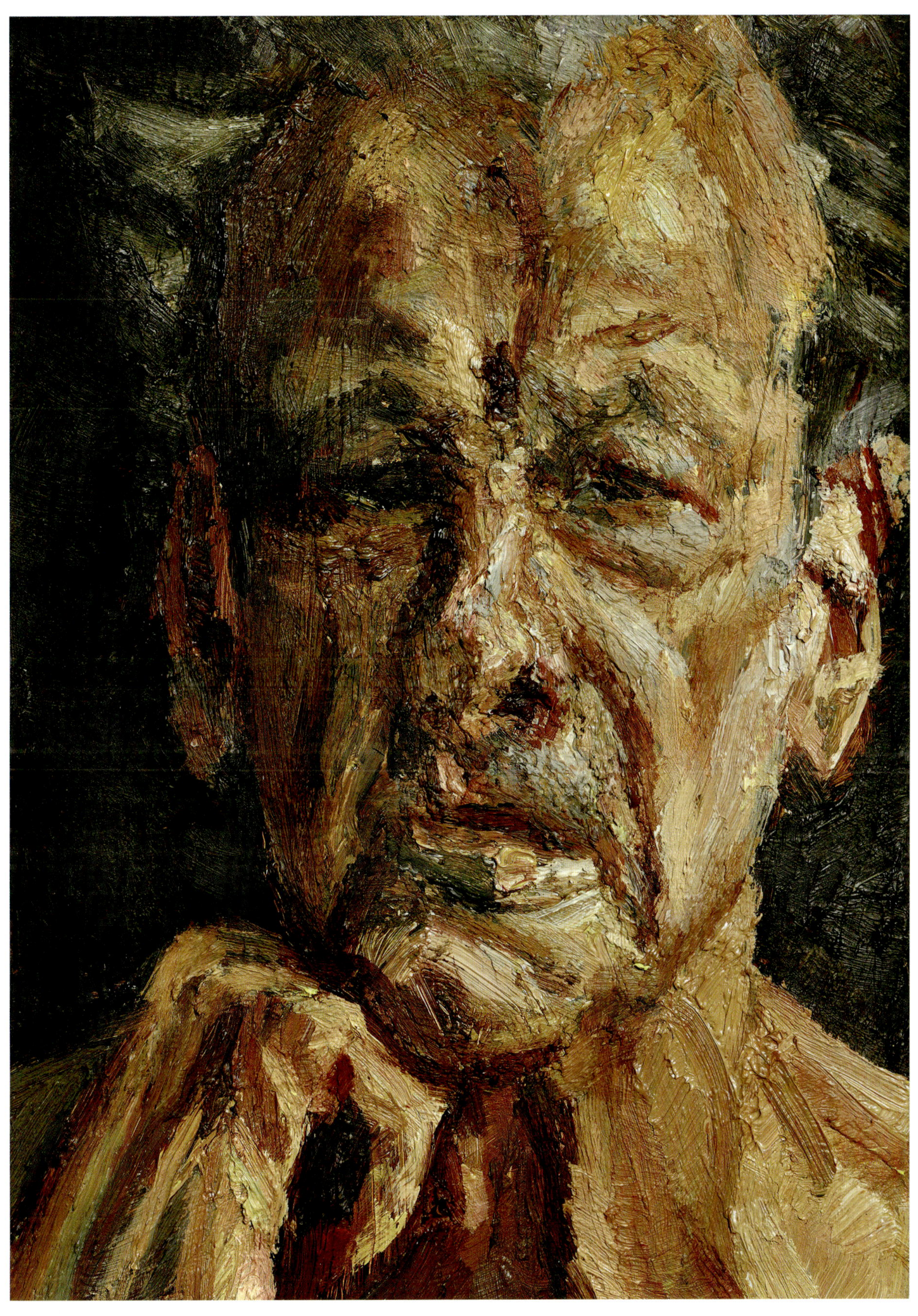

Lucian Freud
Self-Portrait Reflection, 2003

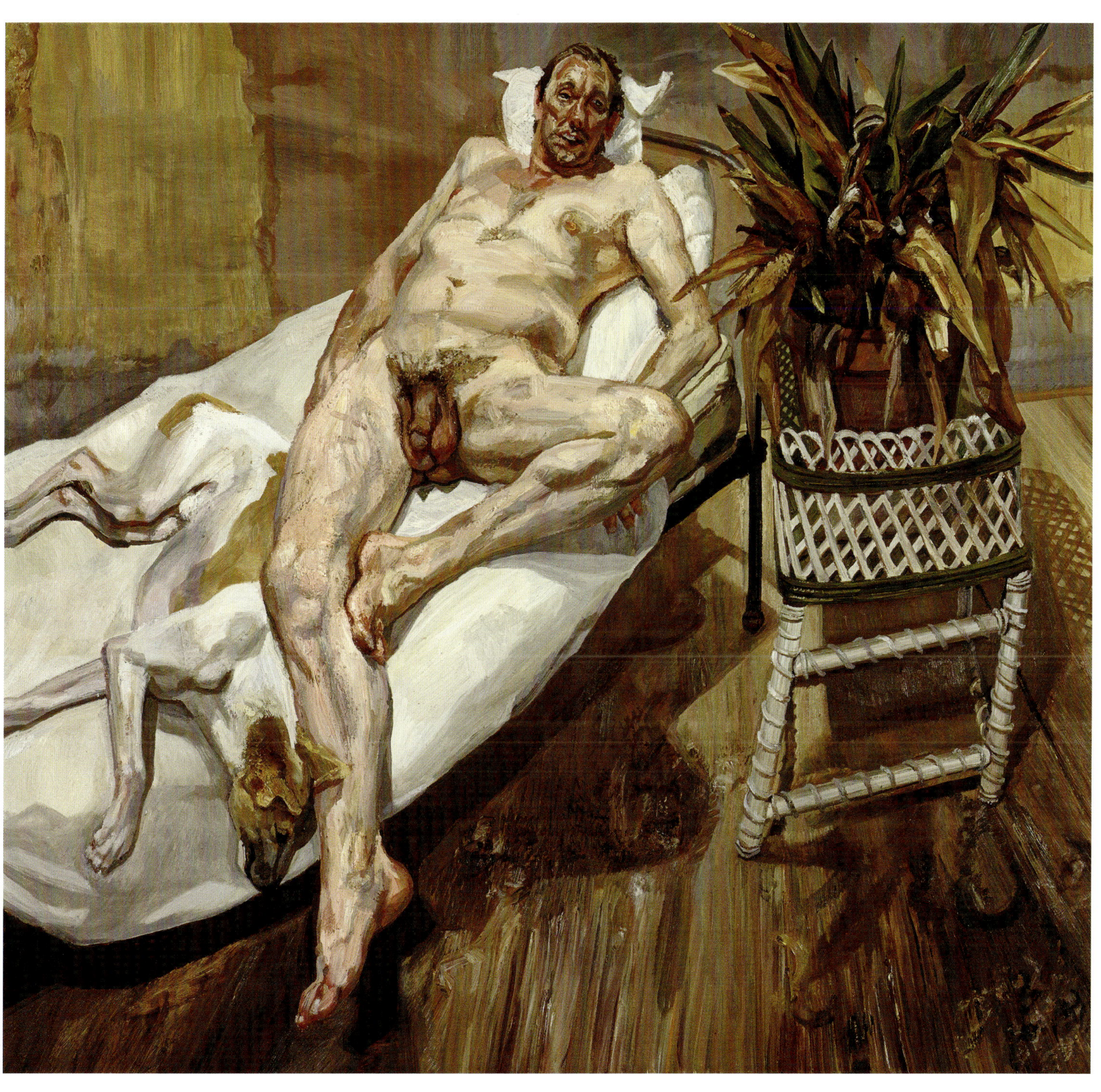

Lucian Freud
David and Eli, 2003–4

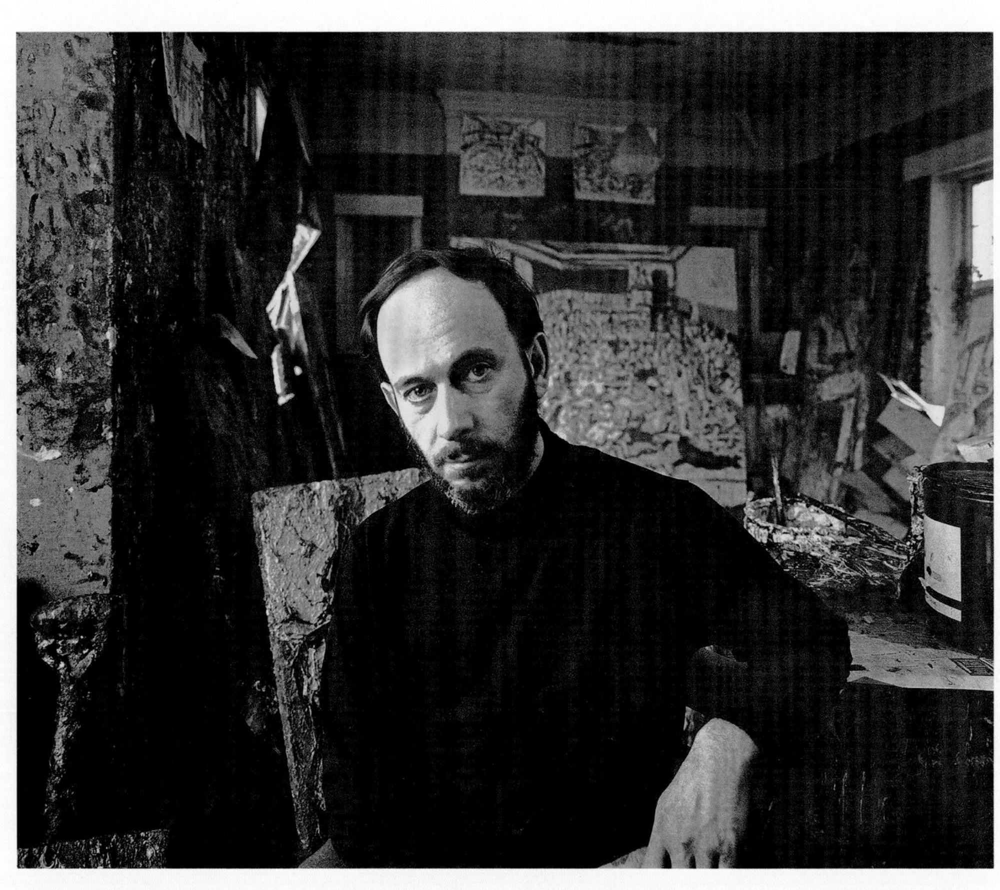

Leon Kossoff, 1972.
Children's Swimming Pool, 12 O'clock, Sunday Morning, September (1971) is partly visible behind the artist at right. Photo: Mark Gerson

LEON KOSSOFF

Leon Kossoff was born in London on December 7, 1926. His parents were first-generation Russian Jewish immigrants who ran a bakery in East London, where he spent his childhood and attended Hackney Downs School. In 1939 the school was evacuated to Norfolk, and he lived temporarily with a family, the Bishops, who encouraged his interest in art.

On his return to London in 1943 Kossoff attended life-drawing classes at Toynbee Hall and Saint Martin's School of Art, before taking up the commercial art course at Saint Martin's (1943–45). His studies were interrupted by a period of national service between 1945 and 1948, when he served in Italy, Holland, Belgium, and Germany with the Royal Fusiliers. Kossoff returned to London and studied at Saint Martin's (1949–53) and the Royal College of Art (1953–56) while also attending evening classes taught by David Bomberg at Borough Polytechnic. At Saint Martin's he met fellow student Frank Auerbach, who became a close friend. The two men sat for each other until 1957. In 1953 Kossoff married Rosalind (also known as Peggy), who would model for him consistently throughout his career, as has the painter John Lessore.

In the early 1950s Kossoff worked on paintings of St. Paul's Cathedral and city building sites, developing a painterly style with thickly applied, constantly reworked layers of paint in characteristic earth colors. He also made his first drawings and paintings of his parents, whom he continued to portray over the following decades, as in the charcoal drawing *Two Seated Figures II* (1980; p. 82) and the resulting painting, *Two Seated Figures No. 2* (1980; p. 83). Kossoff painted the same subjects at different times of the day and in different years, each time registering the specific conditions of light and changes in the surrounding conditions, in the model and in his own stance. Drawing was of primary importance, and his early drawings were intensively worked as he constantly erased and restarted the image. He was to develop a similar process in his paintings, working on board and scraping down the paint with a palette knife before reapplying it.

Kossoff joined the Beaux Arts Gallery, where he had six solo exhibitions between 1957 and 1963. Throughout the 1960s he taught at Regent Street Polytechnic, Chelsea School of Art, and Saint Martin's. He moved to a studio in Willesden Junction, on the edge of a vast industrial landscape of railway lines, where he executed numerous versions of railway subjects, made at different times of the day and year, such as *Willesden Junction, Morning in October* (1971; p. 79). These pictures bring to the fore light, space, movement, and vistas, encapsulating the painter's fascination with the pulsating life and material force of the railway system. Kossoff has continued to paint a close circle of family and friends, producing pictures in which their presence acquires a solid, material presence, similar to that of the buildings and streets of London, which he has also continually returned to, taking his immediate surroundings as his inspiration.

In 1967 Kossoff began to make drawings of the local swimming pool while his young son David was taking swimming lessons. This led to a series of paintings, including *Children's Swimming Pool, Autumn Afternoon* (1971; p. 78), which mark a transformation in his expansive treatment of space, lightness of handling, and more sparing use of paint, as well as a gradual move away from earth colors toward a wide variety of brighter colors. These paintings are part of a large number of "crowd scenes" painted over the years, in which Kossoff masterfully creates a sense of space while bringing together multiple forms within a single picture.

In the mid-1970s Kossoff began to paint the Kilburn Underground station, focusing on the elevated railway bridge, the people and traffic on surrounding roads, and the entrance to the station, as in *Booking Hall, Kilburn Underground* (1987; p. 84). These large-scale scenes typically relied on extensive charcoal drawings made on location, recording the changing light and mood. The unidealized nude also assumed a greater importance, and he began to paint his long-standing model Fidelma at this time, concentrating on the movement and presence of the figure.

In 1987 Kossoff began a series of paintings of the imposing Christ Church, Spitalfields, which he worked on until 1994. Initially he employed a square format in which the spire is depicted at close range and severely foreshortened, before exploring other viewpoints and the unique quality of the building in different light and weather conditions, as in *Christ Church, Spitalfields, Morning* (1990; p. 85). Paintings of the Embankment Underground station followed, with the artist concentrating on a flower stall at the entrance and the crowds of Londoners entering and leaving the station.

Kossoff represented Britain at the centenary edition of the Venice Biennale in 1995, and a major exhibition at Tate Gallery followed in 1996. In 2000 exhibitions of Kossoff's drawings and paintings after Nicolas Poussin were presented at the J. Paul Getty Museum, the Los Angeles County Museum of Art, and the National Gallery of Australia, Canberra. Kossoff had drawn since childhood from the old masters in the National Gallery, London, and his love for their work has remained a constant, as they connect to realms of invention and composition that are a continuous source of fascination and provide a link to the past. In 2007 *Leon Kossoff: Drawing from Painting* at the National Gallery, London, brought together more than sixty paintings, drawings, and prints made after works by Cézanne, Constable, Degas, Goya, Poussin, Rembrandt, Rubens, Titian, Velázquez, and Veronese.

Since 2008 Kossoff has produced an ongoing series of charcoal and pastel drawings of Arnold Circus, on the Boundary Estate in East London—recording dog walkers, cyclists, and women with prams throughout the changing seasons—as well as making drawings and paintings of the cherry tree in his own garden. These works were shown in the exhibition *Leon Kossoff: London Landscapes* at Annely Juda Fine Art, London, and L.A. Louver, Los Angeles, in 2013–14.

Kossoff continues to live and work in London.

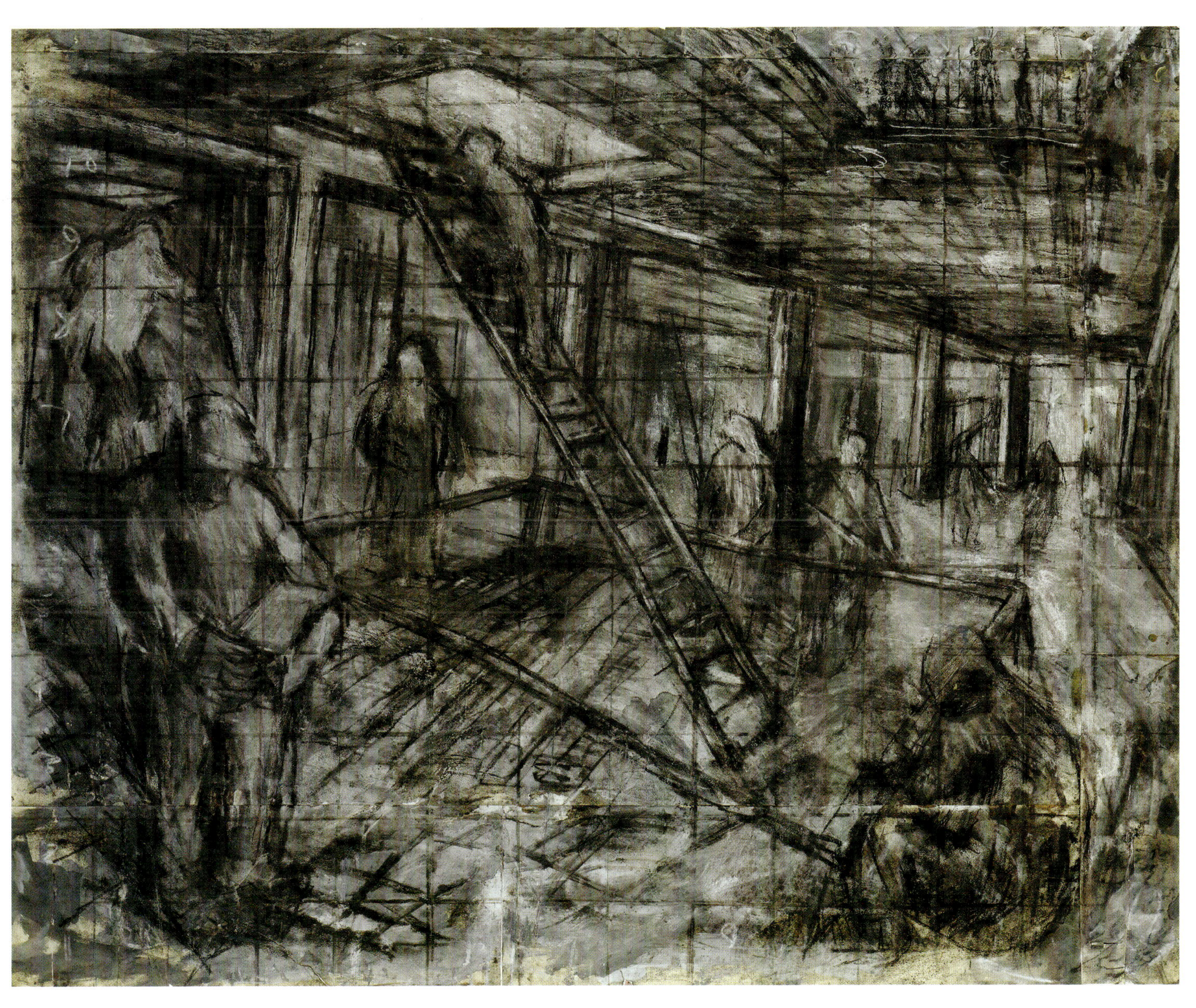

Leon Kossoff

Building Site, Oxford Street, 1952

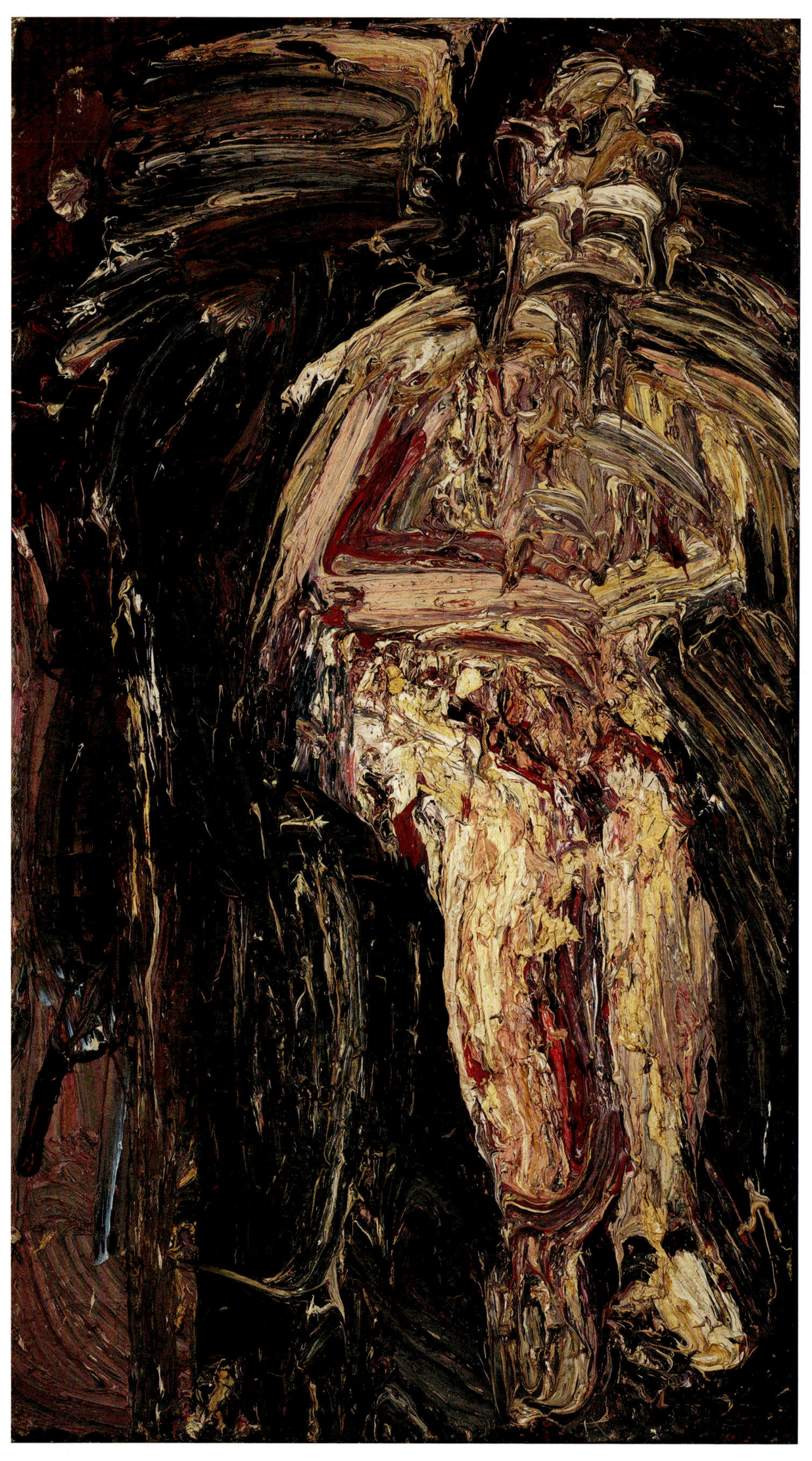

Leon Kossoff
Man in a Wheelchair, 1959–62

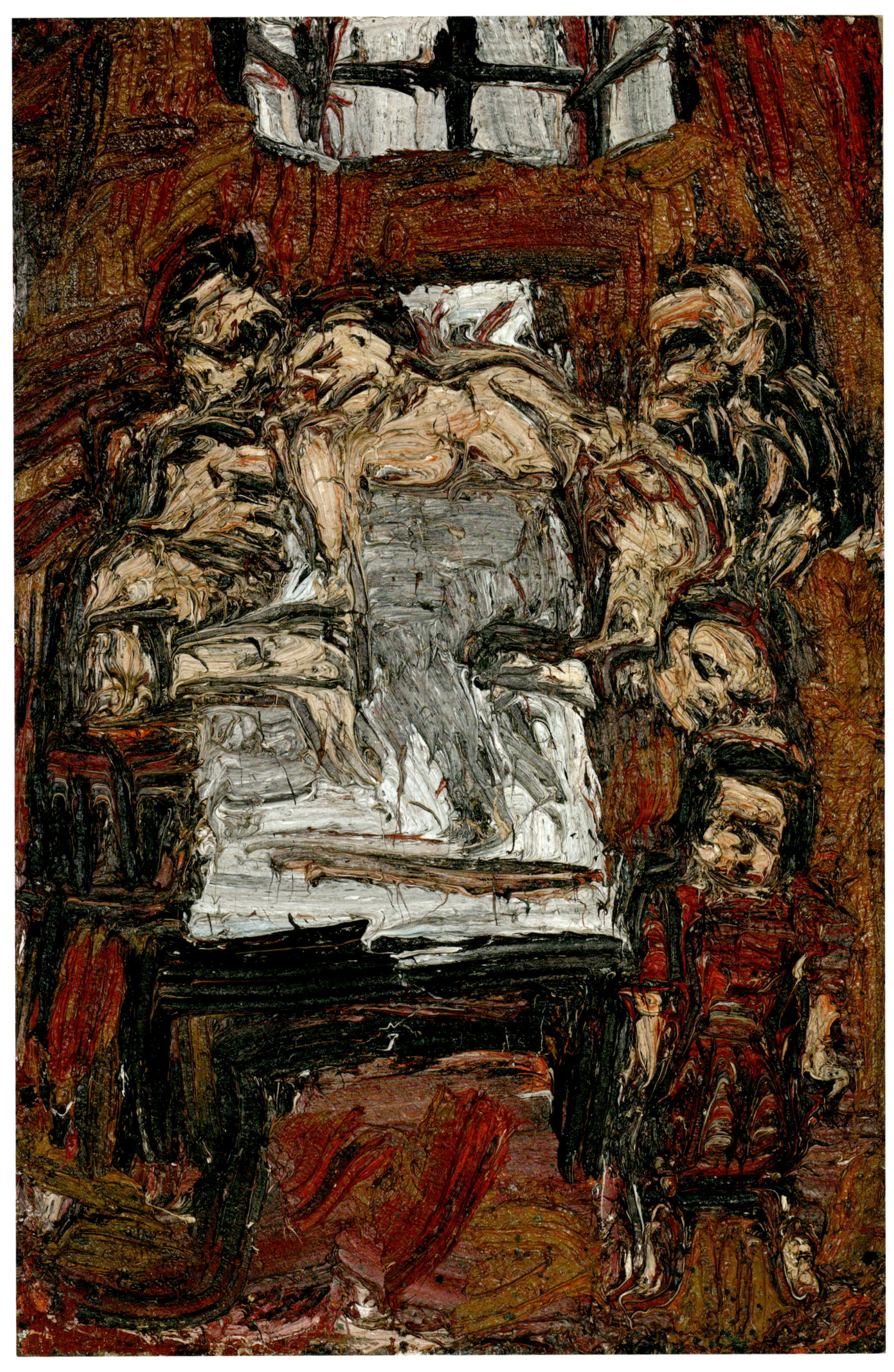

Leon Kossoff

Woman III in Bed, Surrounded by Family, 1965

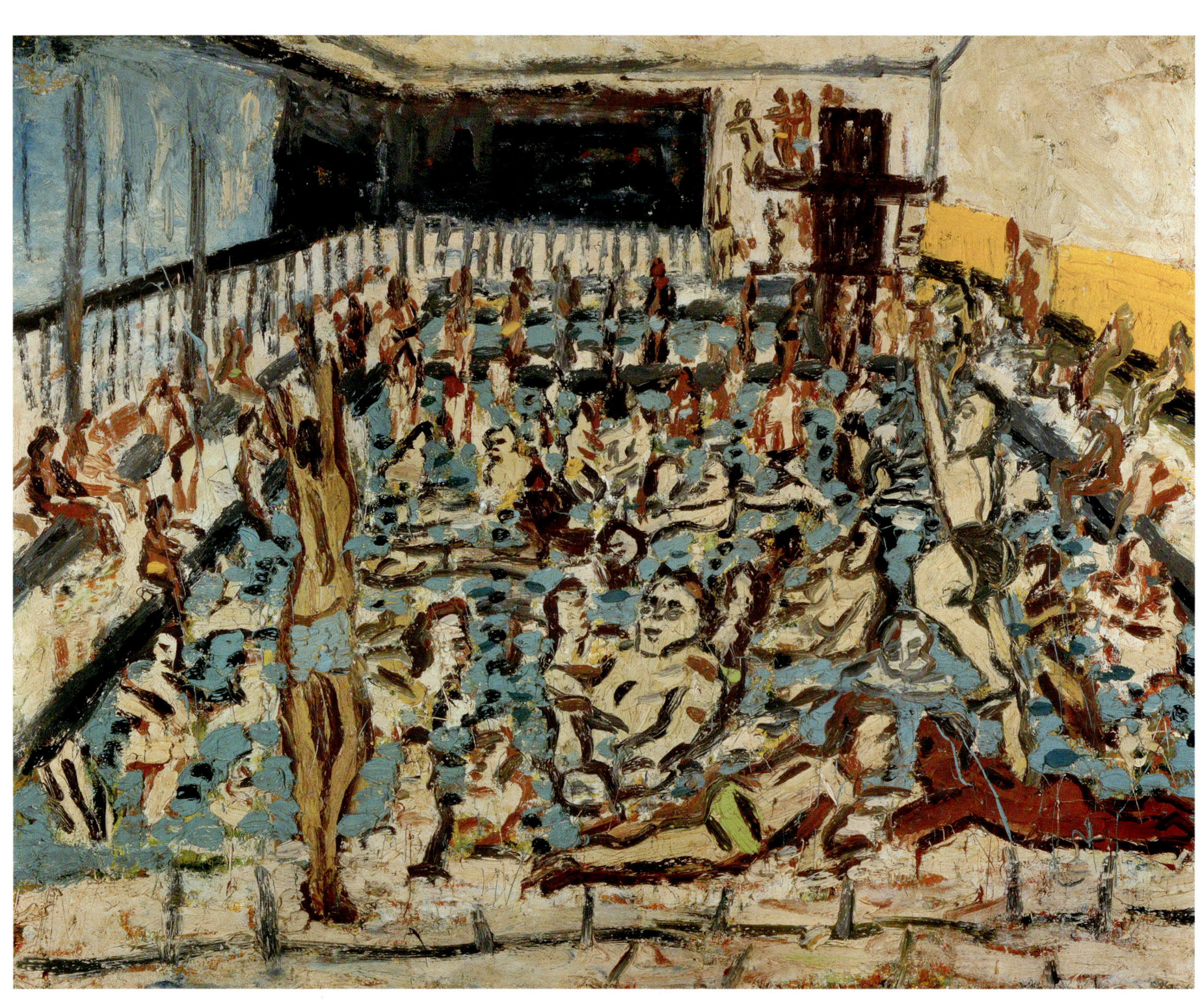

Leon Kossoff

Children's Swimming Pool, Autumn Afternoon, 1971

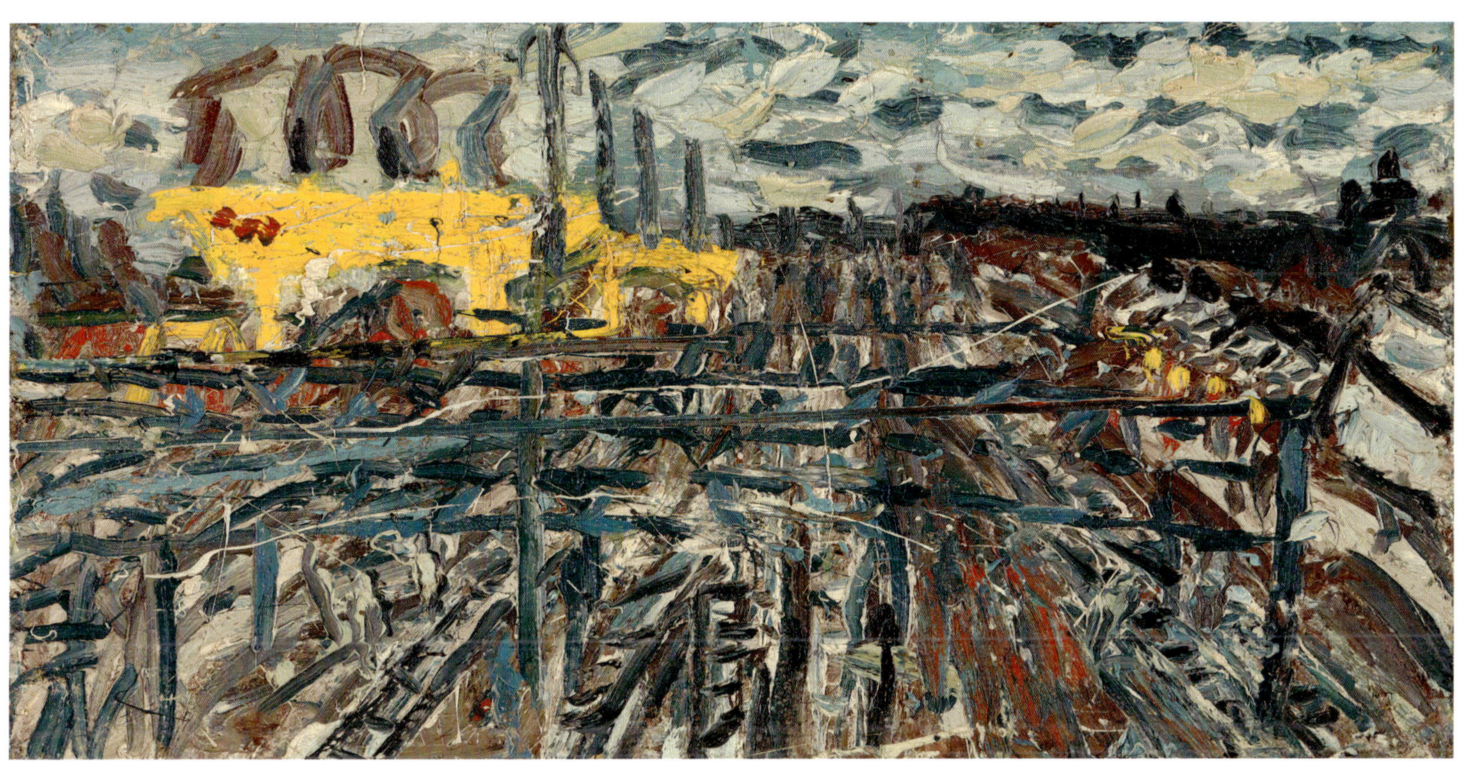

Leon Kossoff
Willesden Junction, Morning in October, 1971

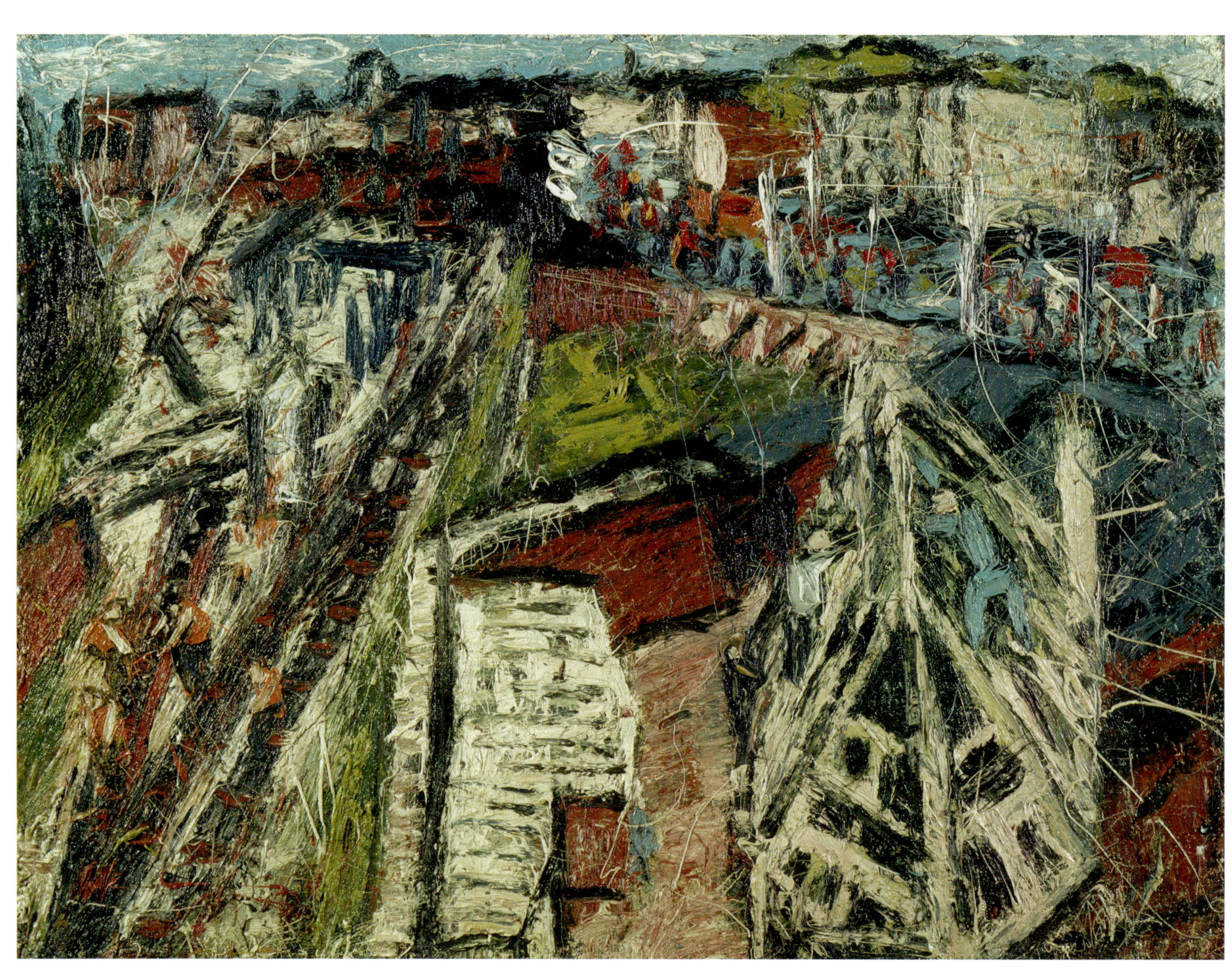

Leon Kossoff

Demolition of the Old House, Dalston Junction, Summer 1974, 1974

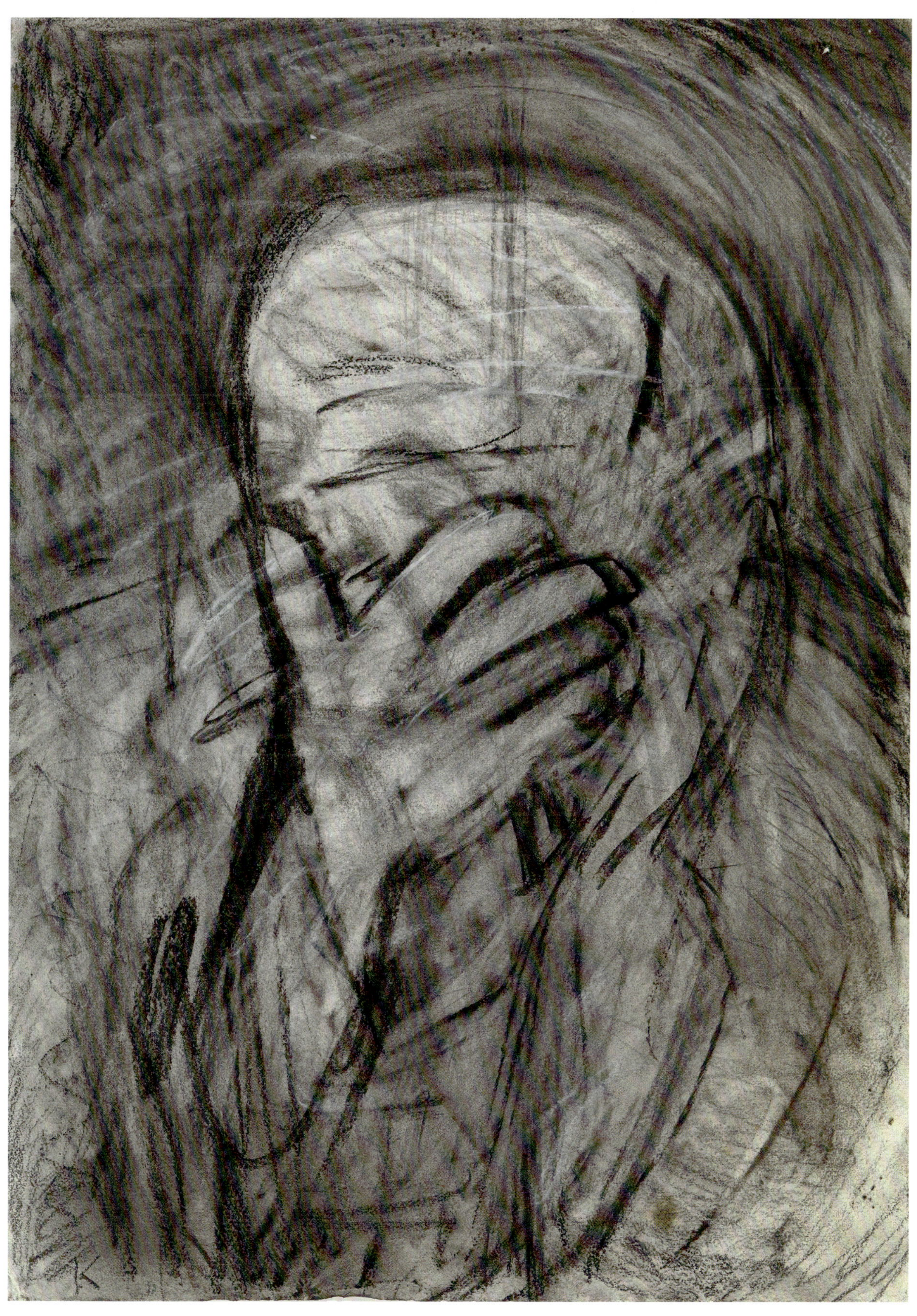

Leon Kossoff
Father Resting, 1977

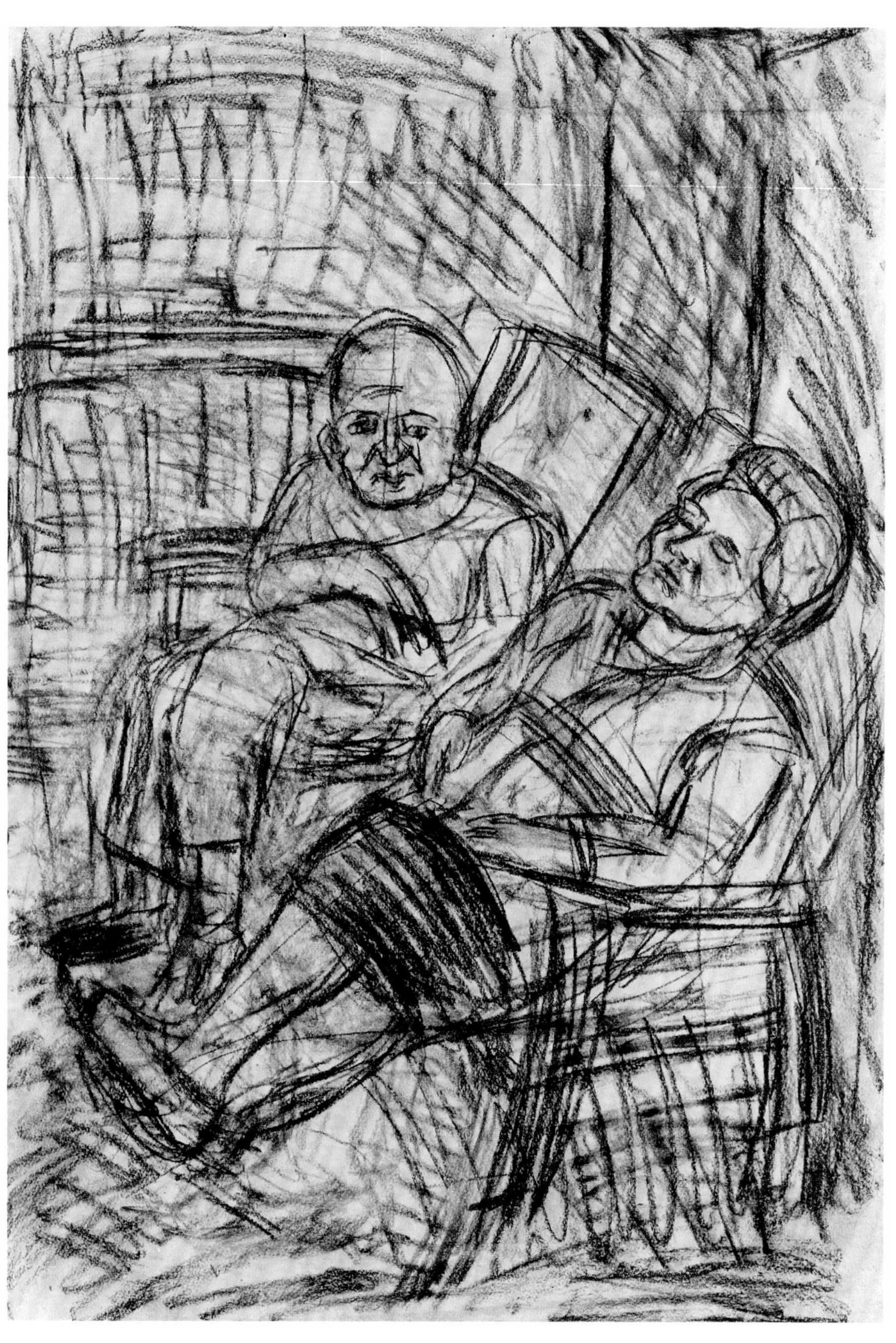

Leon Kossoff
Two Seated Figures II, 1980

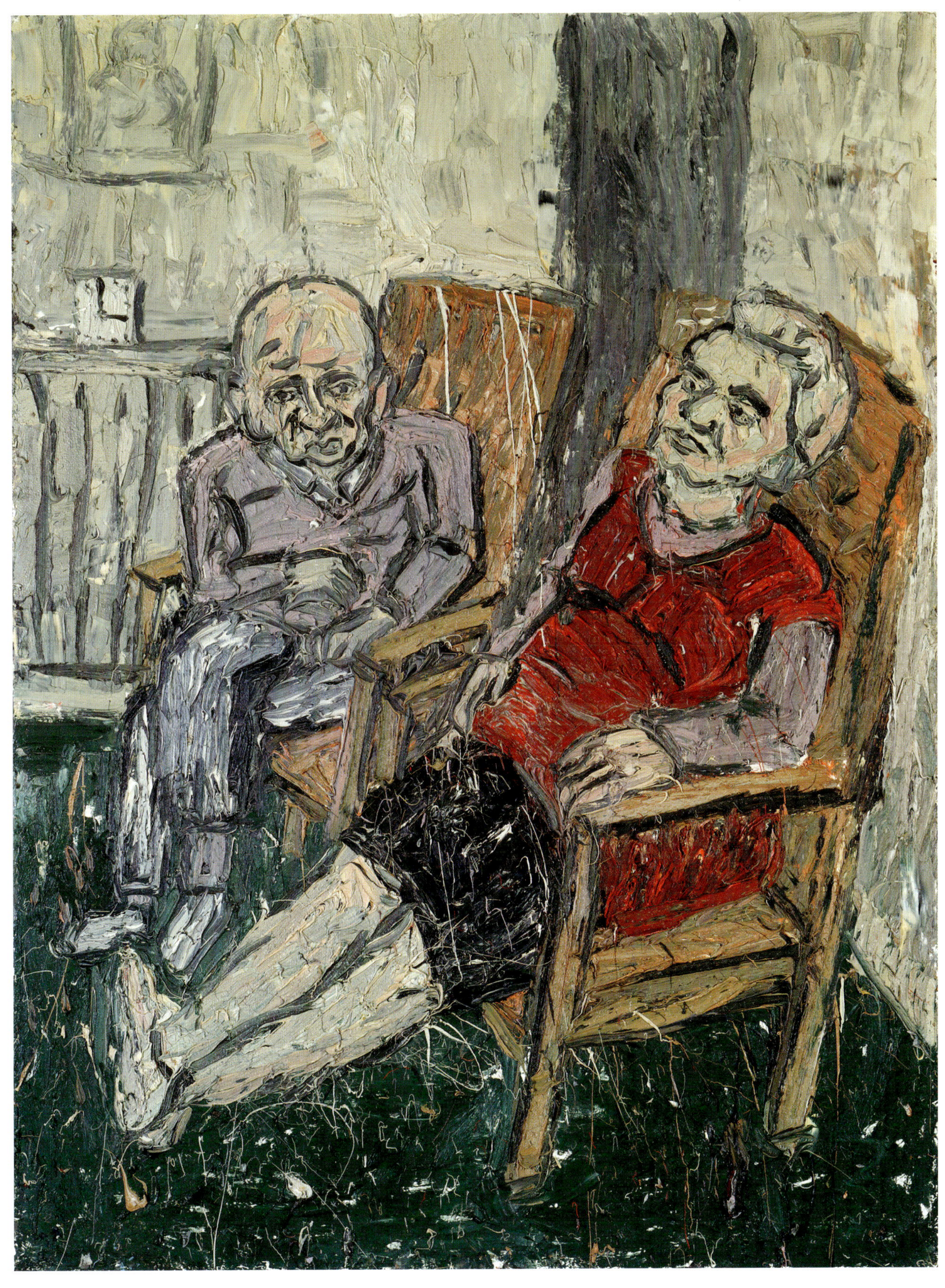

Leon Kossoff

Two Seated Figures No. 2, 1980

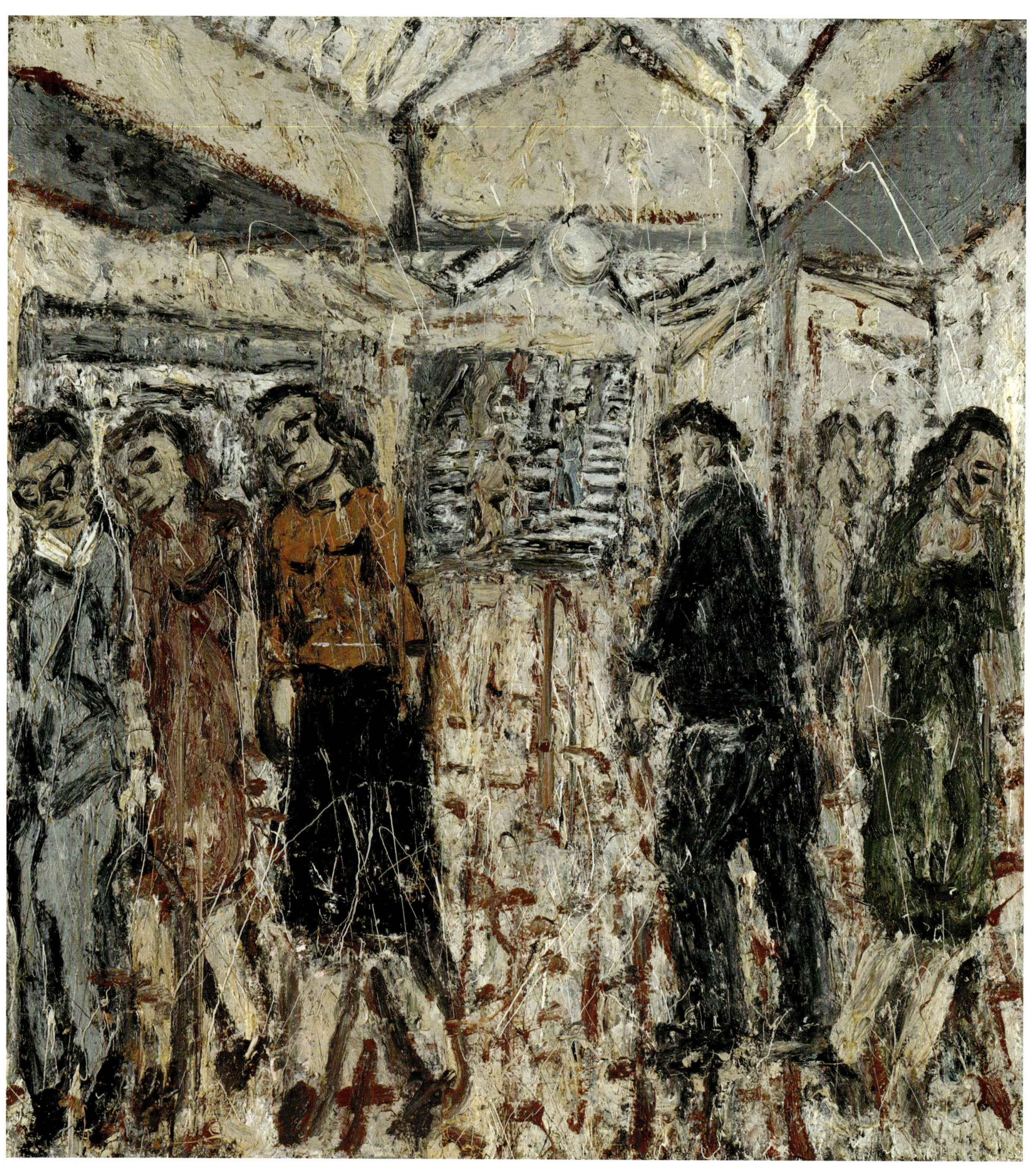

Leon Kossoff

Booking Hall, Kilburn Underground, 1987

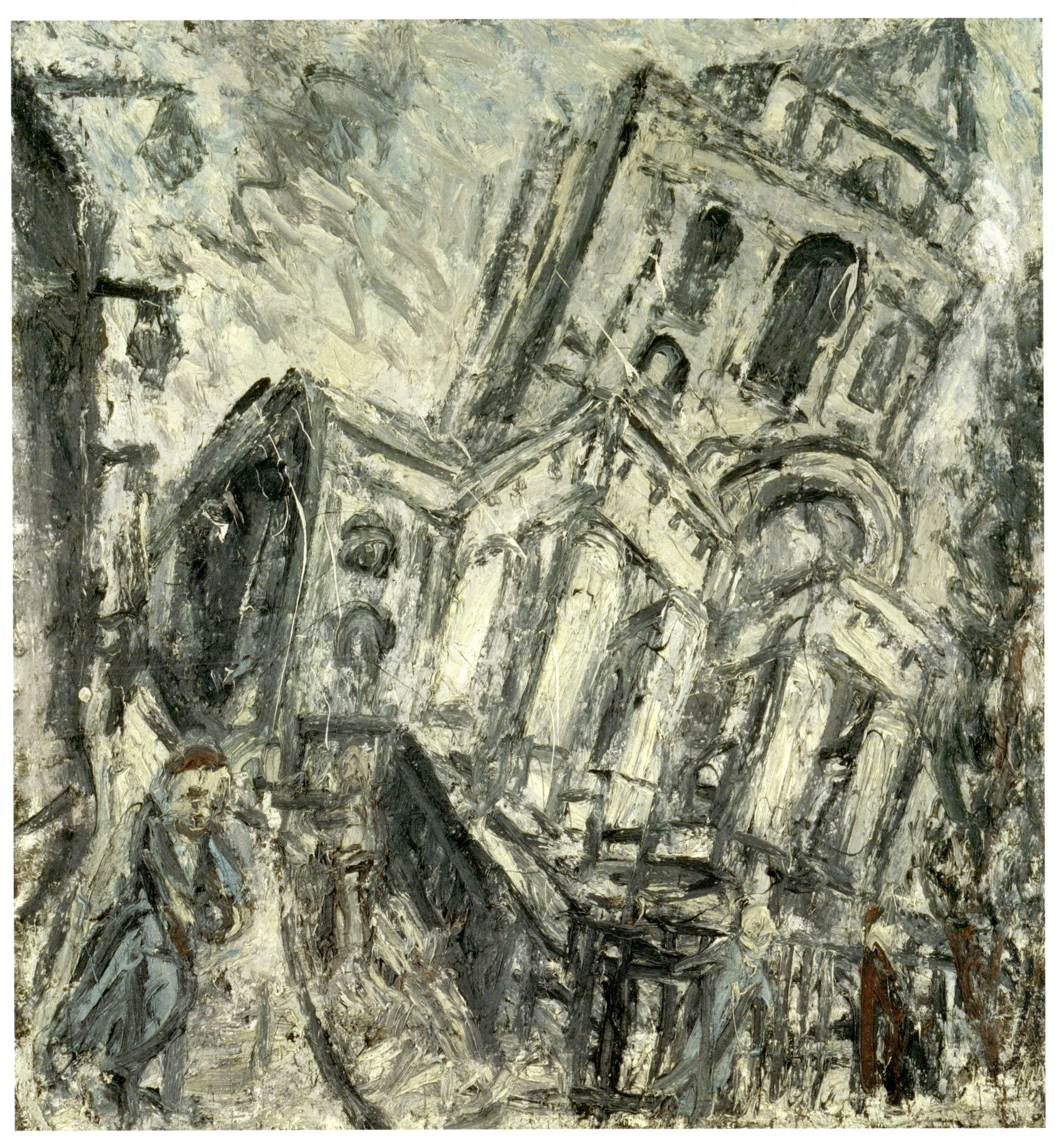

Leon Kossoff

Christ Church, Spitalfields, Morning, 1990

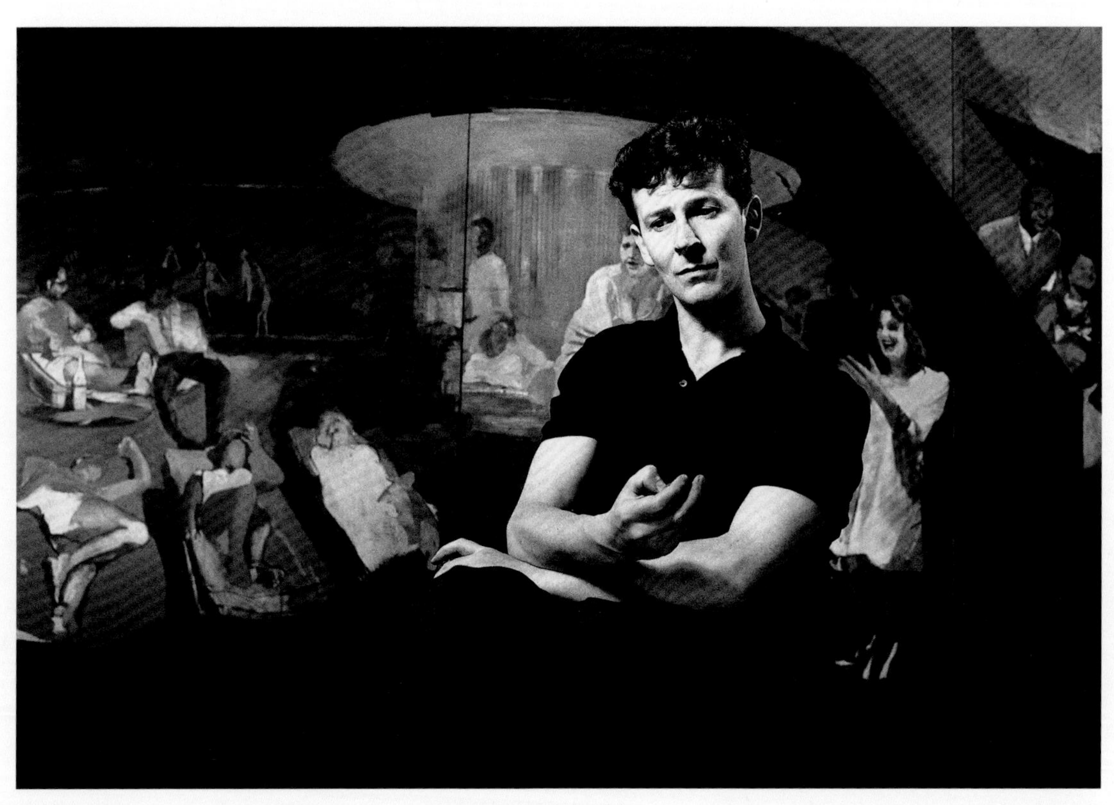

Michael Andrews, 1963.
All Night Long (1963–64) is in progress in the background.
Photo: Jorge Lewinski

MICHAEL ANDREWS

Michael Andrews was born in Norwich on October 30, 1928. His mother, Gertrude, and his father, Thomas, an agent with a local life insurance society, were devout Methodists. During his last year of school he attended Saturday morning classes at Norwich School of Art, studying oil painting under Frank William Leslie Davenport.

On leaving school in 1947, Andrews undertook a period of national service, the last nineteen months of which he spent in Egypt. Returning to England in 1949, he enrolled at the Slade School of Fine Art, where he was taught by William Coldstream, Lucian Freud, and William Townsend. Two paintings made in response to a student assignment set by Coldstream—*August for the People* (1951; University College London), which won second prize in the Slade Summer Competition, and *A Man Who Suddenly Fell Over* (1952; p. 88)—marked the beginning of his interest in the subject of human behavior and self-consciousness.

In 1953 Andrews was awarded the Rome Scholarship but returned to Britain after six months, unable to settle in Italy. The same year he participated in two group exhibitions in London, *Four Young Artists*, at the Beaux Arts Gallery, and *Young Painters*, at the Institute of Contemporary Arts. His first solo exhibition was presented at the Beaux Arts Gallery in 1958. During this period he concentrated on portraits of his friends and contemporaries, including the artist John Lessore, as well as party scenes, developing his characteristic combination of meticulous observation with imaginative elements and implied narrative.

In 1960 he began working on *The Family in the Garden* (1960–62; Lisbon, Fundação Calouste Gulbenkian), at the time his largest and most ambitious composition to date. This work signaled a transition from his interest in the individual to more complex studies of social interactions and group dynamics. The following year Andrews returned to London, where his social circle included Frank Auerbach, Francis Bacon, Peter Blake, Lucian Freud, and David Hockney. He made two paintings of the Colony Room, a Soho drinking club frequented by the group. *Colony Room I* (1962; p. 2) features portraits of Bacon and Freud among the crowd. The subject of the social gathering as a theatrical and dramatic device, in which people perform and are judged, continued to occupy Andrews throughout the 1960s. He painted further party scenes from both recollection and imagination, incorporating portraits of people he knew and drawing imagery from the media, fashion, pop music, literature, and cinema. The color supplement to the *Sunday Times* (launched in 1962) became a key source of topical photographs and glossy advertising images.

Between 1958 and 1966 Andrews taught at Norwich School of Art, Chelsea College of Art, and the Slade, where his colleagues included Harold Cohen and R. B. Kitaj. He met his wife, June Keeley, during this period, and their daughter, Melanie, was born in 1970. The same year he completed the first of seven distinctive paintings in the series Lights (1970–75; p. 91), which addressed his personal and philosophical concern with self-consciousness, conceiving of the floating gas balloon as a symbol of the ego. Scenes of cityscapes, ocean liners, piers, and bridges are depicted from an aerial perspective and realized in thin layers of acrylic paint, applied with a spray gun. The last four paintings in the series were exhibited at the Anthony d'Offay Gallery, London, in 1974. Lights was followed in the late 1970s by School, a series of brightly colored paintings of fish, which returned to the theme of group behavior and social conformity.

In 1975 Andrews made the first of many regular holidays to Glenartney, in Perthshire, Scotland. It was there, in the summer of 1976, that the photographer Jean-Loup Cornet took a picture of the artist swimming with his daughter. Andrews liked the photograph so much that years later he decided to base a painting on it: *Melanie and Me Swimming* (1978–79; p. 92). He included the rocks above the pool, which did not appear in the photograph, painting them from memory. While in Glenartney he participated in deerstalking. Over the next decade he made twenty-five paintings of deer hunts in the vast highland landscape. Throughout this series, which he titled Holiday, he sought to emphasize the relationship between humankind and the environment.

A retrospective was organized by the Arts Council in 1980–81 at the Hayward Gallery, London; the Fruitmarket Gallery, Edinburgh; and the Whitworth Gallery, Manchester. In 1977 he moved to East Anglia, first living in Suffolk and then, beginning in 1981, in the village of Saxlingham Nethergate, near Norwich, where he worked on two versions of the village green, titled *SAX A.D. 832* (first version 1982; second version 1983). After a trip to Uluru (also known as Ayers Rock), in central Australia, in 1983, he produced several panoramic landscapes exploring the vast scale and spiritual significance of the site, which is sacred to the Anangu Aboriginal people. The works reflect his interest in landscapes imprinted with human history and experience. In some of these paintings, such as *Permanent Water Mutidjula, by the Kunia Massif (Maggie Springs, Ayers Rock)* (1985–86; private collection), he mixed soil taken from the area into the paint. A traveling exhibition dedicated to the Ayers Rock series and other landscapes was organized by the Whitechapel Art Gallery in 1991.

Between 1988 and 1993 Andrews worked on a series of portraits, beginning with a self-portrait. Andrews moved back to London in 1992 and began a series of studies of the Thames while convalescing from cancer treatment. The third of his four Thames paintings, *Thames Painting, the Estuary* (1994–95; p. 93), combined photographs taken by the artist with visual references to various sites spanning one hundred years. It was his last finished painting. Andrews died in London on July 19, 1995.

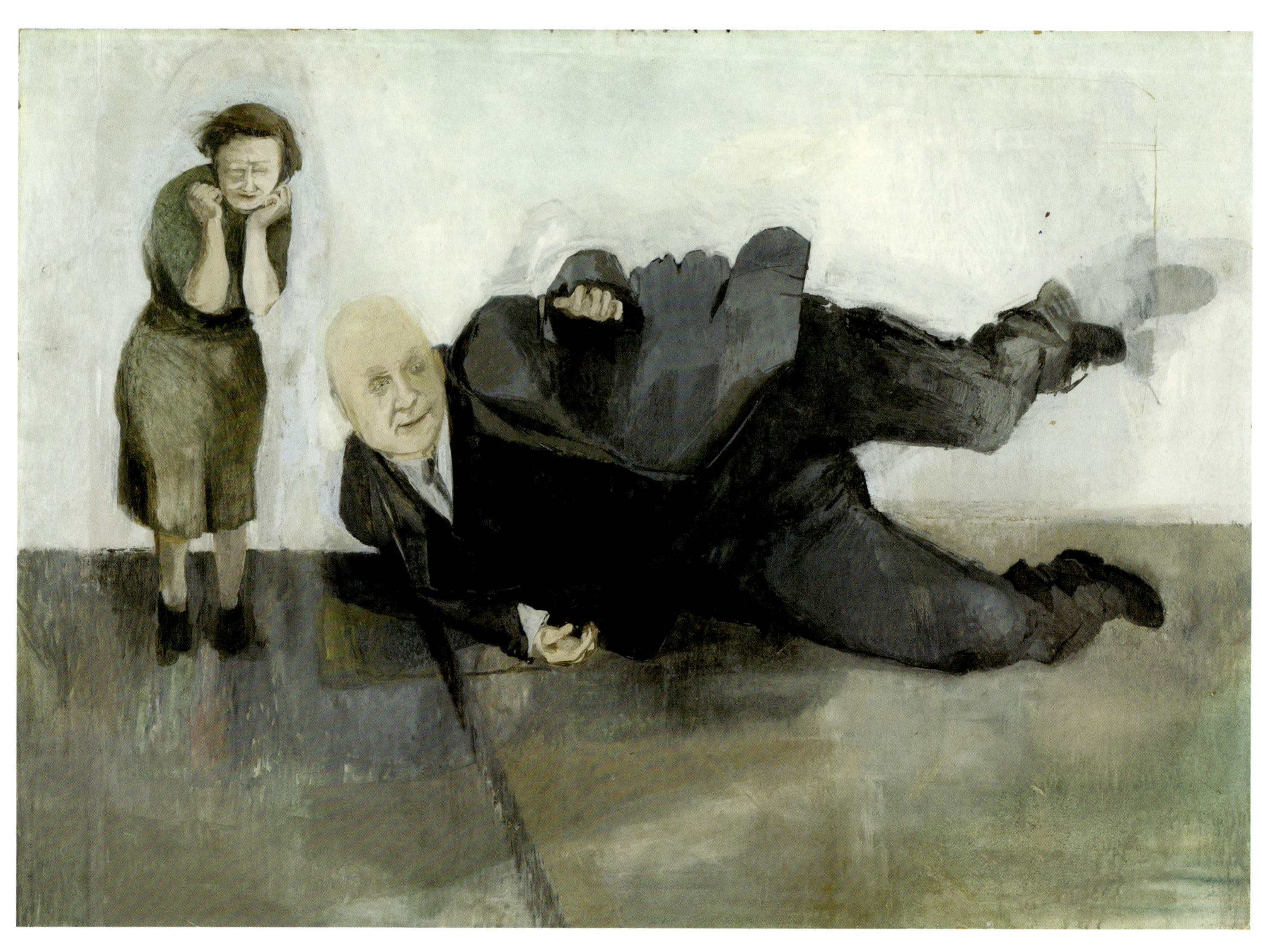

Michael Andrews

A Man Who Suddenly Fell Over, 1952

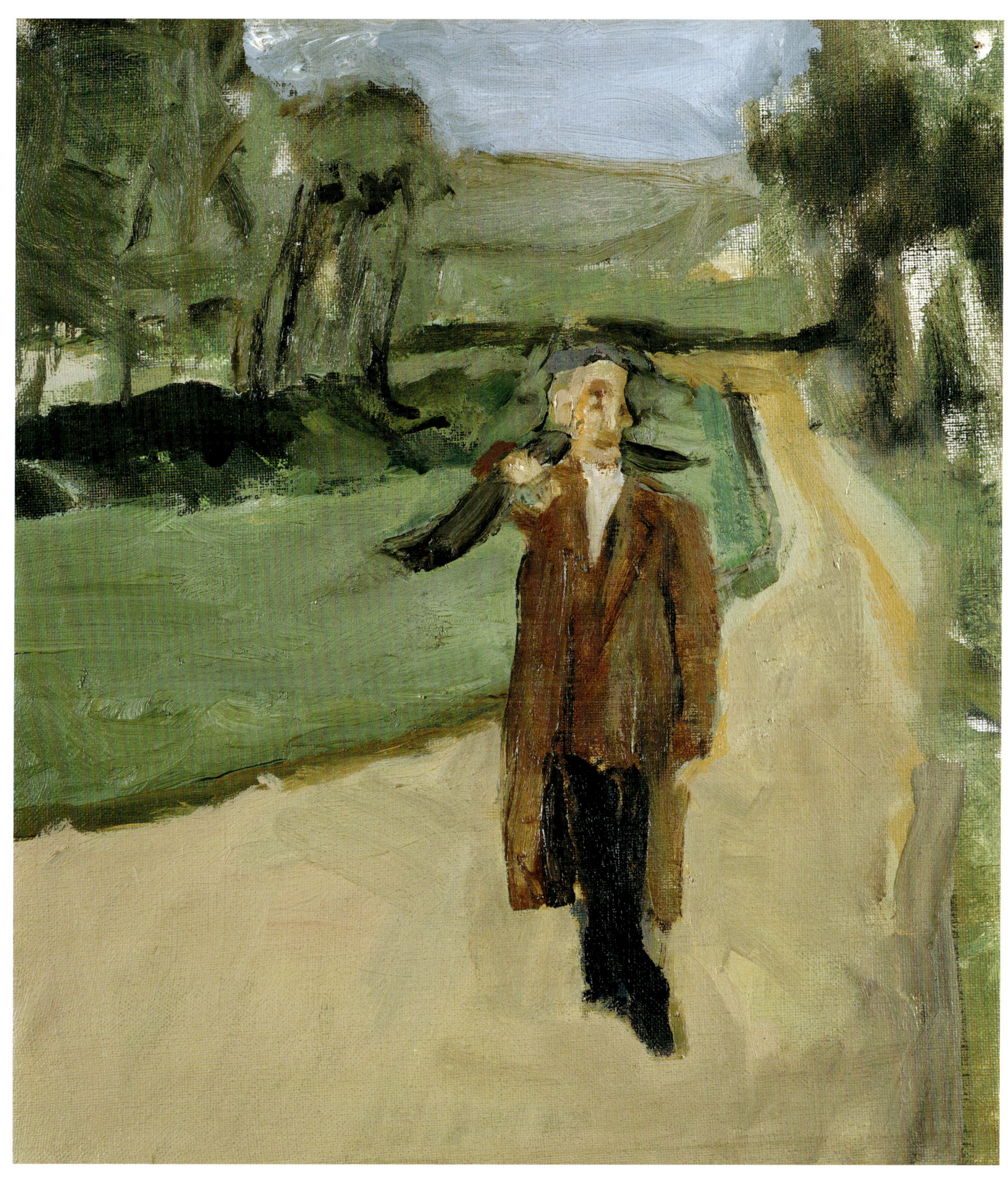

Michael Andrews
Study for a Man in a Landscape (Digswell), 1959

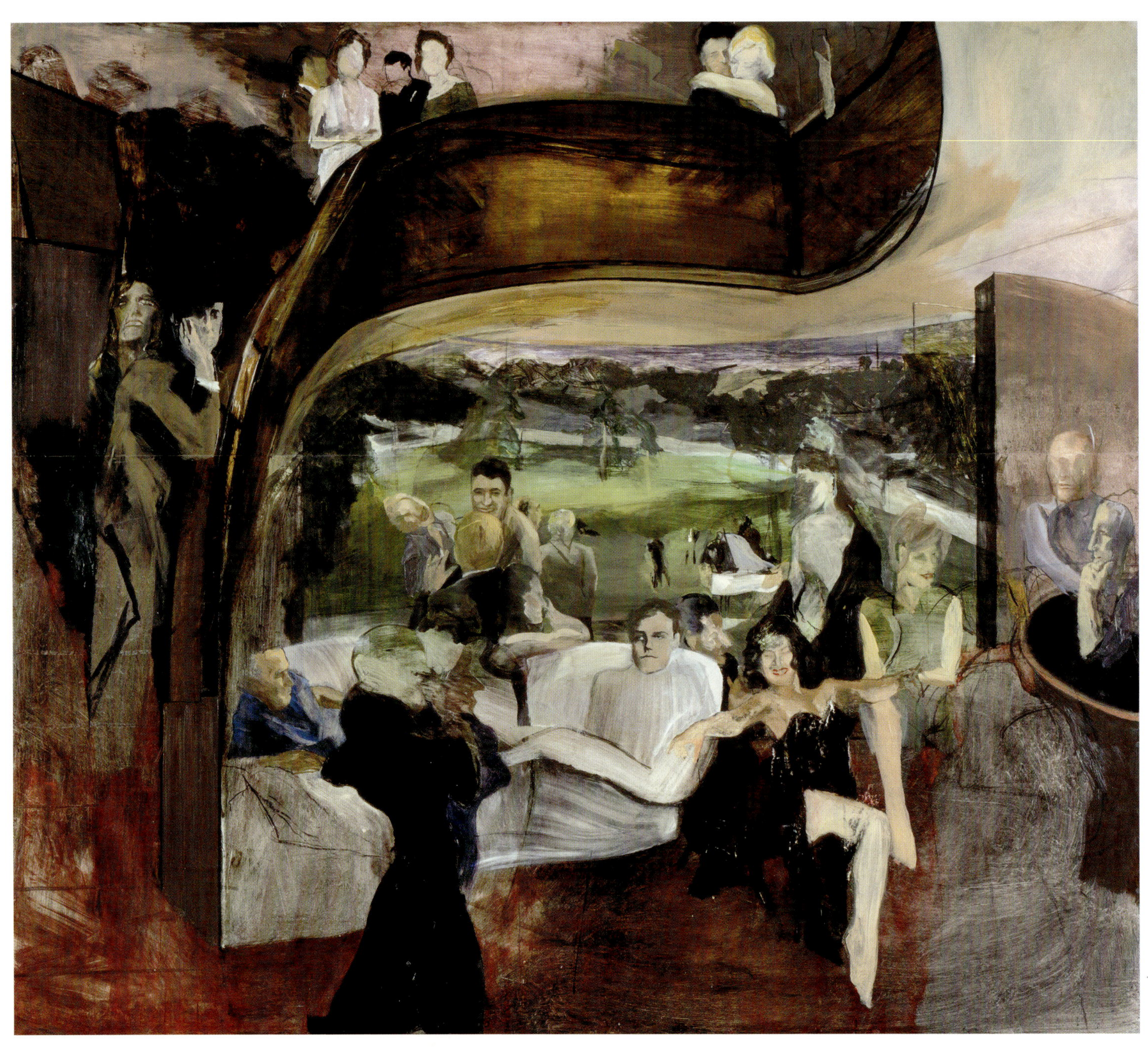

Michael Andrews
The Deer Park, 1962

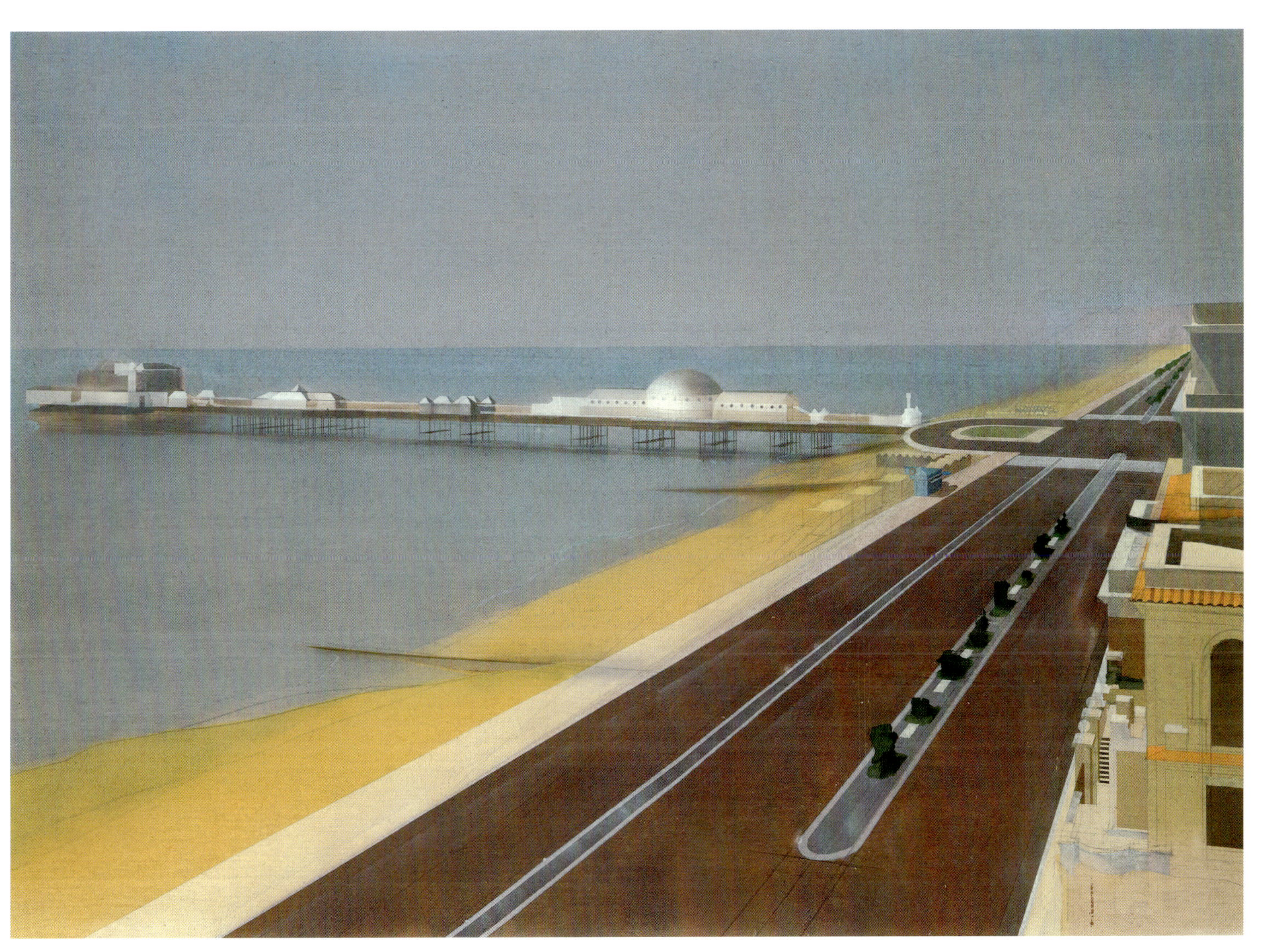

Michael Andrews
Lights IV: The Pier and the Road, 1973

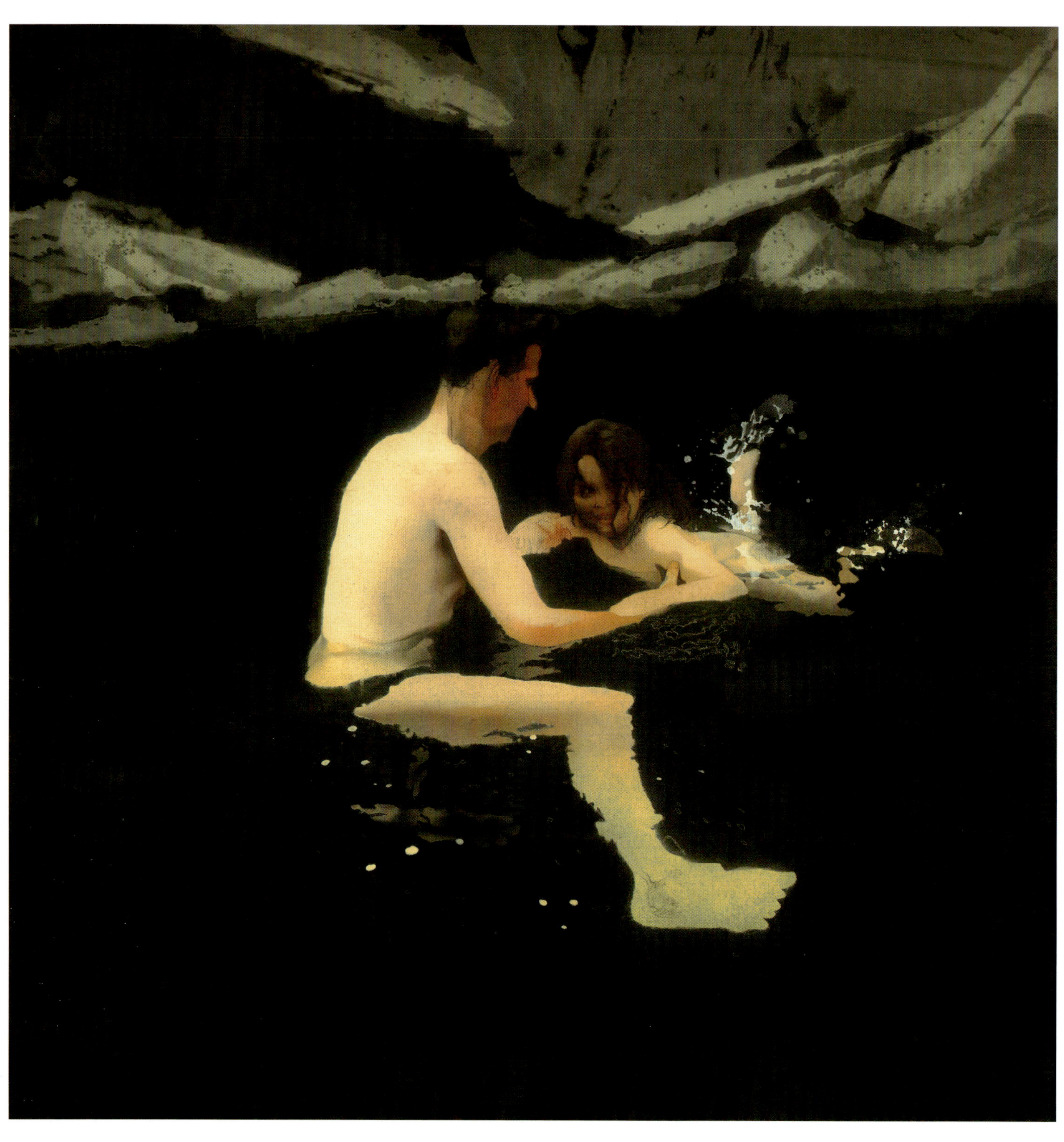

Michael Andrews
Melanie and Me Swimming, 1978–79

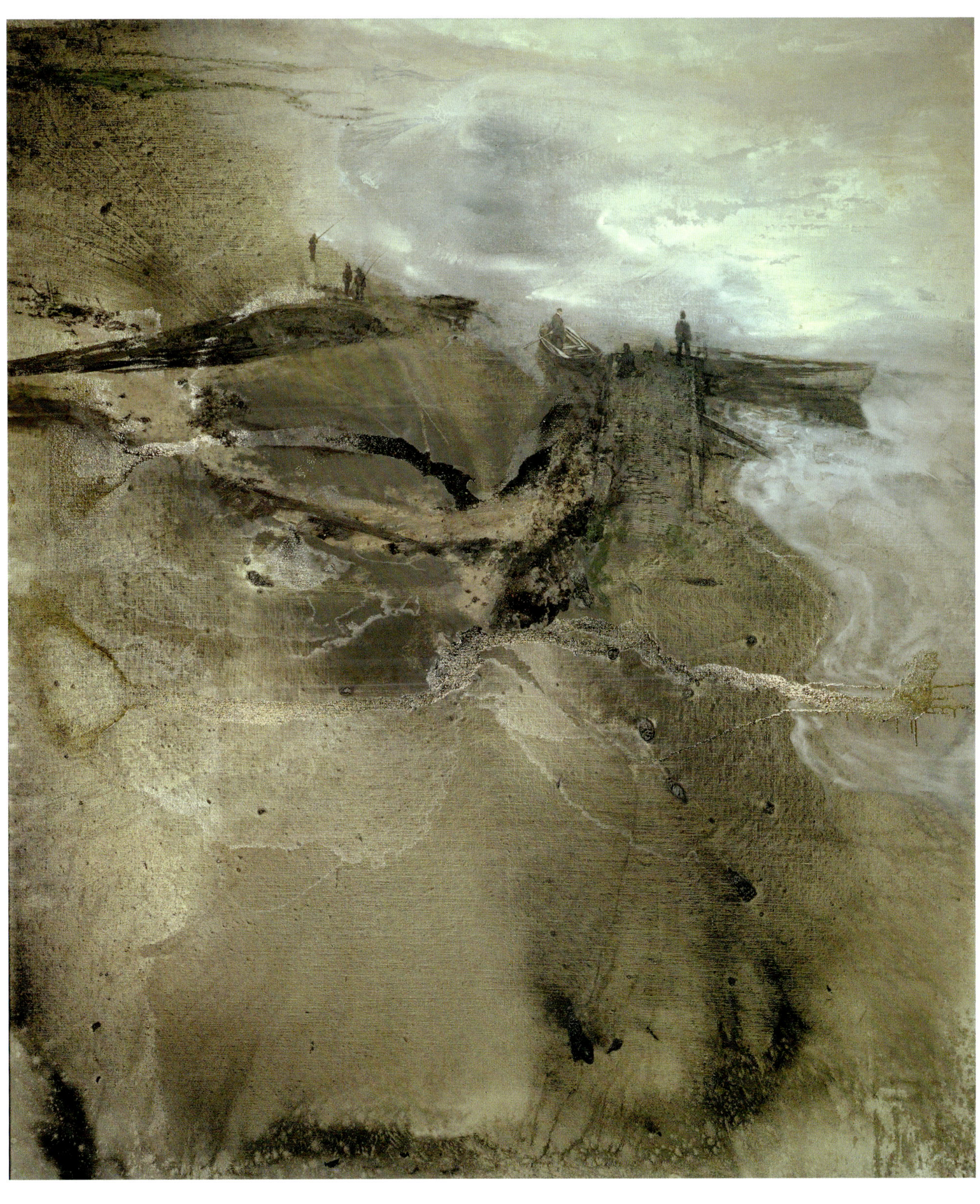

Michael Andrews
Thames Painting, the Estuary, 1994–95

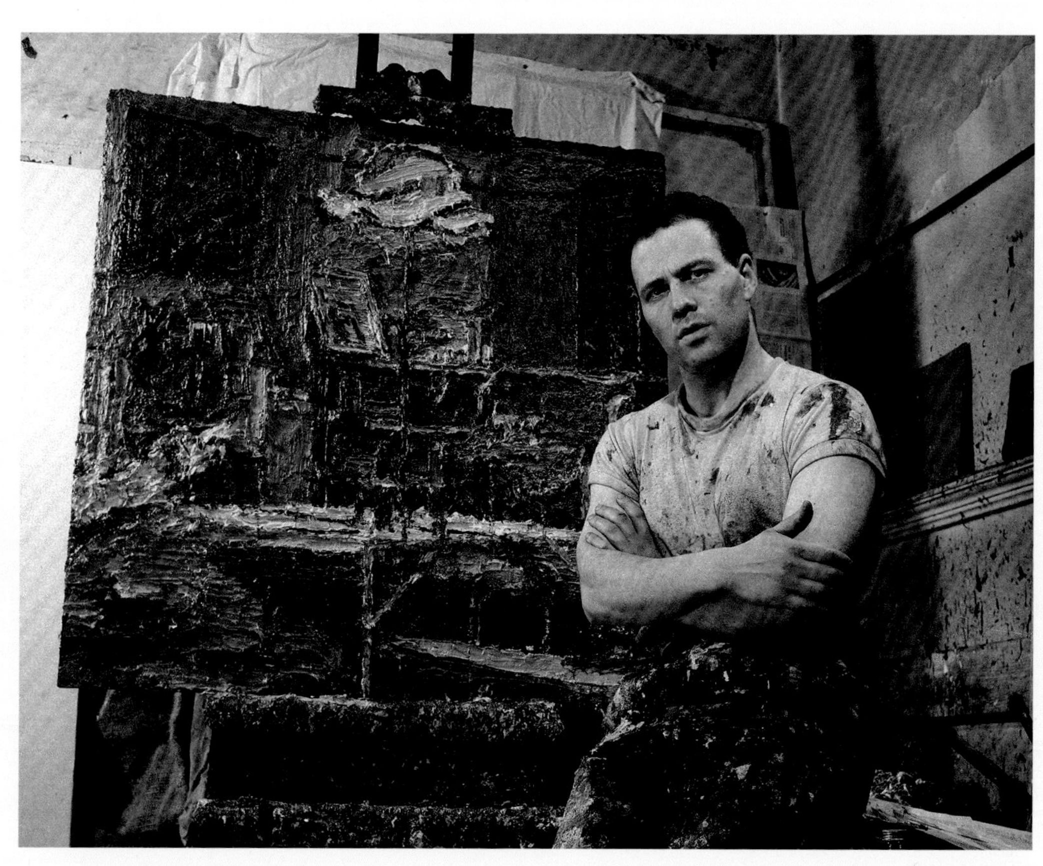

Frank Auerbach, 1963.
The Sitting Room (1964) is in
progress in the background.
Photo: Jorge Lewinski

FRANK AUERBACH

Frank Auerbach was born in Berlin on April 29, 1931, to Jewish parents. His father, Max Auerbach, was a lawyer and his mother, Charlotte Nora Auerbach, a former art student. In April 1939, just before his eighth birthday, Auerbach was sent to England to escape Nazism under the sponsorship of the writer Iris Origo. He attended the Bunce Court School, near Faversham, in Kent, which was evacuated to Shropshire during the war. It was a boarding school for both English children and Jewish refugees. His parents remained behind in Germany and later died in the concentration camps.

On leaving school, Auerbach moved to London and studied full-time at Borough Polytechnic in 1948, before beginning at Saint Martin's School of Art (1948–52) and the Royal College of Art (1952–55). He then attended evening classes at Borough Polytechnic with David Bomberg, who encouraged students to pursue intense expressions "stripped of all irrelevant matter." During this period Auerbach developed a friendship with fellow student Leon Kossoff. In 1954 Auerbach moved to Kossoff's former studio in Mornington Crescent, Camden Town, where he has worked ever since.

While studying painting, Auerbach also performed in small theaters in London. At the age of seventeen he met Estella (Stella) Olive West while they were both acting in a production of Peter Ustinov's *House of Regrets* at the Torch Theatre. He moved into the basement room of her house in Earl's Court, and she began to pose for him. Referred to as E.O.W. in his titles, Stella became the model for many of his early nudes and female heads, such as *E.O.W. Nude* (1953–54; p. 97) and *Head of E.O.W.* (1959–60; p. 100). During this period Auerbach also painted urban landscapes and building sites in post–World War II London, recording the deterioration, excavation, and renewal of the city in works such as *Oxford Street Building Site 1* (1959–60; p. 99).

Auerbach's diploma exhibition at the Royal College of Art was seen by the dealer Helen Lessore, who included his work in the summer exhibition at the Beaux Arts Gallery and subsequently, in 1956, presented his first solo exhibition at the gallery. He was criticized for his thick application of paint but found support from the art critics John Berger and David Sylvester, among others. Around this time he became friends with Michael Andrews, Francis Bacon, and Lucian Freud.

Between 1955 and 1968 Auerbach taught at various schools and art colleges, including Camberwell College of Arts, Ealing Technical College and School of Art, and the Slade School of Fine Art. He met the professional model Juliet Yardley Mills (J.Y.M.) at Sidcup College of Art in 1957. Capable of sustaining awkward poses for many hours, she sat for numerous drawings and paintings over a period of forty years, including *J.Y.M. Seated No. 1* (1981; p. 114). In 1958 he married Julia Wolstenholme, a fellow student at the Royal College of Art. Their son, Jacob (Jake), was born that year.

Beginning in the 1960s Auerbach employed brighter colors and a more dynamic technique, pushing paint around the canvas with fingers, brushes, and tools. He began to scrape down entire canvases rather than work on top of previous unsuccessful attempts, thus beginning the entire image afresh at each session. He also began working on the subject of Camden Town and the environs of his studio. Primrose Hill became a key motif in the 1970s, and he produced many versions of the subject at different times of the year using bold, directional brushstrokes. For practical reasons he worked on these large canvases in the studio, from drawings made outside in the early morning or late evening.

A retrospective was organized by the Arts Council in 1978, beginning at the Hayward Gallery, London, and touring to the Fruitmarket Gallery, Edinburgh. The same year Auerbach's wife, Julia, their son, Jake, and the art historian Catherine Lampert began sitting for portraits regularly. Though Auerbach's portraits have focused largely on a core group of friends and family, a total of twenty people posed between 1978 and 1985, most for only one or two works. The art historian and businessman David Landau and the art critic William Feaver are among the artist's longtime sitters.

Auerbach's international standing was confirmed when he received the Golden Lion award (with Sigmar Polke) at the 1986 Venice Biennale. This was followed by exhibitions in Amsterdam (Van Gogh Museum, 1989) and St. Louis (Saint Louis Art Museum, 1990). In 1995 the National Gallery, London, presented an exhibition of Auerbach's drawings and paintings based on works from the collection, including pictures by Rembrandt van Rijn, Peter Paul Rubens, and Titian.

During the 2000s a retrospective was held at the Royal Academy of Arts (2001), followed by an exhibition of the building site paintings at the Courtauld Gallery (2009–10), both in London. Auerbach began to depict interior views of the studio, such as *In the Studio IV* (2013–14; London, Marlborough Fine Art), alongside his familiar landscapes of North London. A major exhibition was organized at the Kunstmuseum Bonn and Tate Britain, London (2015–16), with works selected by the artist and Lampert. On this occasion Jake Auerbach made a film titled *Frank*, documenting his father's responses to seeing the works included in the exhibition, some of which he had not seen for as long as sixty years.

Auerbach continues to live and work in London.

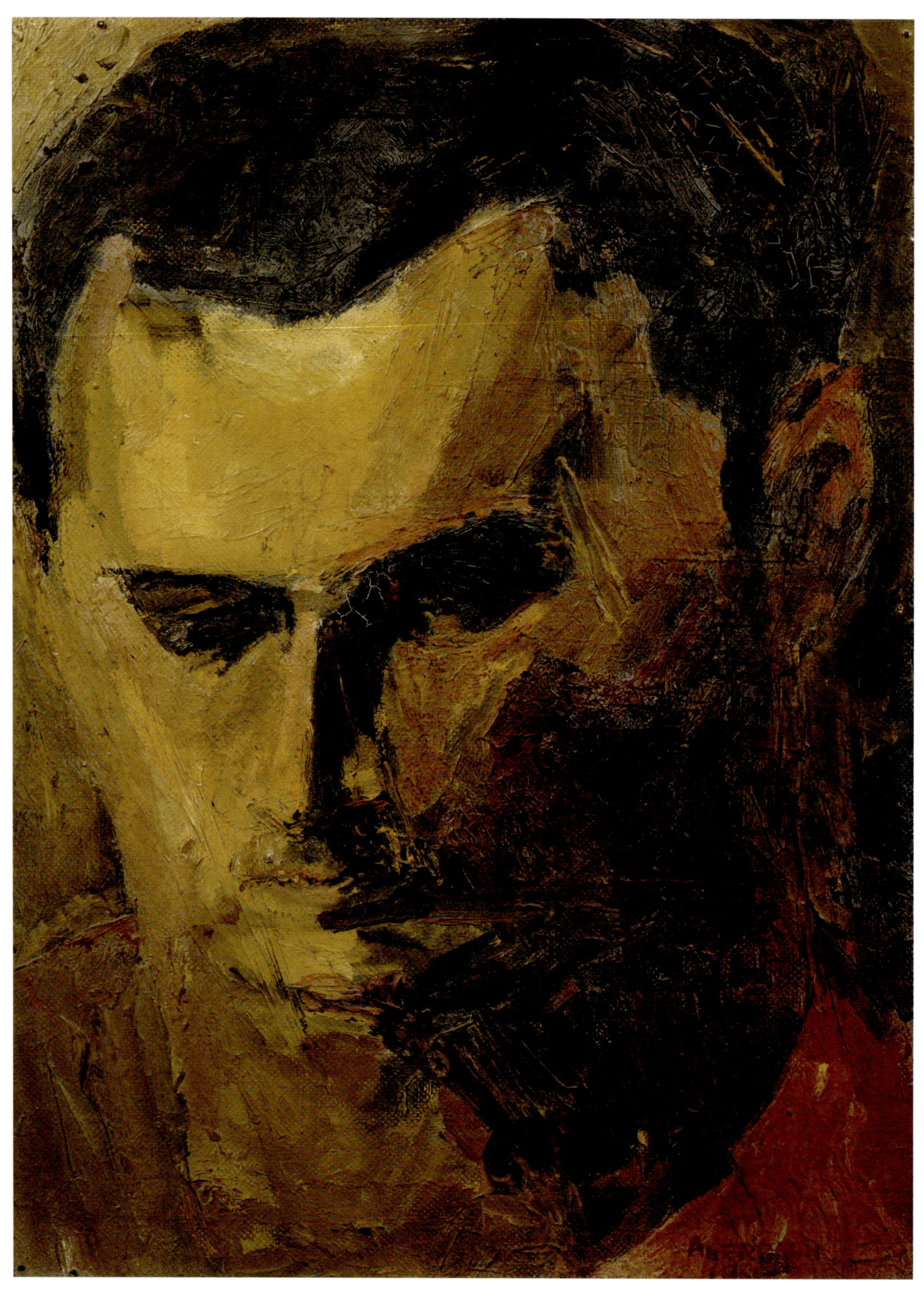

Frank Auerbach
Portrait of Leon Kossoff, 1951

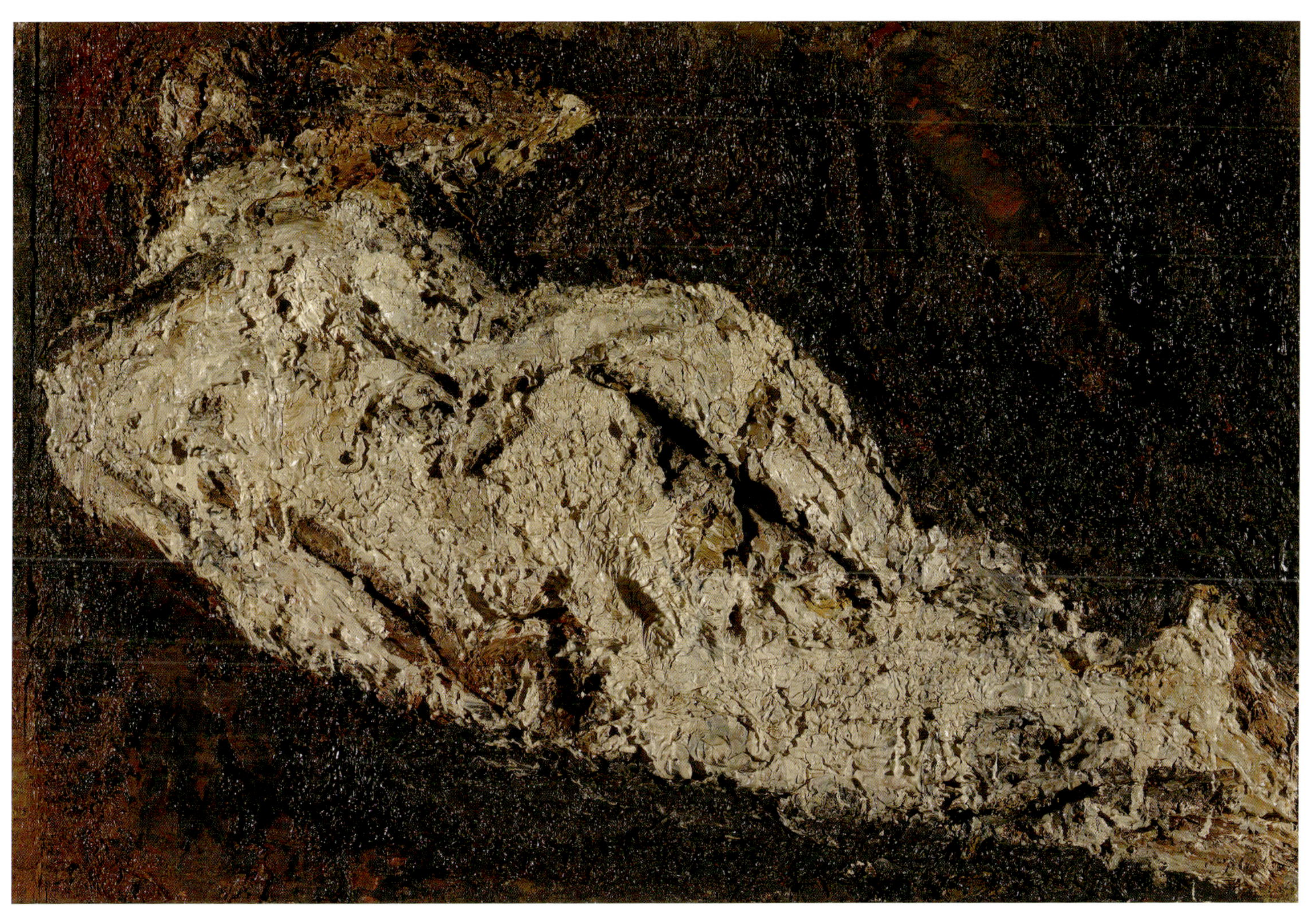

Frank Auerbach
E.O.W. Nude, 1953–54

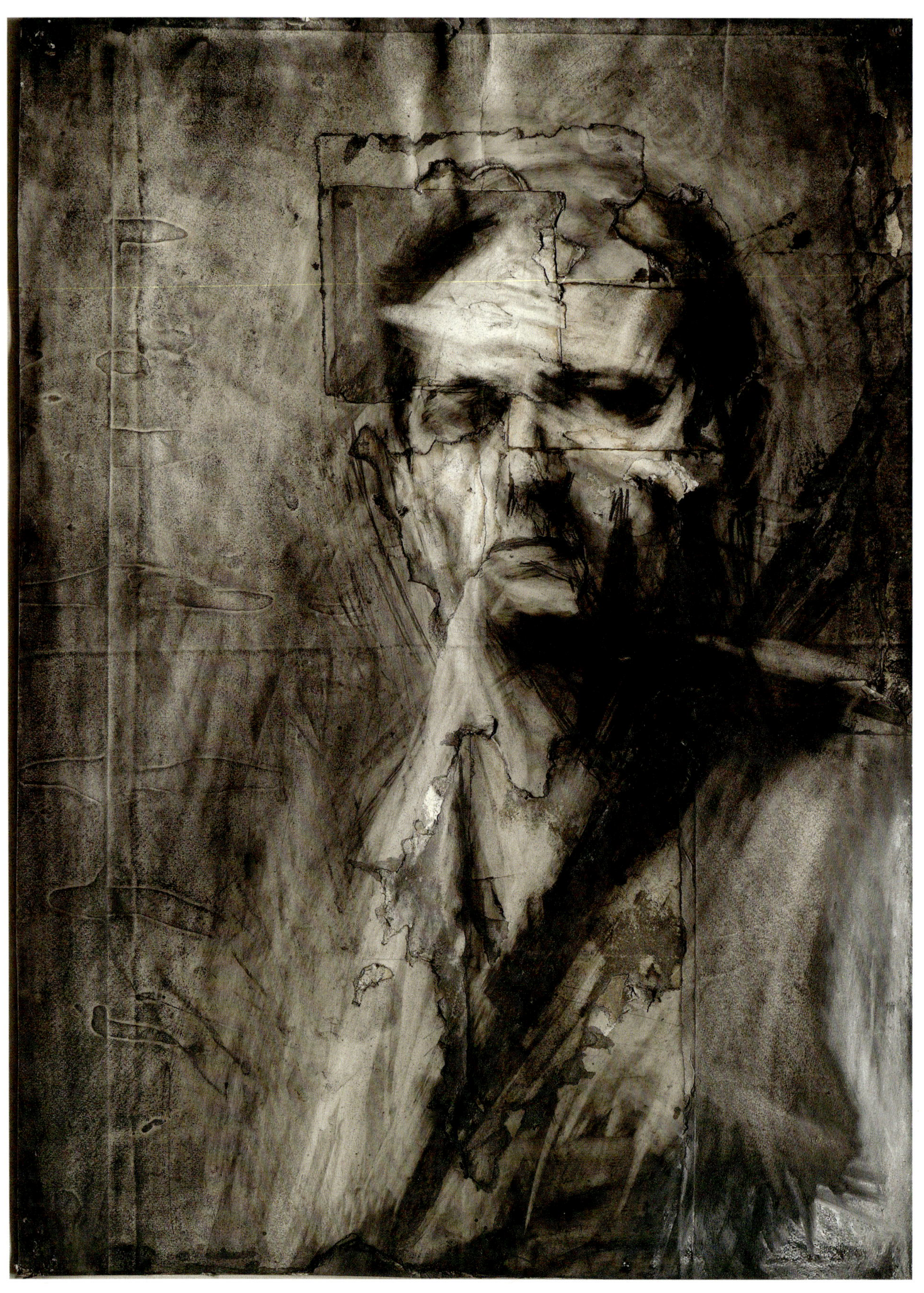

Frank Auerbach
Self-Portrait, 1958

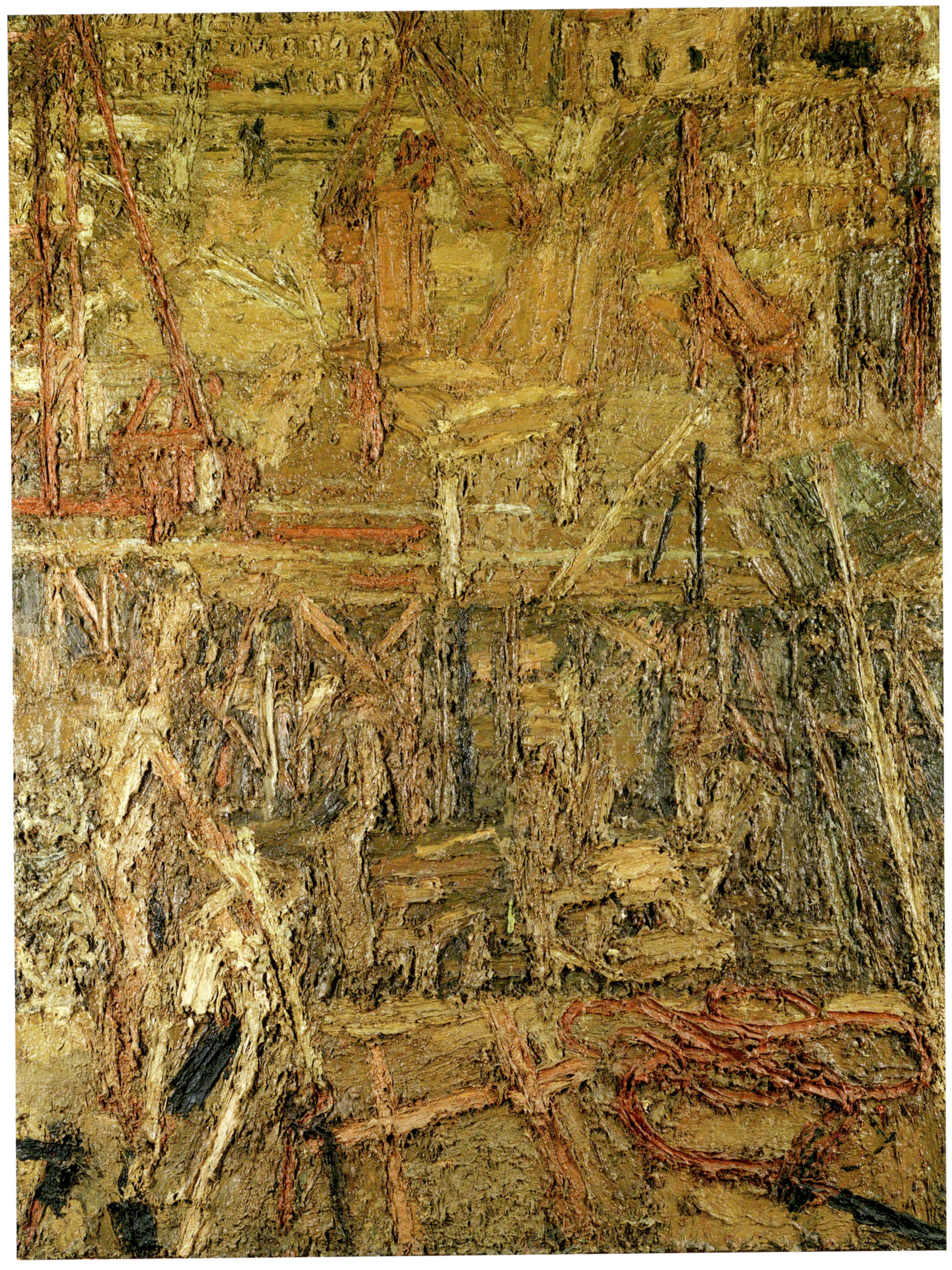

Frank Auerbach
Oxford Street Building Site I, 1959–60

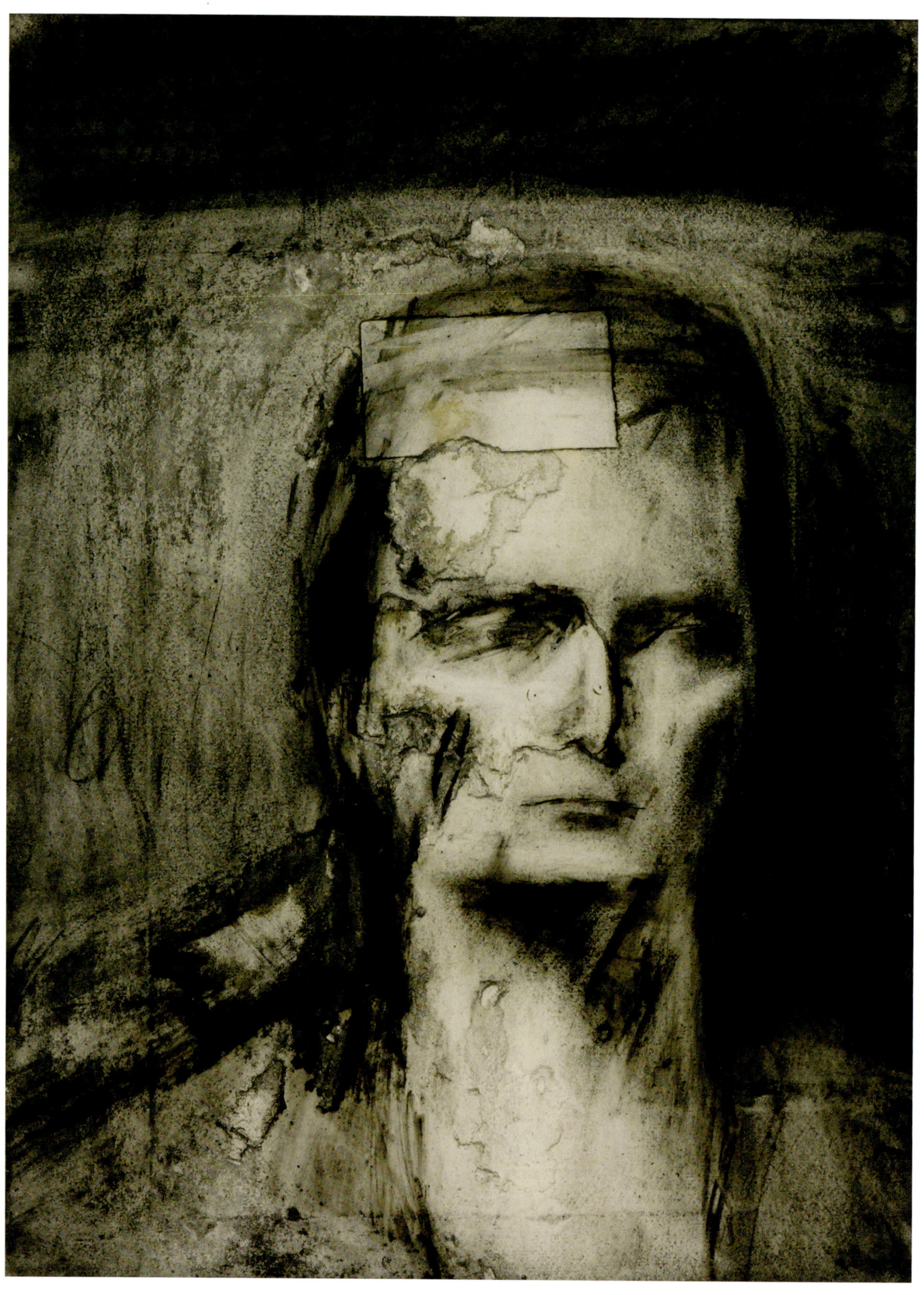

Frank Auerbach
Head of E.O.W., 1959–60

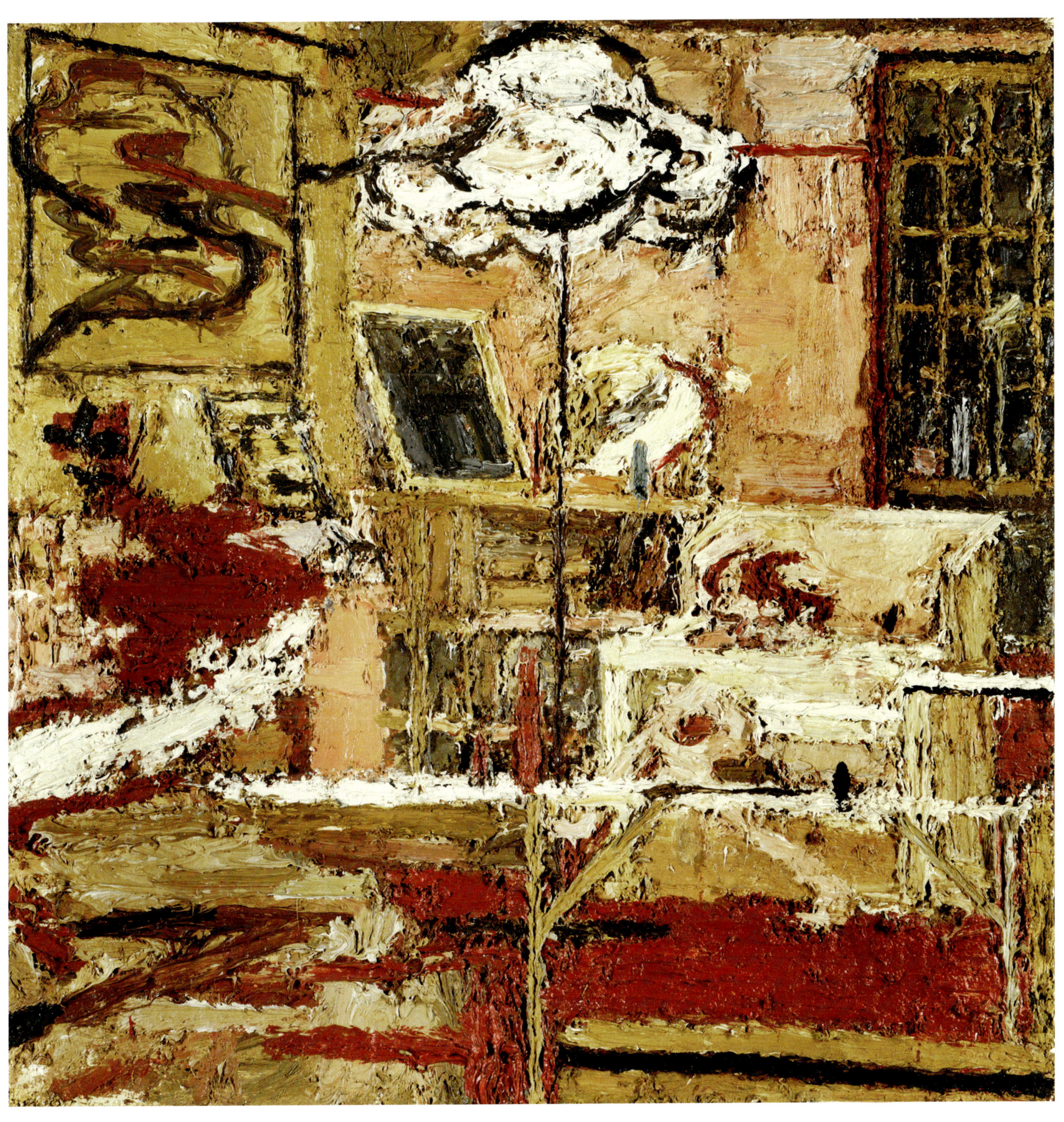

Frank Auerbach
The Sitting Room, 1964

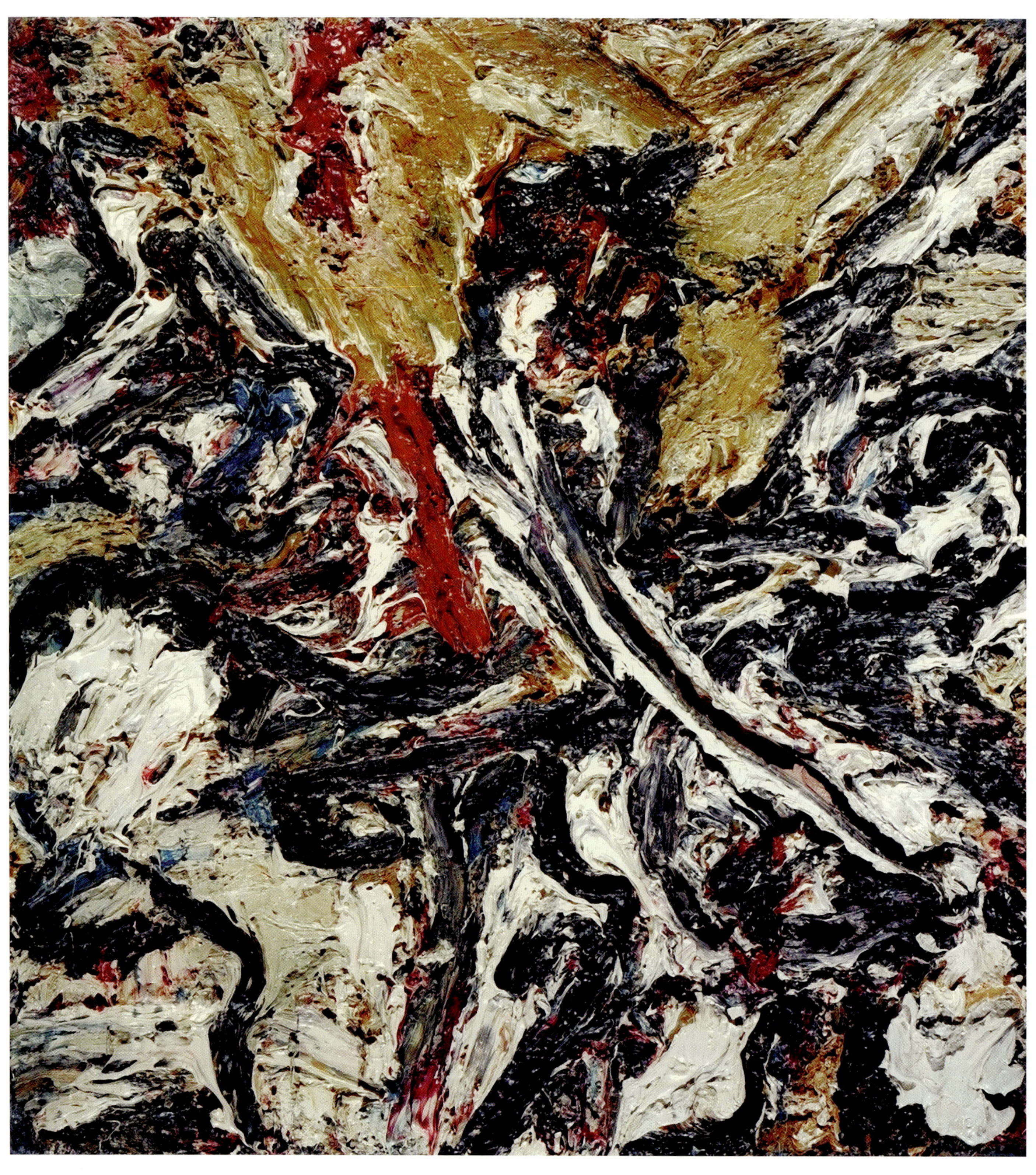

Frank Auerbach
Study after Titian II, 1965

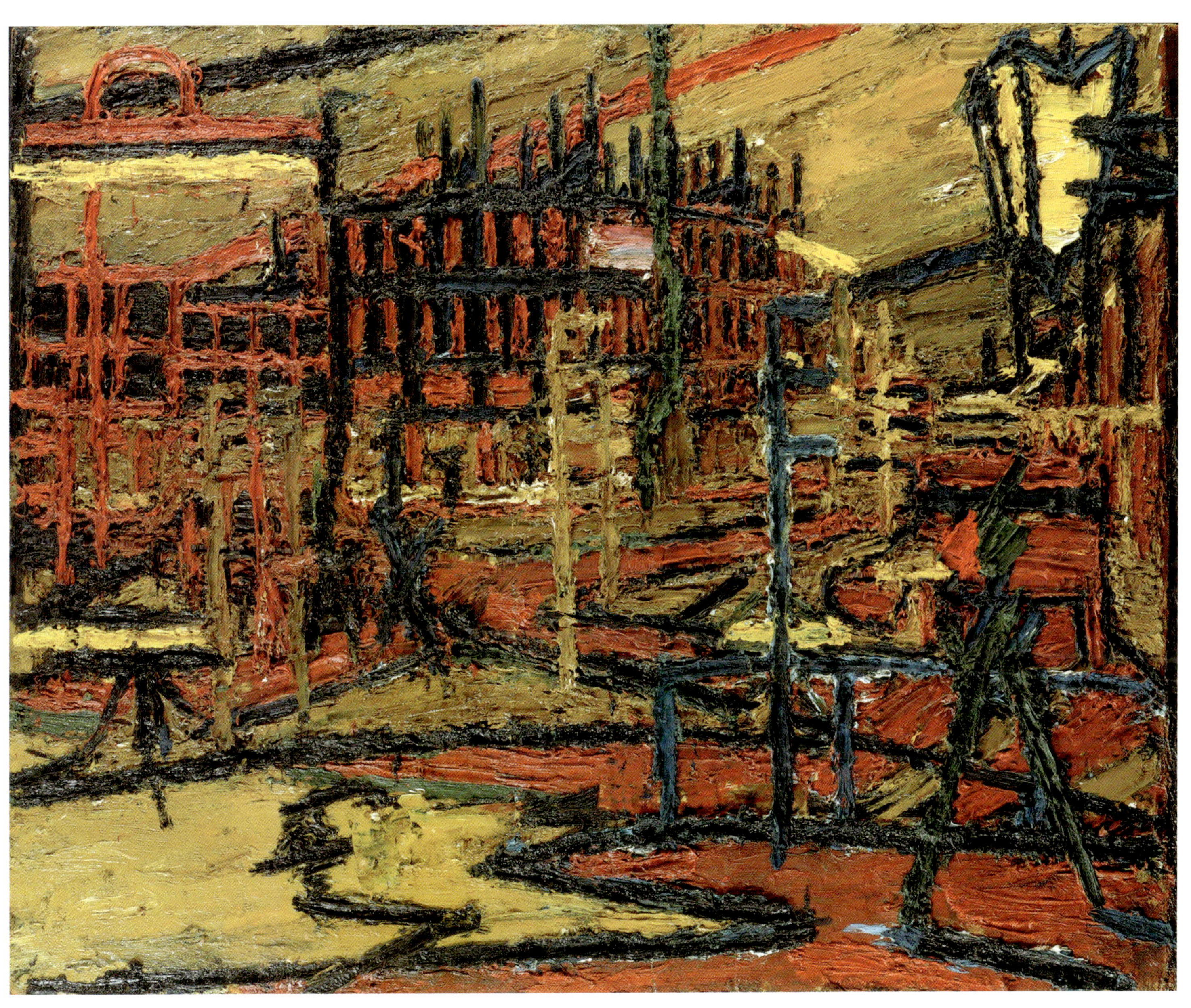

Frank Auerbach
Mornington Crescent with the Statue of Sickert's Father-in-Law, 1966

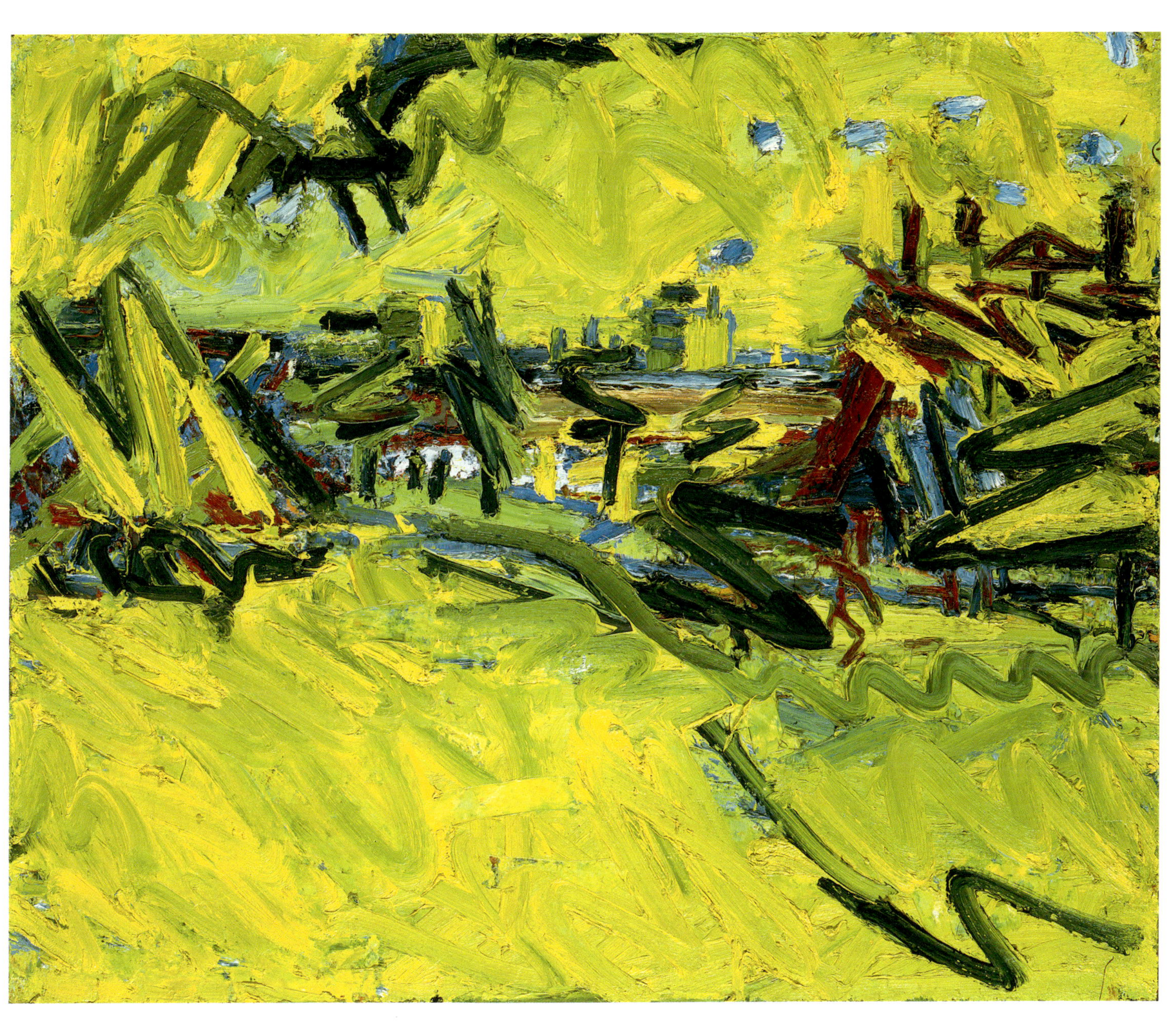

Frank Auerbach

The Origin of the Great Bear, 1967–68

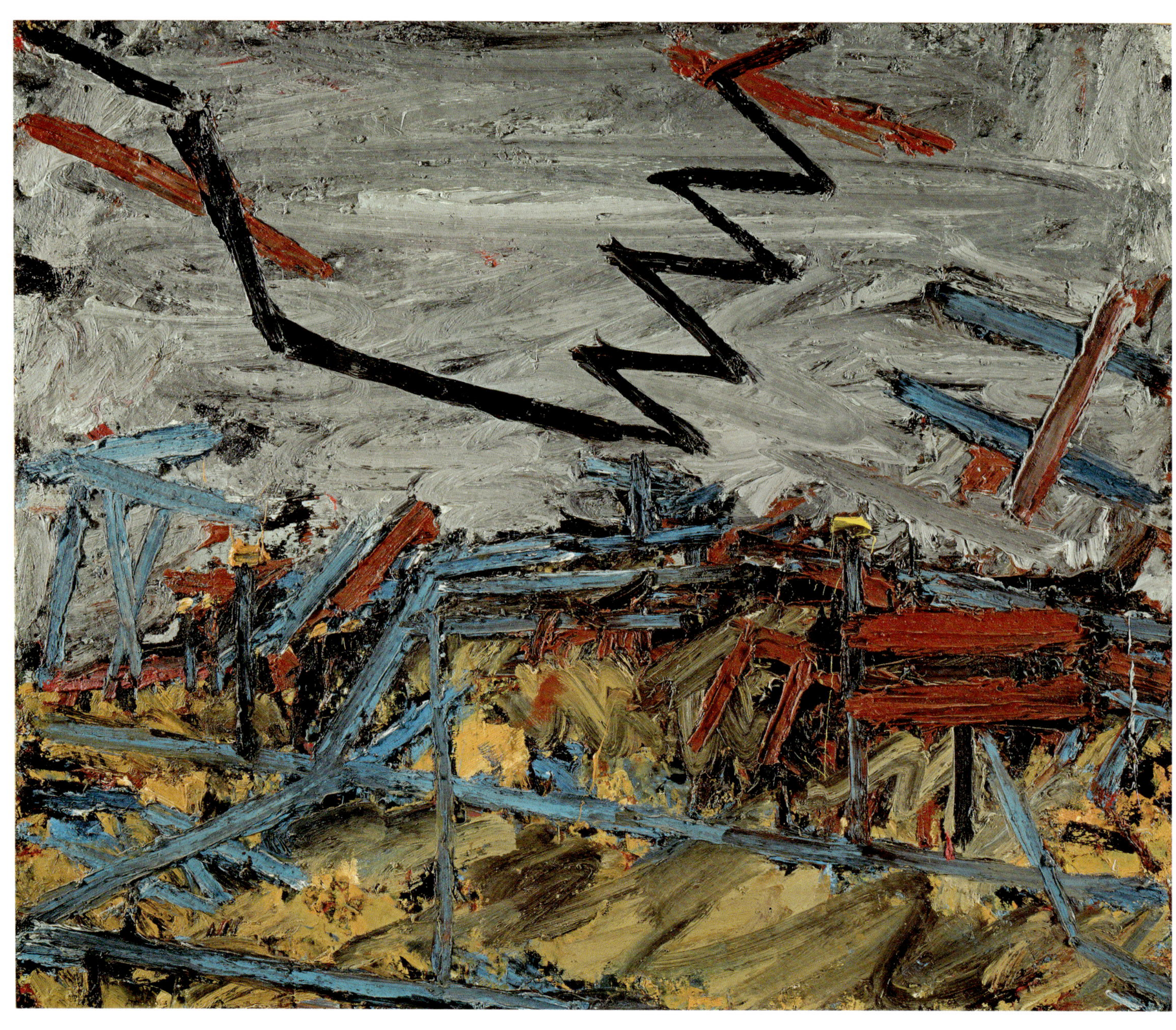

Frank Auerbach
Primrose Hill, 1967–68

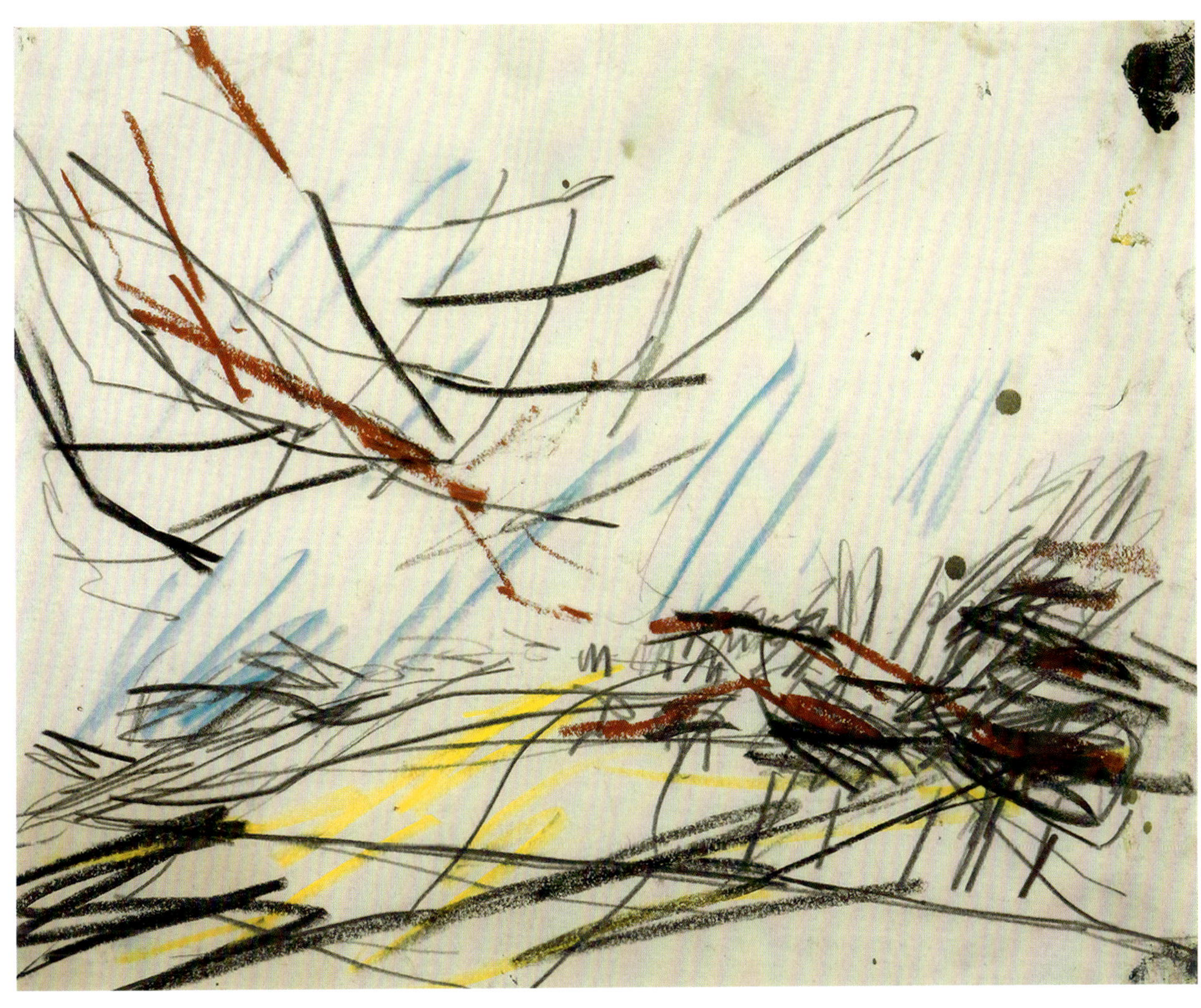

Frank Auerbach
Working Drawing for "Primrose Hill," 1968

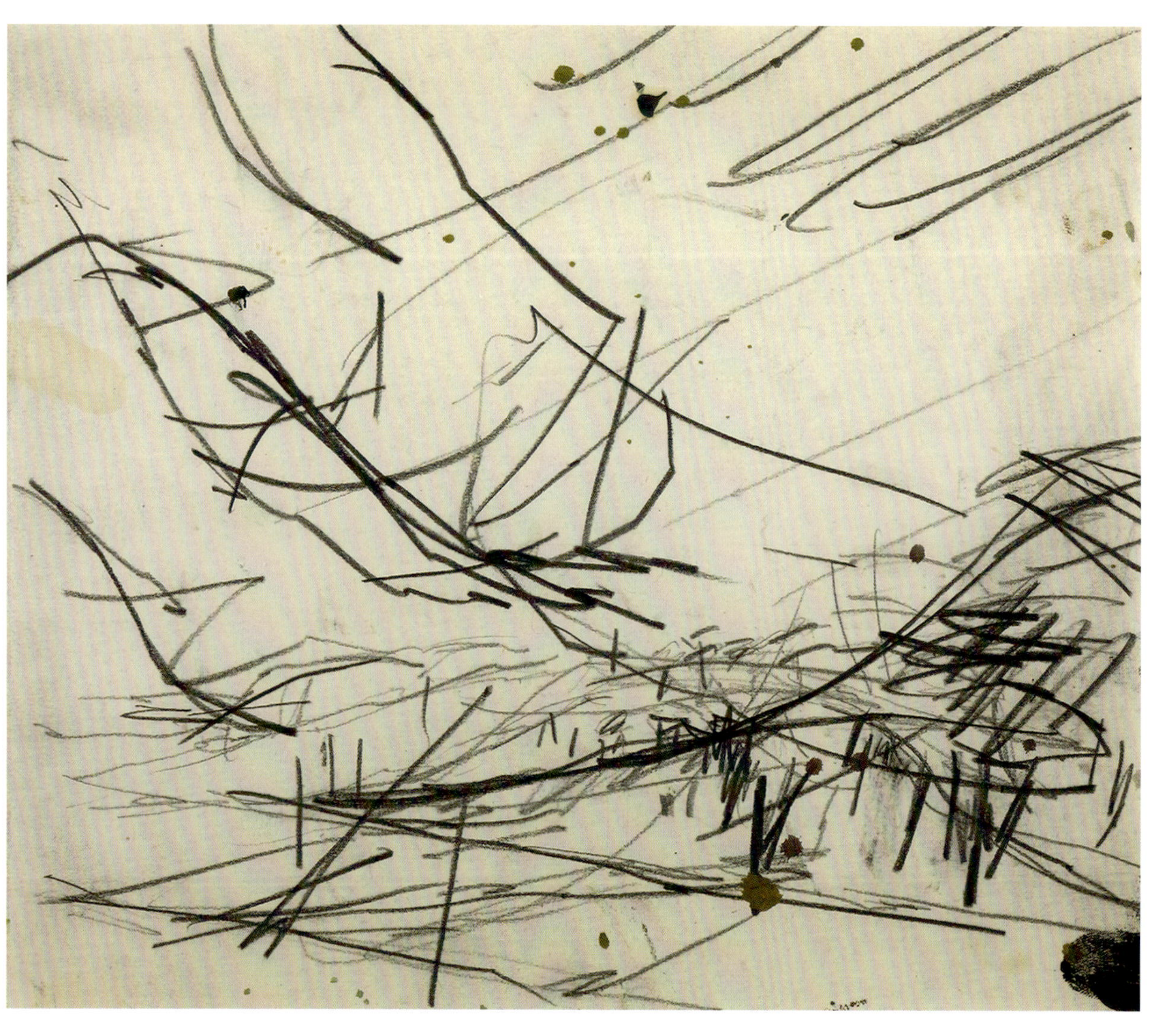

Frank Auerbach
Working Drawing for "Primrose Hill," 1968

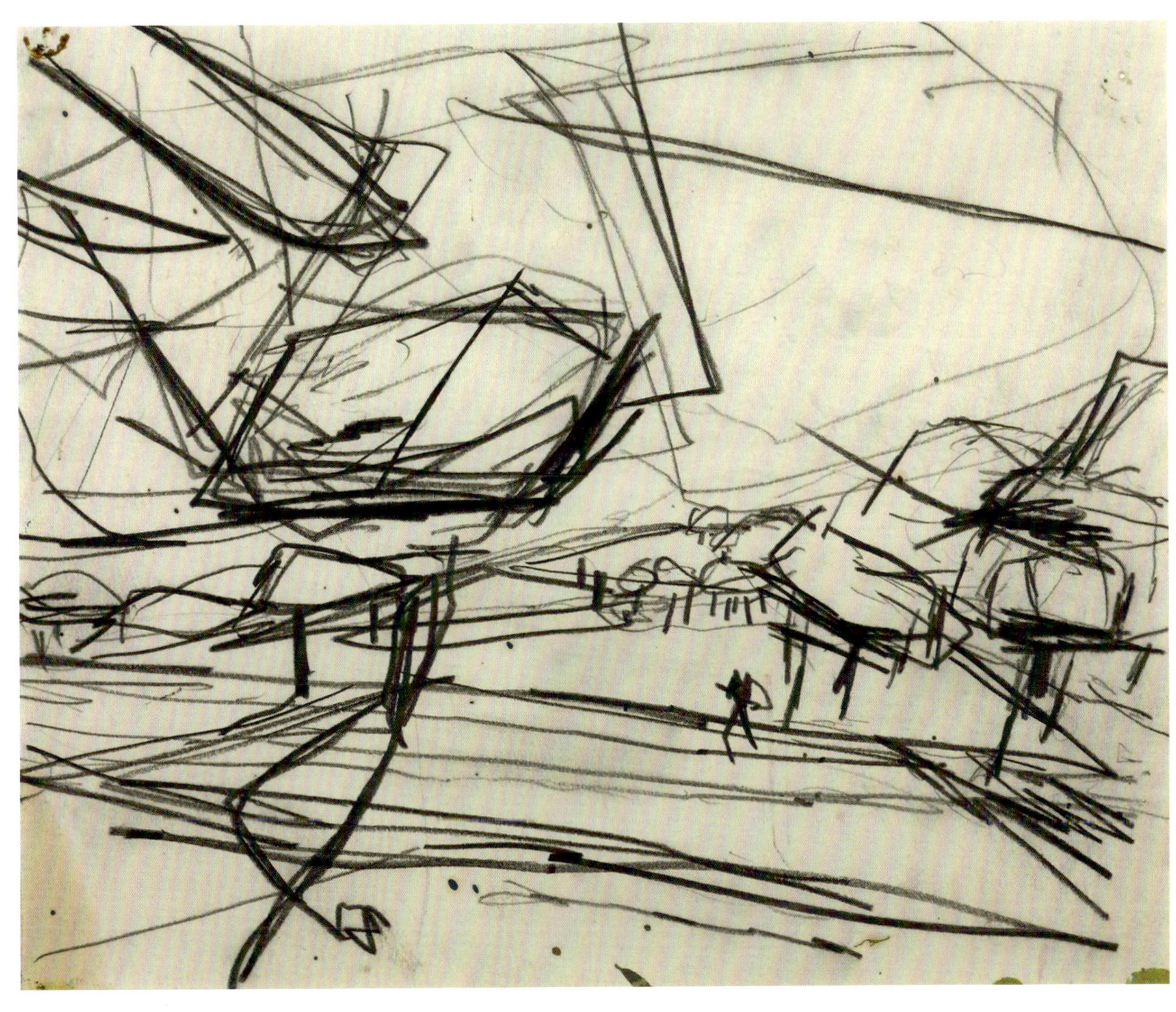

Frank Auerbach
Working Drawing for "Primrose Hill," 1968

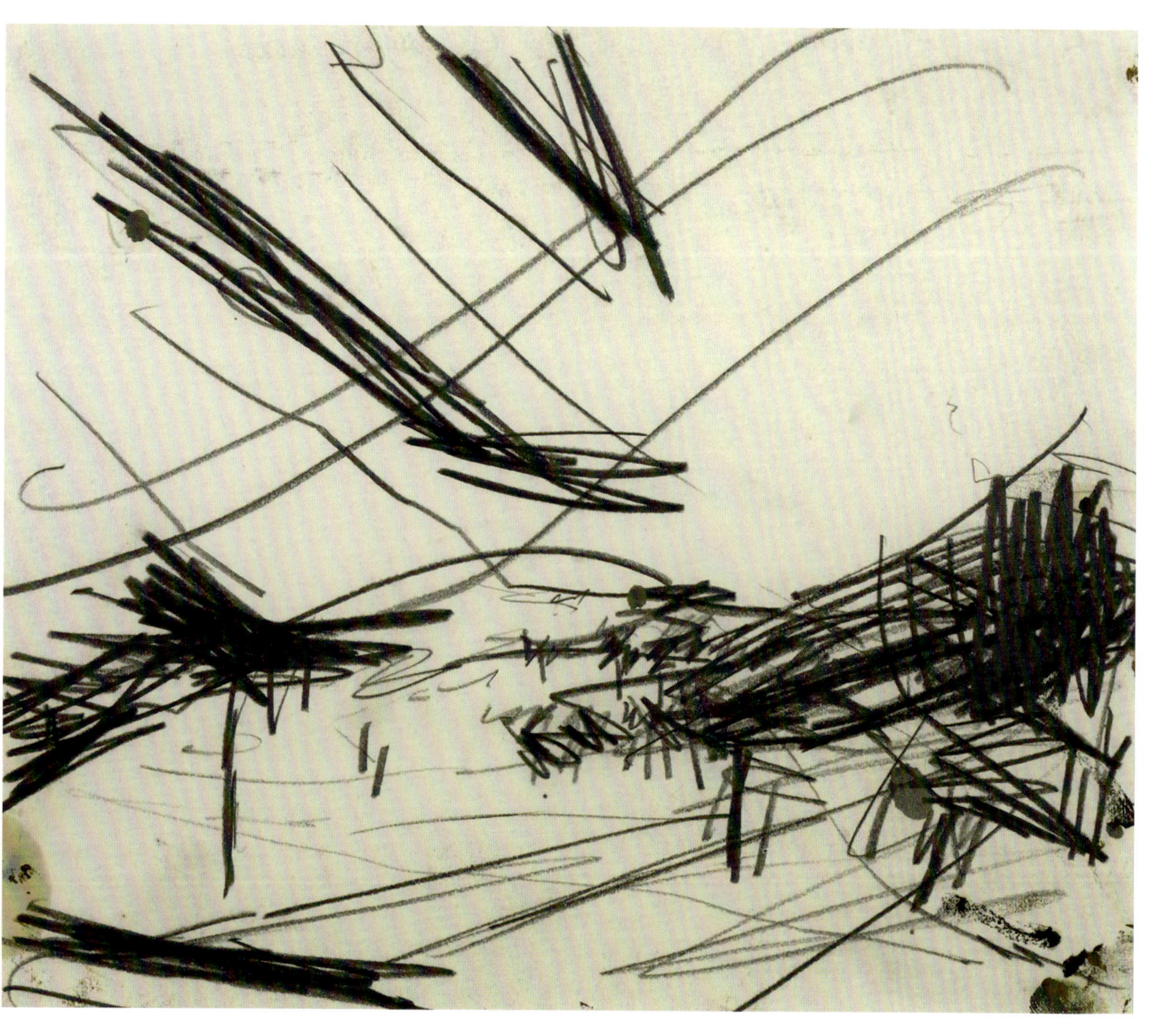

Frank Auerbach

Working Drawing for "Primrose Hill," 1968

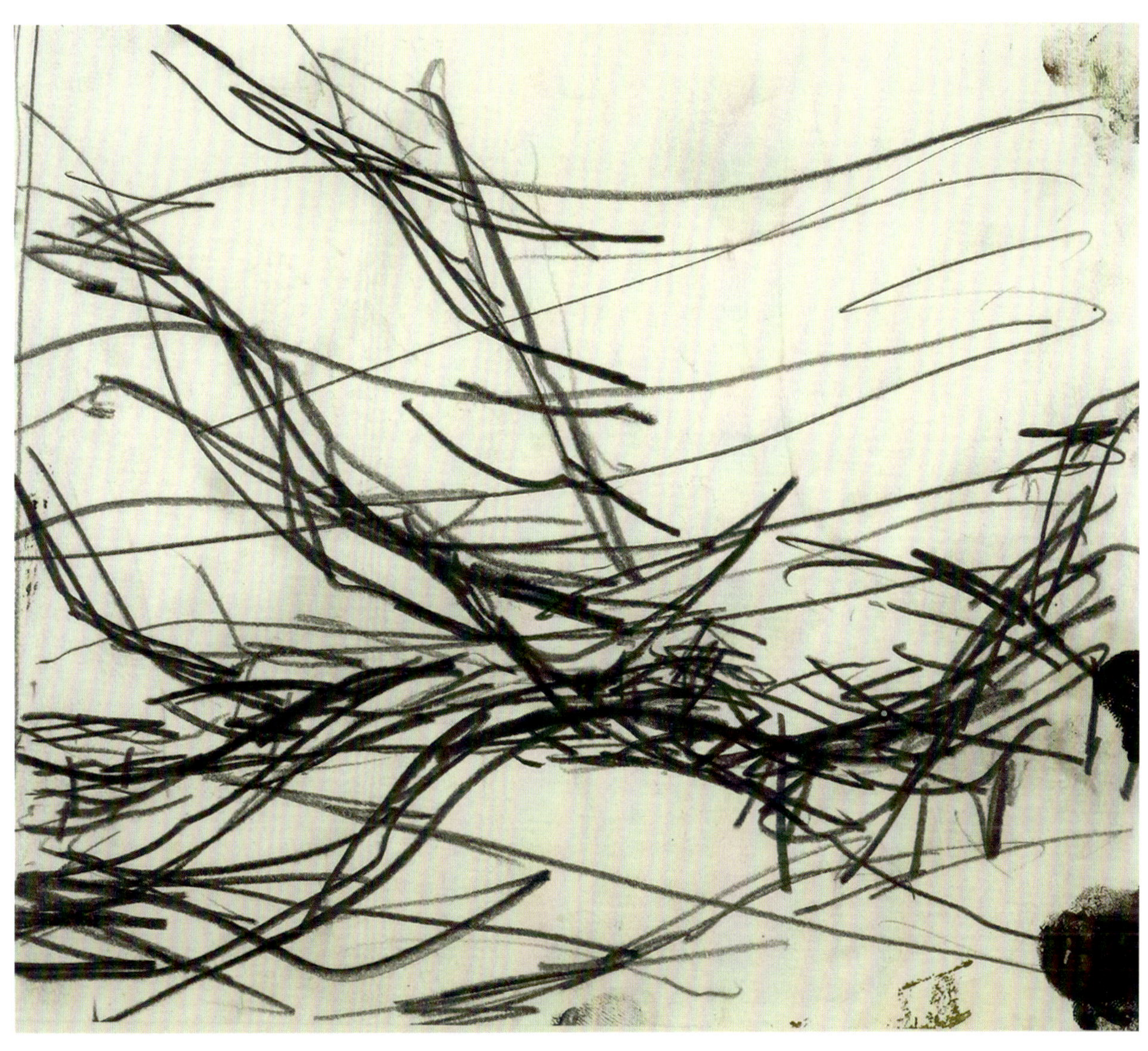

Frank Auerbach
Working Drawing for "Primrose Hill," 1968

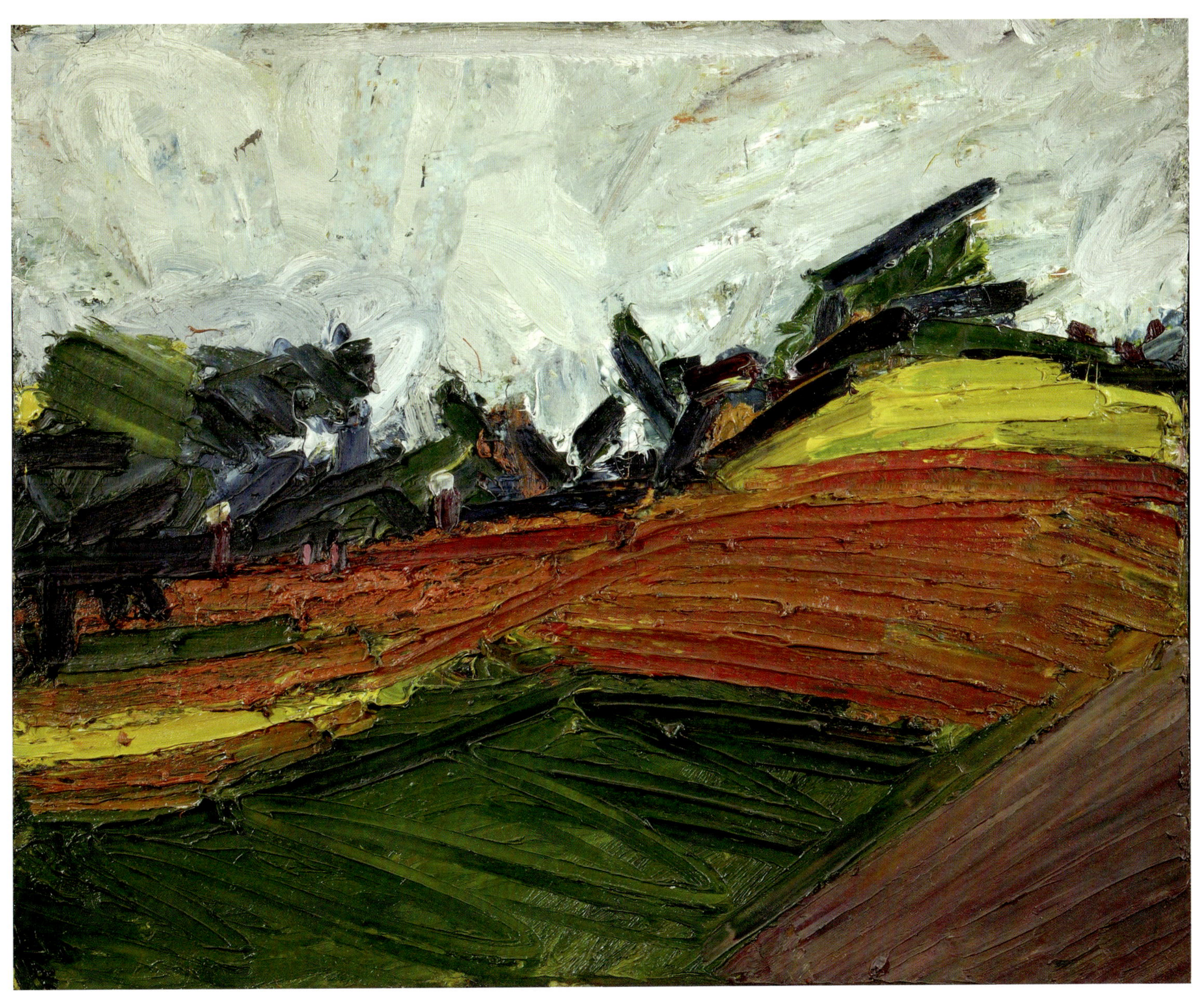

Frank Auerbach
Primrose Hill, 1971

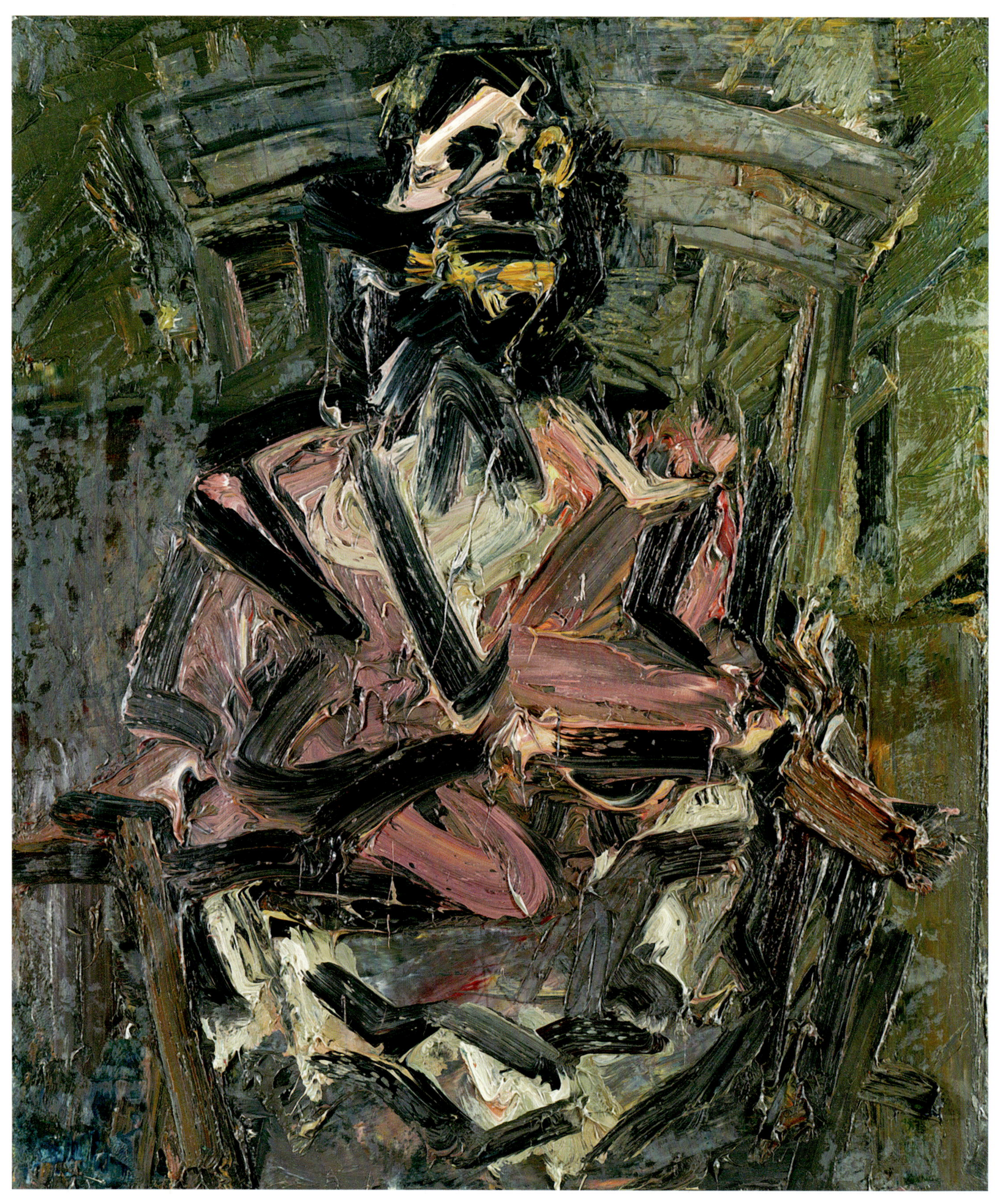

Frank Auerbach
J.Y.M. Seated No. 1, 1981

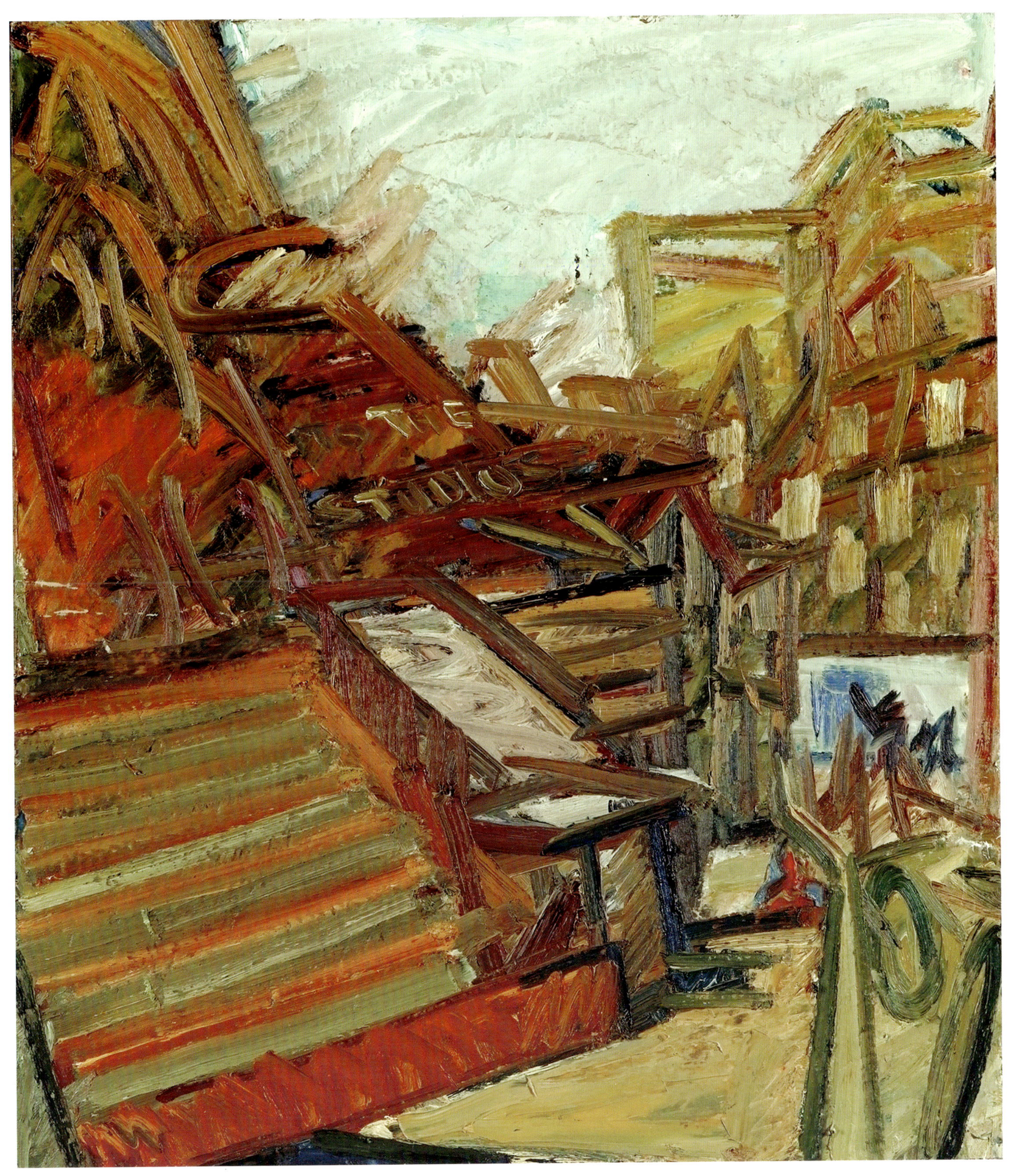

Frank Auerbach

To the Studios, 1990–91

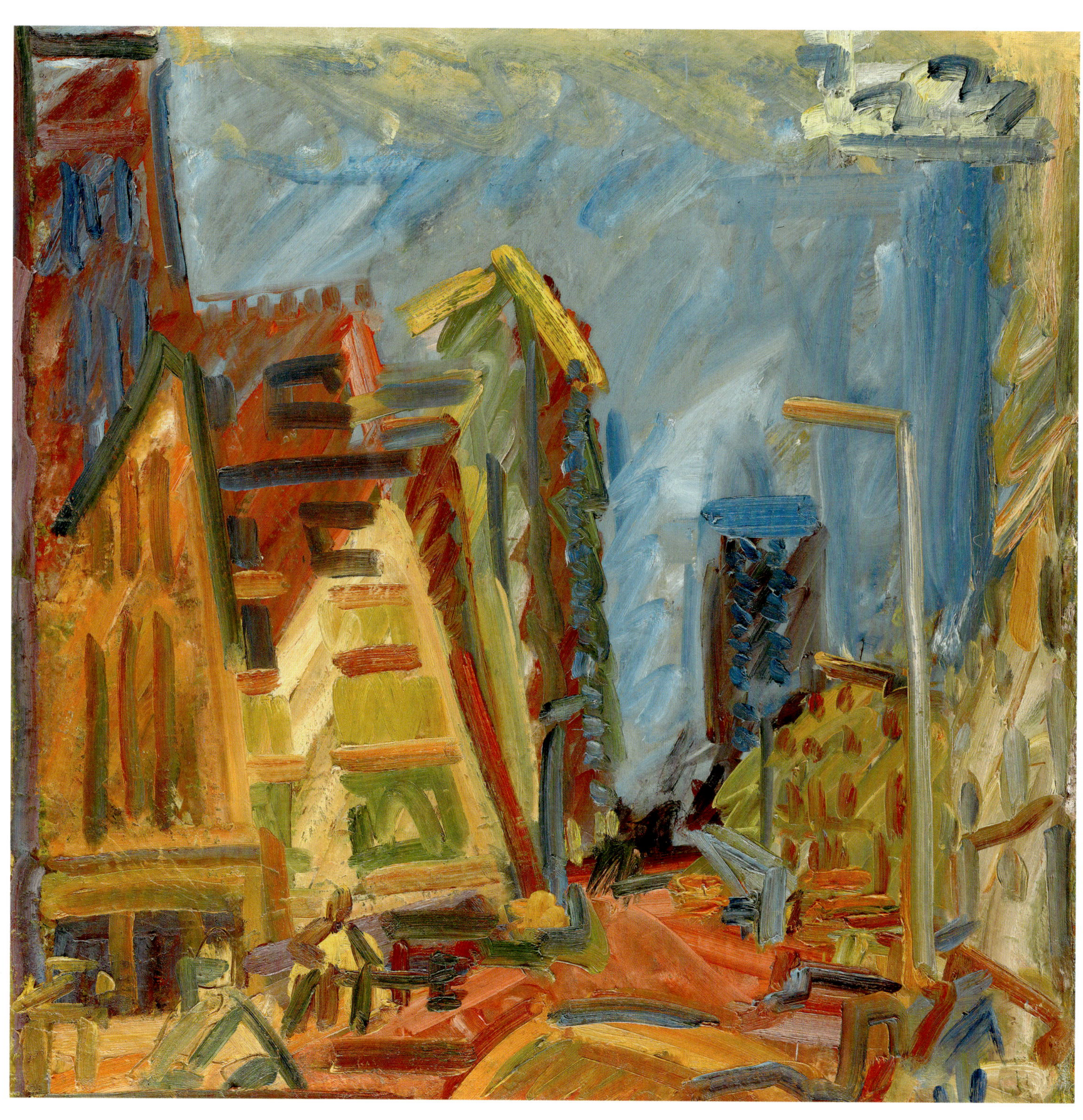

Frank Auerbach
Mornington Crescent—Summer Morning, 2004

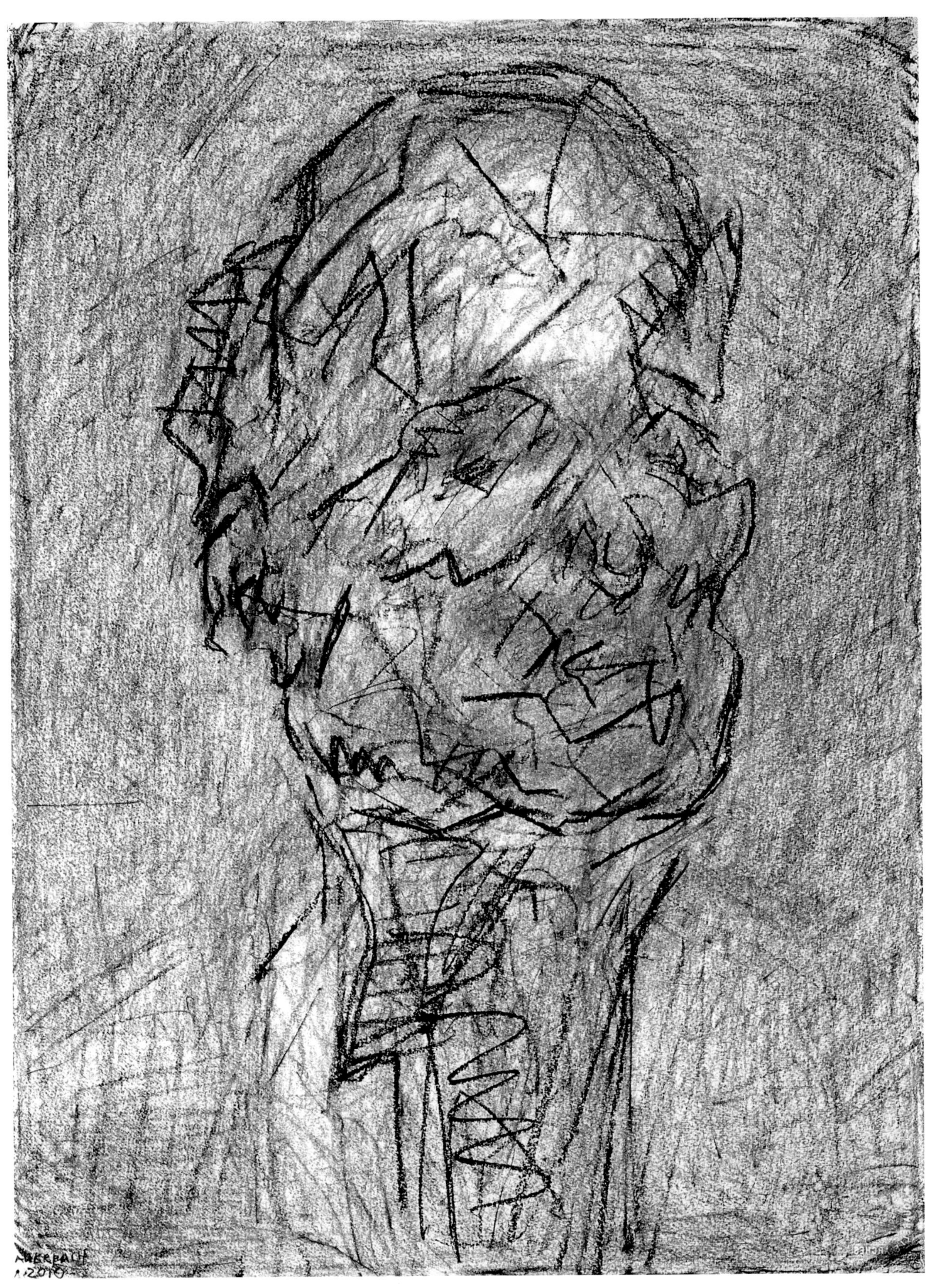

Frank Auerbach
Self-Portrait II, 2010

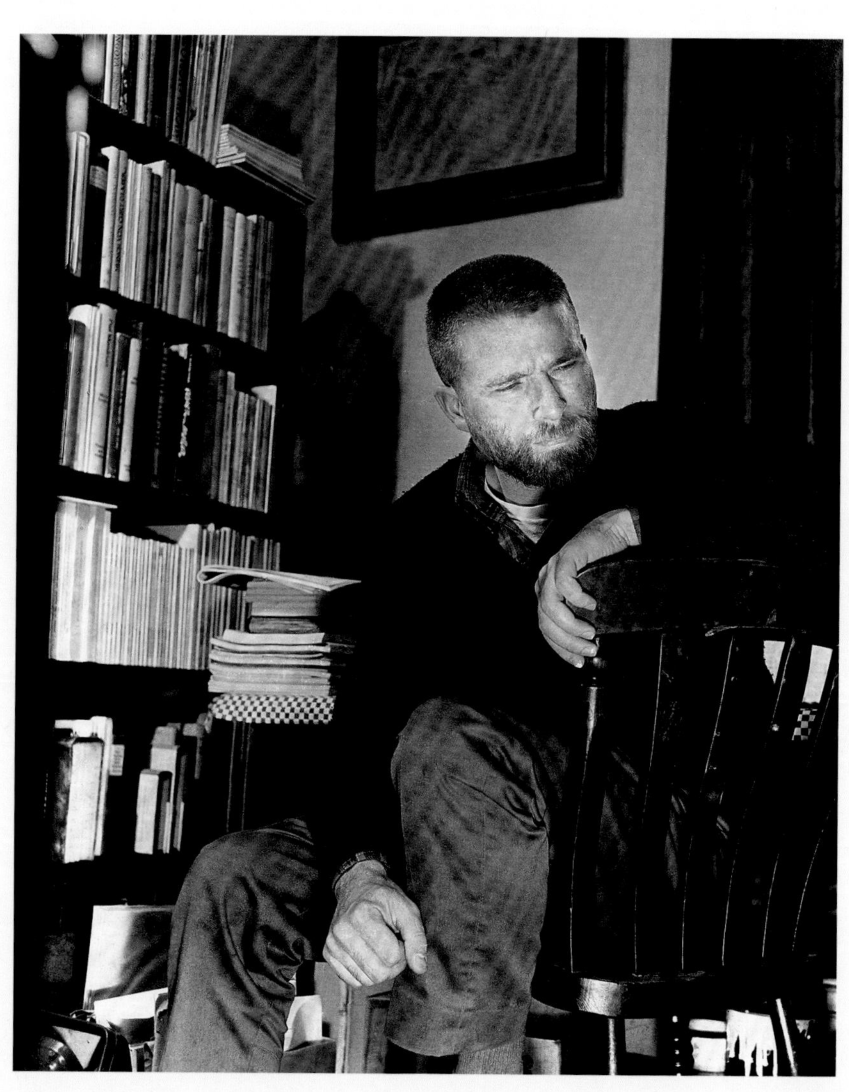

R. B. Kitaj, 1963.
Photo: Jorge Lewinski

R. B. KITAJ

Ronald Brooks Kitaj was born in Cleveland on October 29, 1932. His father, Sigmund Benway, was Hungarian, and his mother, Jeanne Brooks, was the American-born daughter of Russian Jewish immigrants. His parents divorced shortly after he was born, and in 1941 his mother married Walter Kitaj, a Viennese refugee and chemist. As a child R. B. Kitaj was taken to art classes at the Cleveland Museum of Art. He attended high school in Cleveland until 1949.

In the early 1950s Kitaj sailed to Cuba, Mexico, and South America as a merchant seaman. Between assignments he studied painting at Cooper Union, New York (1950–51, 1952), and spent time in Europe, where he attended the Academy of Fine Art, Vienna, and saw works by Gustav Klimt and Egon Schiele. It was there that he met Elsi Roessler, an American art student, whom he married in 1953. Kitaj was conscripted into the American army in 1956 and posted to AFCE headquarters at Fontainebleau, France. On his discharge from the army, Kitaj moved to England to attend the Ruskin School, Oxford (1958–59), and the Royal College of Art (1959–61), where he became friends with fellow student David Hockney. He was still at the Royal College of Art when he began *The Murder of Rosa Luxemburg* (1960; p. 121). His son Lem was born in Oxford in 1958, and in 1964 he adopted a daughter, Dominie.

During the early 1960s Kitaj concentrated on paintings combining figurative imagery with abstraction and bright color. His first solo exhibition, titled *Pictures with Commentary, Pictures without Commentary*, was held at Marlborough Fine Art, London, in 1963. The paintings and accompanying catalogue contained references to a wide variety of literature, influenced by Aby Warburg's interdisciplinary approach to art history. It was around this time that Kitaj met Michael Andrews, Frank Auerbach, Francis Bacon, Lucian Freud, Henry Moore, and Leon Kossoff, who were also represented by the gallery. He began to incorporate collage into his paintings, drawing on diverse sources from photography, cinema (a lifelong passion), history, and politics.

In 1965 Kitaj returned to the United States for the first time in nine years for his first exhibition in New York (Marlborough Gallery), where he met Mark Rothko. An exhibition was presented by the Los Angeles County Museum of Art later that year. Between 1967 and 1968 Kitaj taught at the University of California, Berkeley, and renewed his childhood passion for baseball. He completed a group of seven small paintings of baseball players, including *Sisler and Schoedienst* (1967; private collection), which anticipated his later return to life drawing and observation of the human form in their direct portraiture and straightforward subject matter.

Following the death of Elsi, Kitaj moved to Hollywood and taught at the University of California, Los Angeles (1970–71), where he painted very little. He returned to London in 1972 and began working on *The Autumn of Central Paris (after Walter Benjamin)* (1972–73; private collection). He increasingly sought to give expression to a sense of alienation and his preoccupation with his Jewish heritage in multilayered, fragmented compositions, as in the later *Cecil Court, London W.C.2. (The Refugees)* (1983–84; p. 127).

On a visit to Paris in 1975, Kitaj saw works by Edgar Degas at the Petit Palais and was inspired to begin working in pastels. The following year he selected works for the exhibition *The Human Clay* at the Hayward Gallery, London, for the Arts Council of Great Britain. He also led, along with Hockney, a widely publicized campaign for a return to the study of the human figure in art schools. He began to work increasingly from life himself, moving away from complex compositions to more straightforward figure studies such as *Two London Painters: Frank Auerbach and Sandra Fisher* (1979; p. 126).

In the late 1970s Kitaj began a relationship with the American artist Sandra Fisher, and they married in 1983. Their wedding is celebrated in his painting *The Wedding* (1989–93; p. 128). Depicted among the guests are Auerbach, Freud, and Hockney, who was the best man. In 1981 a retrospective was organized at Hirshhorn Museum and Sculpture Garden, Washington, DC, which toured to the Cleveland Museum of Art and the Kunsthalle Düsseldorf. Kitaj's third child, Max, was born in 1984.

During the late 1980s Kitaj underwent a period of growing reclusion and uncertainty in his painting. He continued to read widely in Jewish culture—studying Walter Benjamin, Sigmund Freud, and Franz Kafka—and positioned himself more explicitly as a Jewish artist. In 1989 he published his *First Diasporist Manifesto*, an impassioned text analyzing the Jewish dimension in his art and his position as an outsider. This was followed by an exhibition of Jewish art at the Barbican, *From Chagall to Kitaj* (1990). In 1994 Kitaj's retrospective at the Tate Gallery (touring to the Los Angeles County Museum of Art and the Metropolitan Museum of Art, New York, 1994–95) triggered much negative criticism in relation to his abundant use of text in the galleries. This, combined with the death of Sandra Fisher in 1994, led him to leave London for Los Angeles in 1997. His fourth child, Hougharry Pollen, was born in 1996.

During the early 2000s Kitaj completed more than twenty paintings in the Los Angeles series, which depict the artist and Sandra as winged angels in intimate embraces. The *Second Diasporist Manifesto* was published in 2005 on the occasion of an exhibition at Marlborough Gallery in New York.

Kitaj died in Los Angeles in 2007.

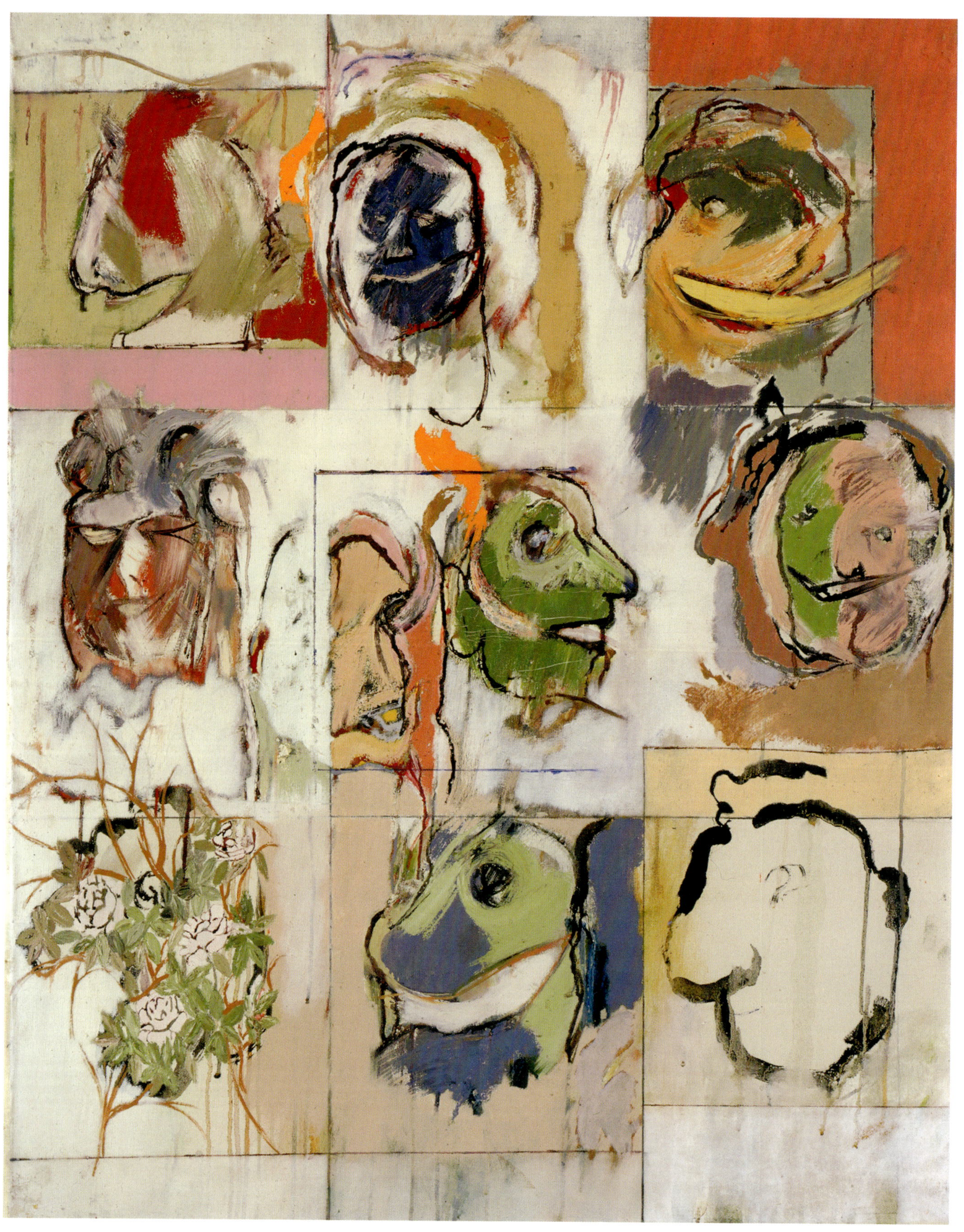

R. B. Kitaj
Erasmus Variations, 1958

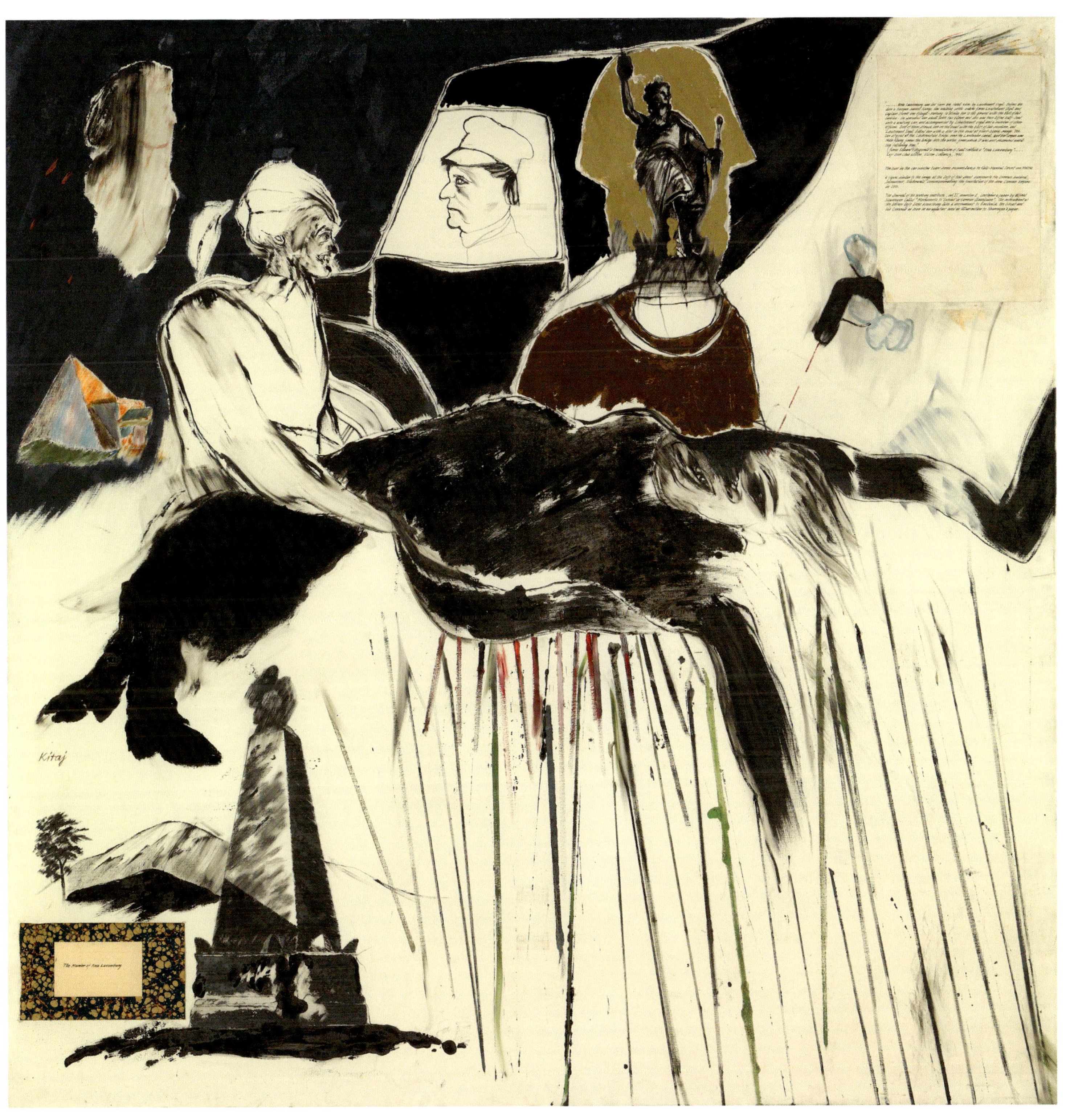

R. B. Kitaj

The Murder of Rosa Luxemburg, 1960

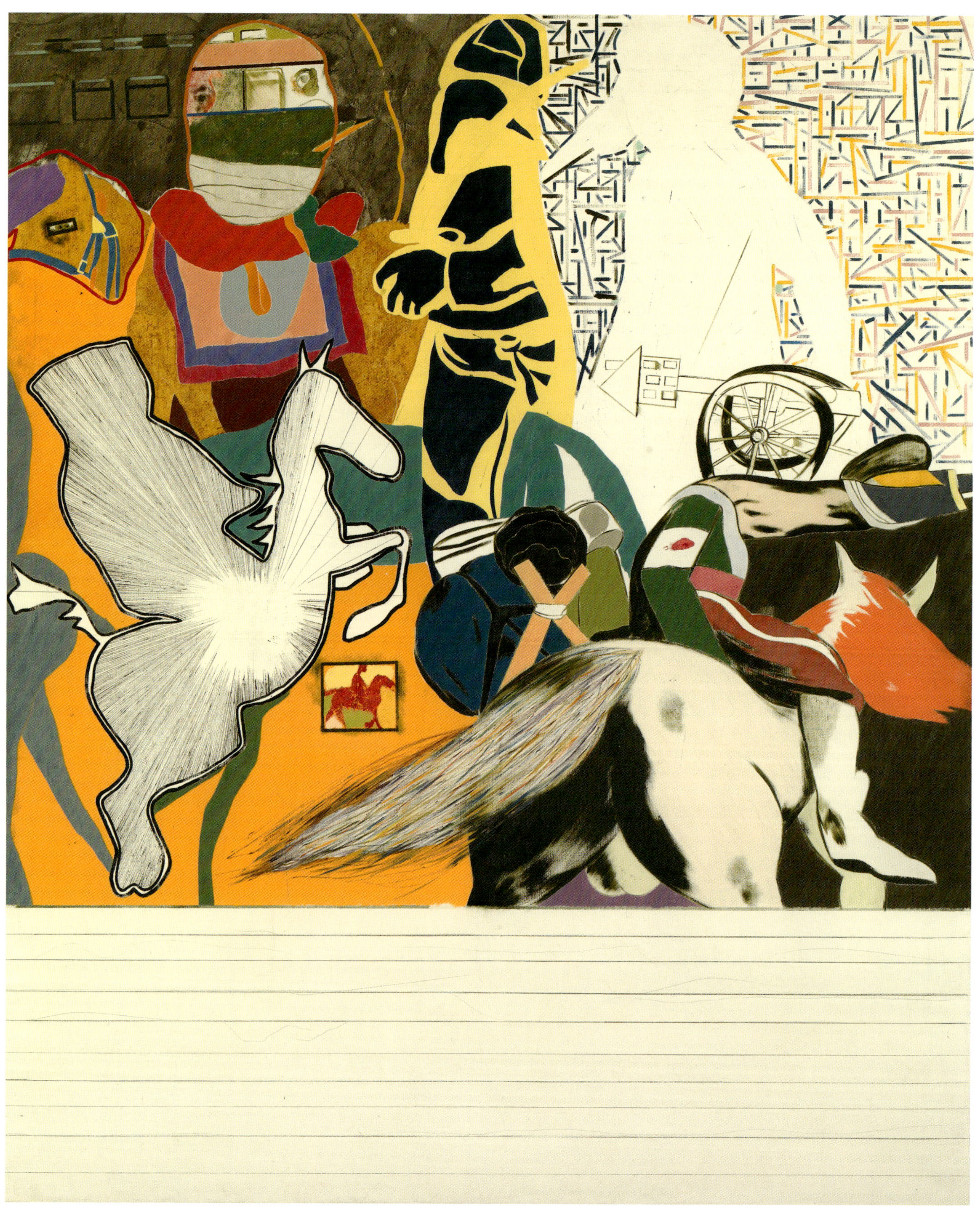

R. B. Kitaj

Isaac Babel Riding with Budyonny, 1962

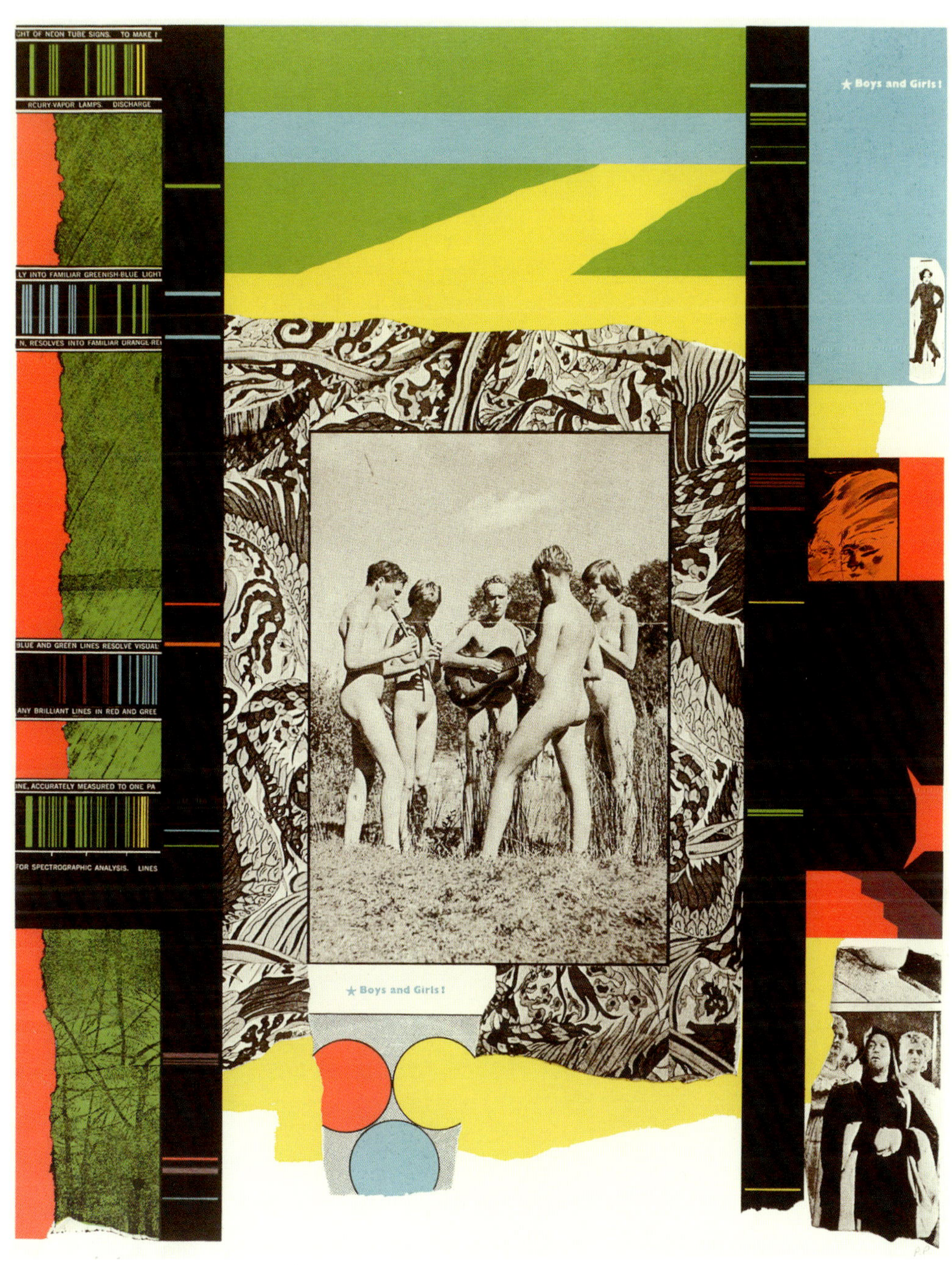

R. B. Kitaj
Boys and Girls!, 1964

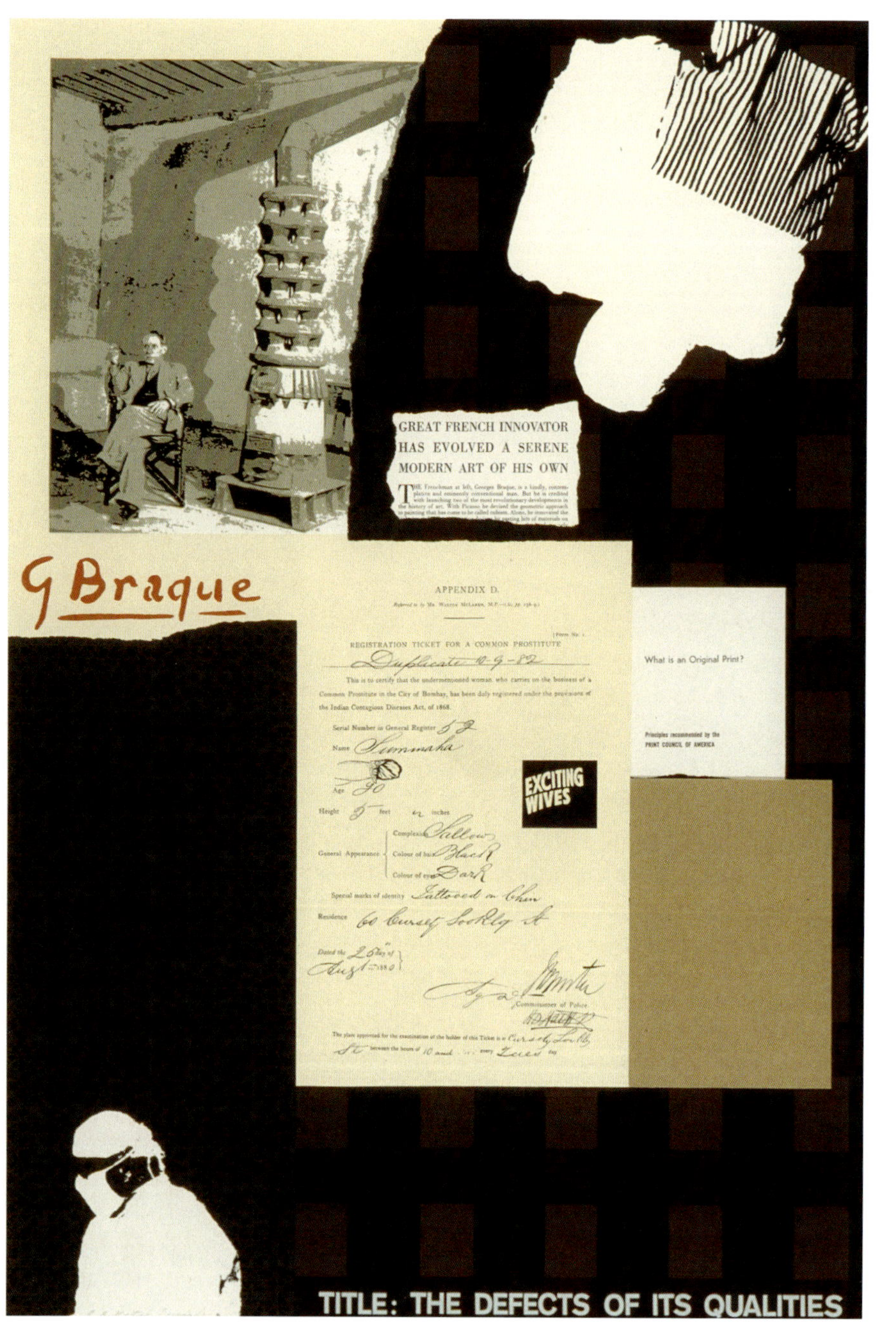

R. B. Kitaj
The Defects of Its Qualities, 1967–68

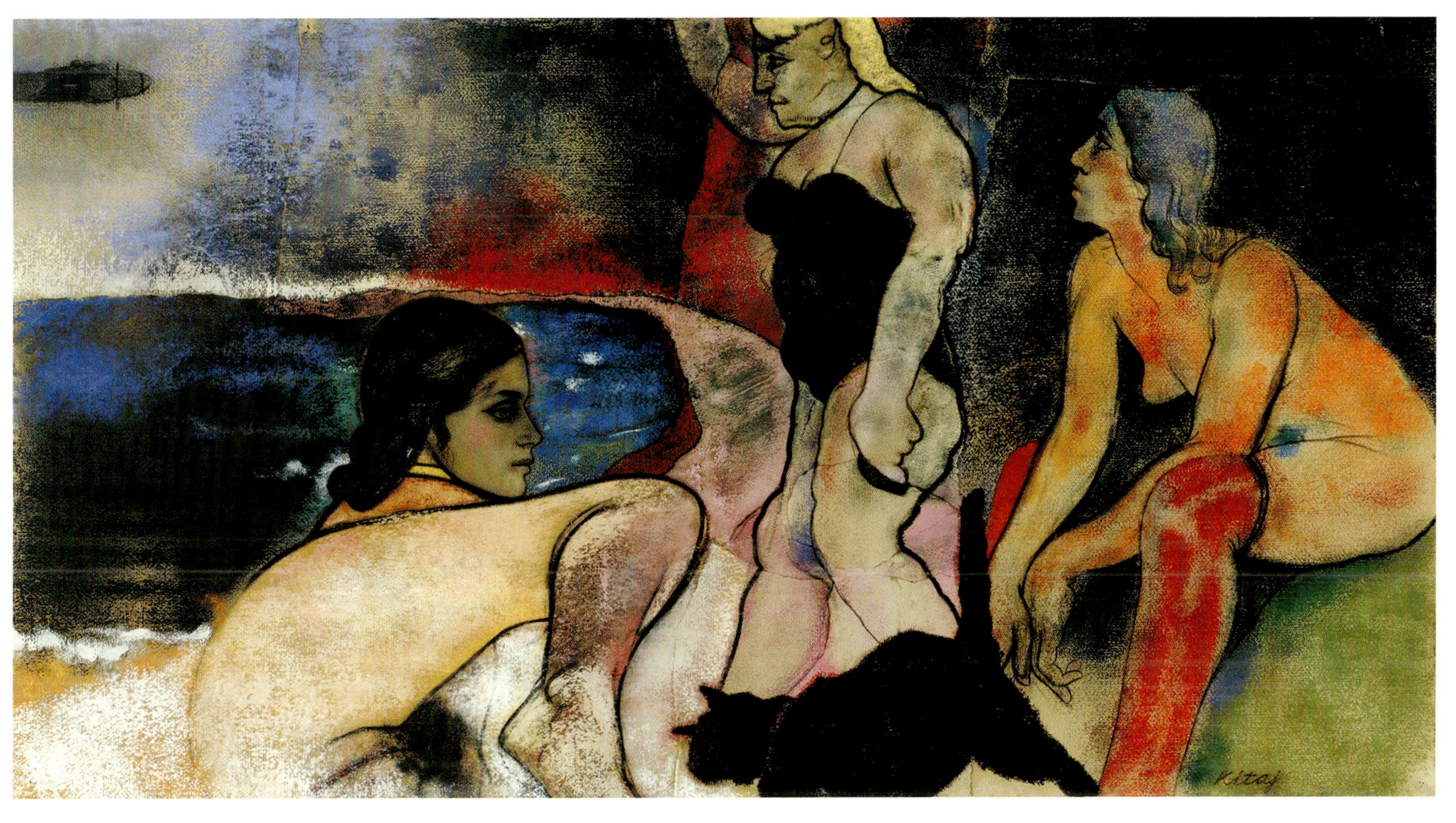

R. B. Kitaj

The Rise of Fascism, 1975–79

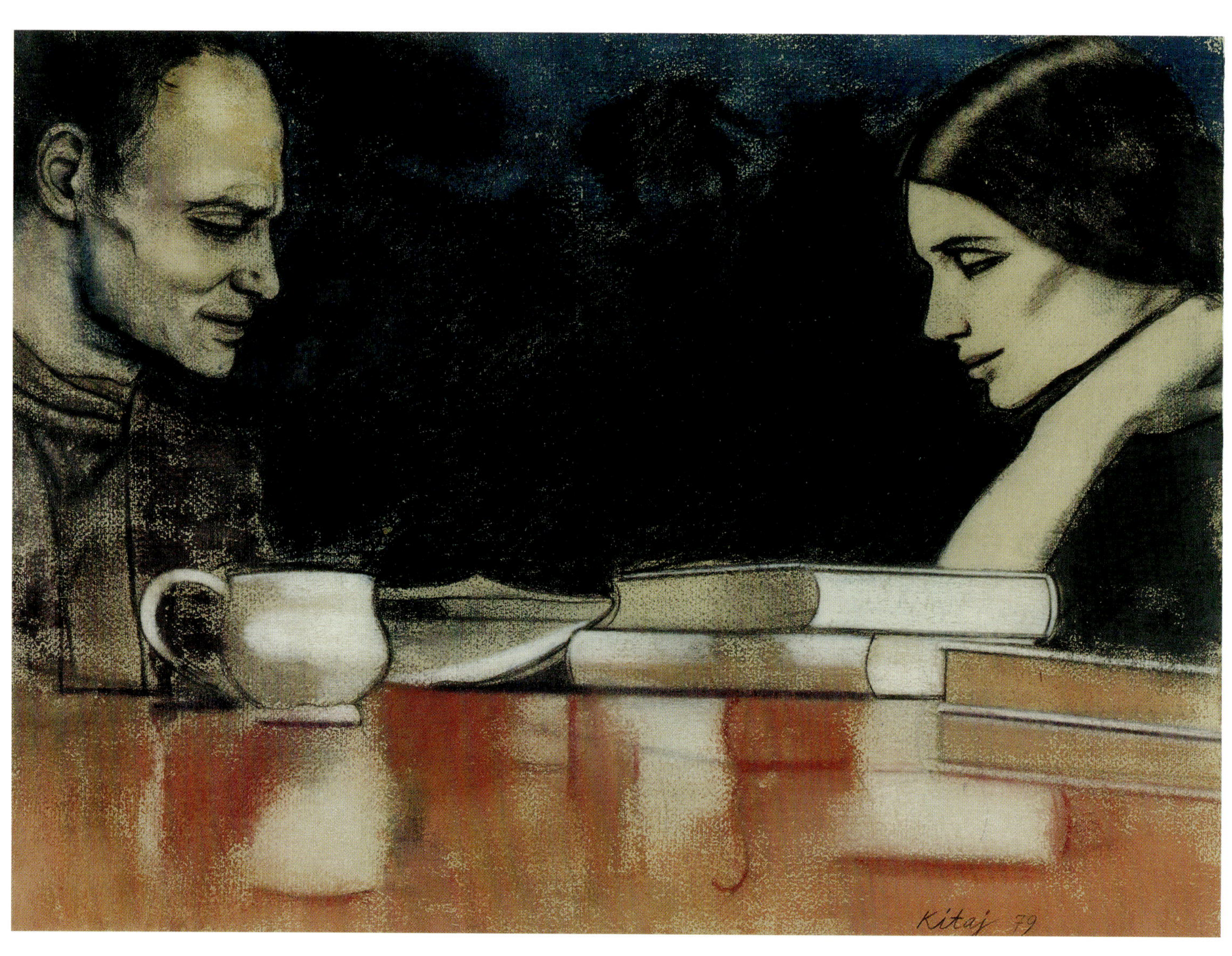

R. B. Kitaj

Two London Painters: Frank Auerbach and Sandra Fisher, 1979

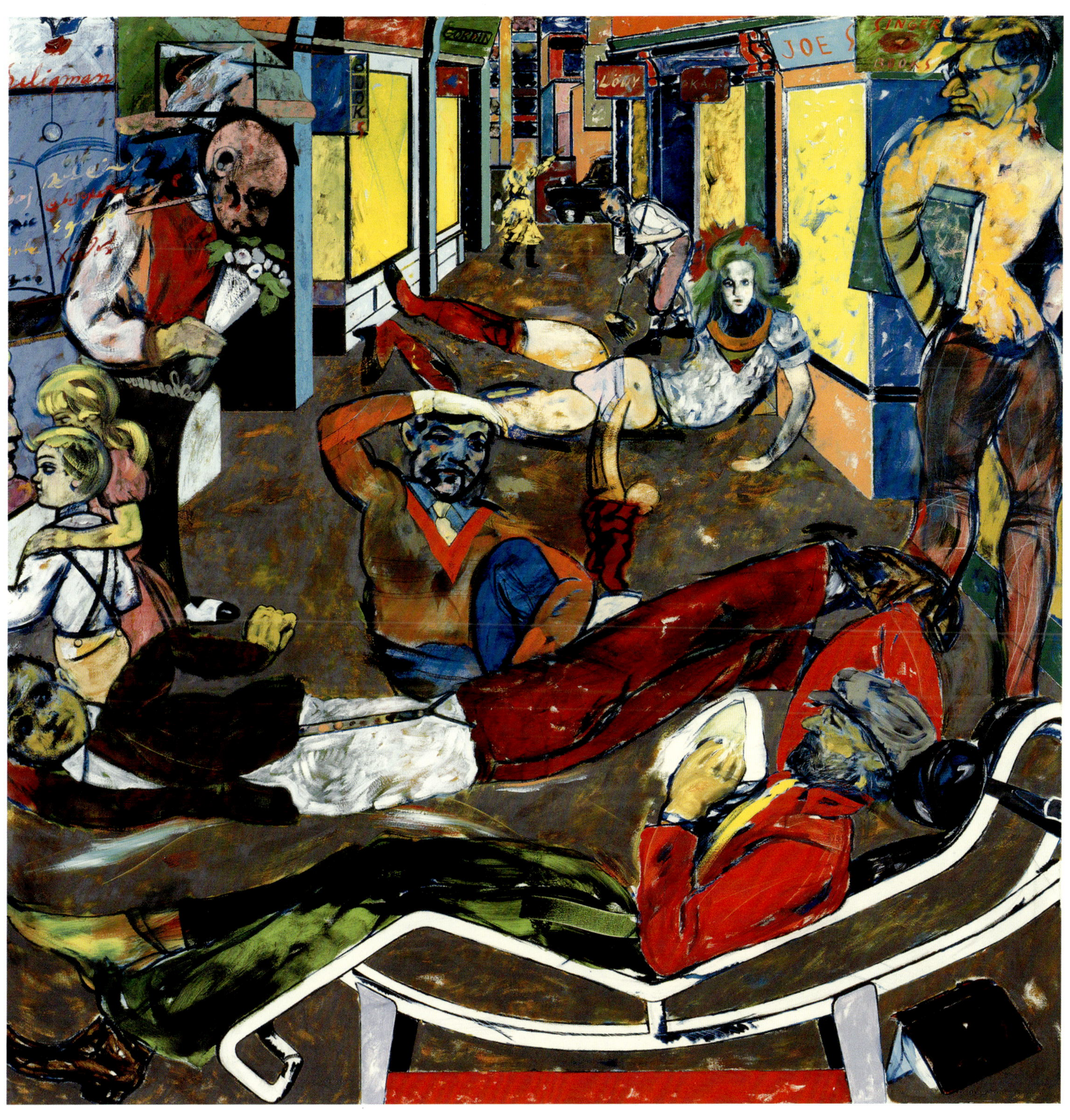

R. B. Kitaj

Cecil Court, London W.C.2. (The Refugees), 1983–84

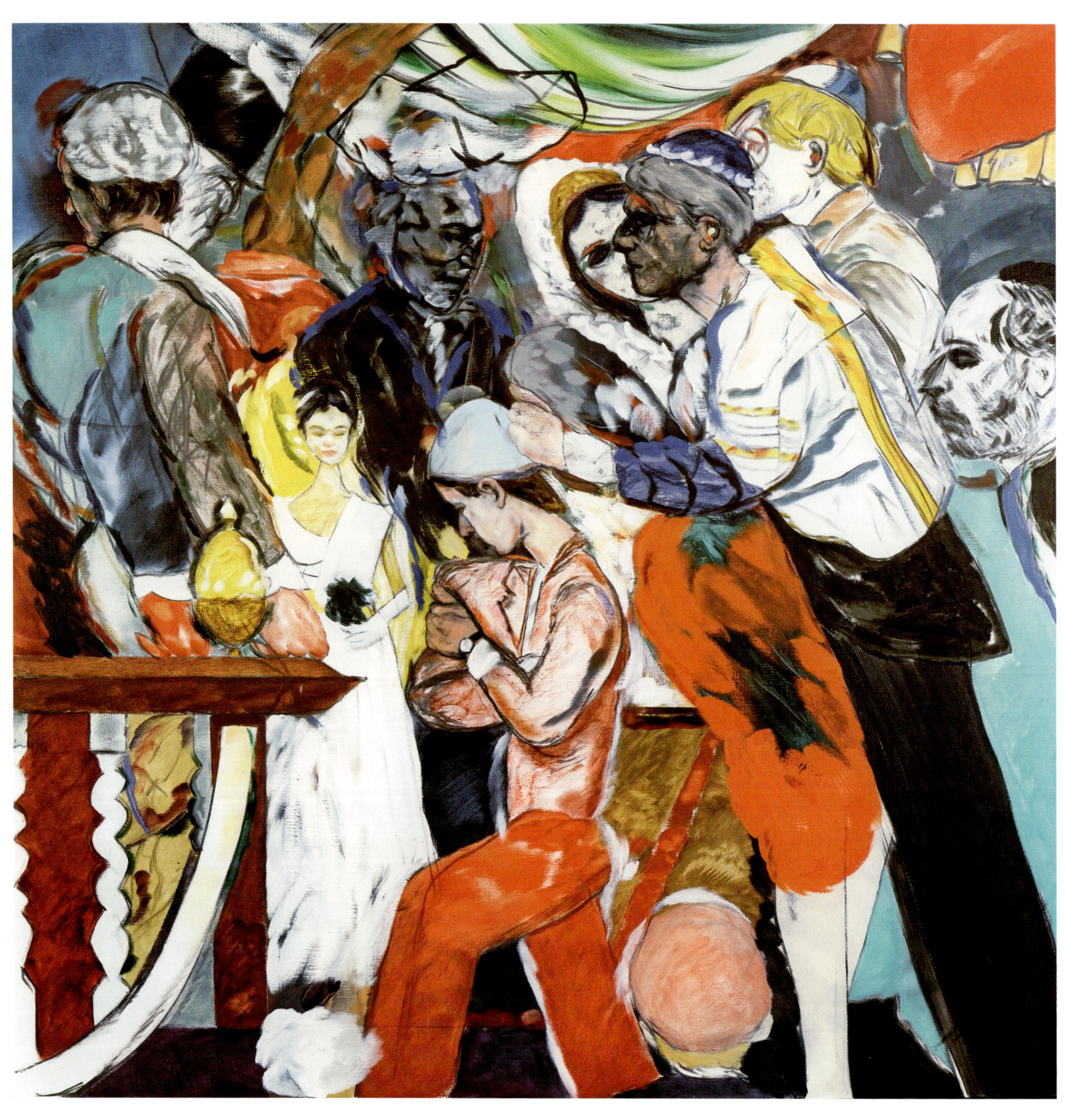

R. B. Kitaj
The Wedding, 1989–93

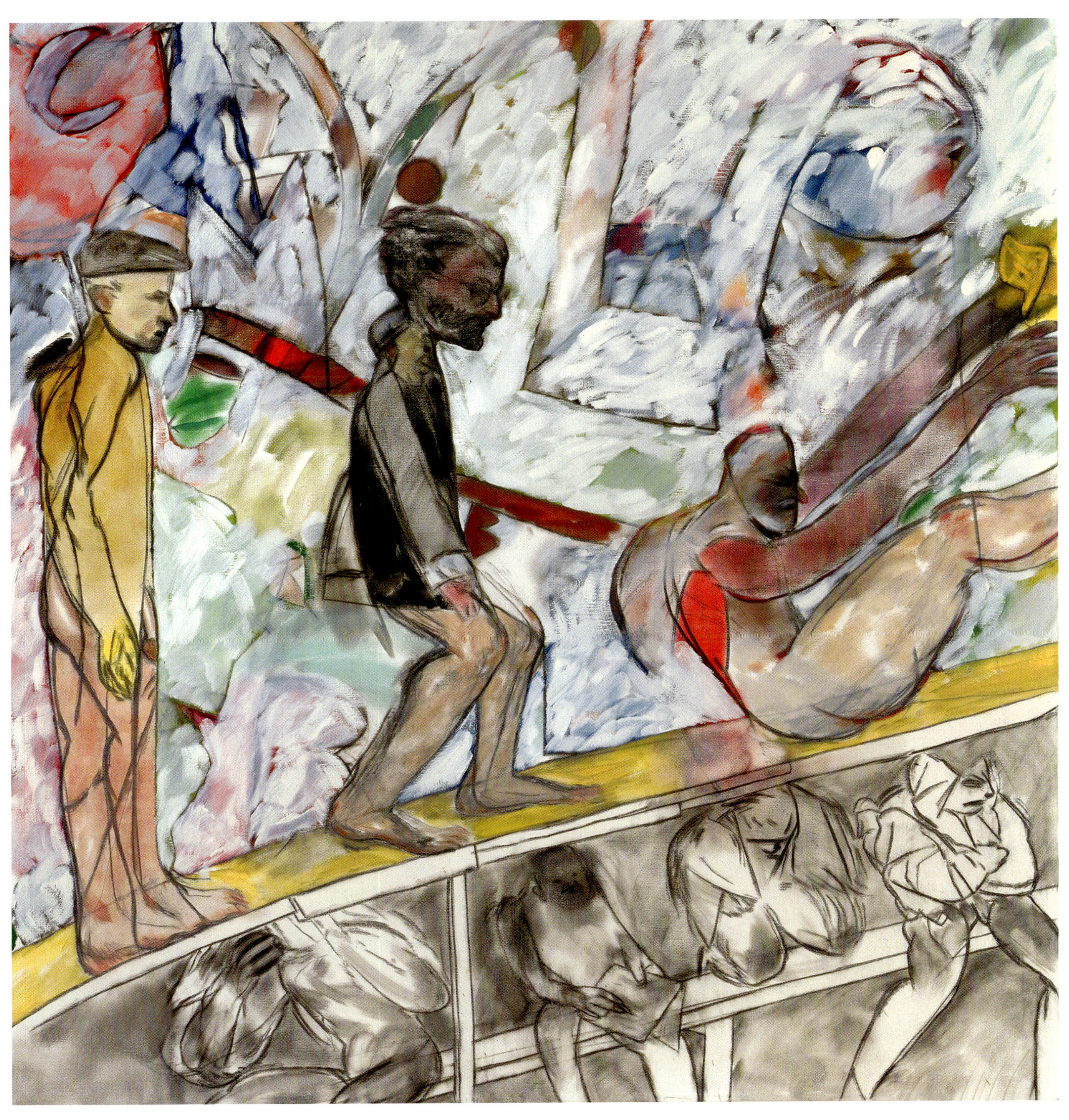

R. B. Kitaj

My Cities (An Experimental Drama), 1990–93

WORKS IN THE EXHIBITION

FRANCIS BACON

Figures in a Garden, ca. 1935
Oil on canvas
74 x 94 cm (29⅛ x 37 in.)
Tate. Accepted by HM Government in lieu of inheritance tax and allocated to Tate 2007
Page 32

Figure in a Landscape, 1945
Oil on canvas
144.8 x 128.3 cm (57 x 50½ in.)
Tate. Purchased 1950
Page 33

Figure in a Landscape, ca. 1952
Oil on paper
33.9 x 26.3 cm (13⅜ x 10⅜ in.)
Tate. Purchased with assistance from the National Lottery through the Heritage Lottery Fund, the Art Fund and a group of anonymous donors in memory of Mario Tazzoli 1998
Page 34

Figure with Meat, 1954
Oil on canvas
129.9 x 121.9 cm (51 1/8 x 48 in.)
The Art Institute of Chicago, Harriott A. Fox Fund, 1956.1201
Page 35

Study for Portrait II (after the Life Mask of William Blake), 1955
Oil on canvas
61 x 50.8 cm (24 x 20 in.)
Tate. Purchased 1979
Page 36

Blue Crawling Figure, No. 1, ca. 1957–61
Oil on paper
34 x 27 cm (13⅜ x 10⅝ in.)
Tate. Purchased with assistance from the National Lottery through the Heritage Lottery Fund, the Art Fund and a group of anonymous donors in memory of Mario Tazzoli 1998
Page 37

Collapsed Figure, ca. 1957–61
Oil on paper
34 x 27 cm (13⅜ x 10⅝ in.)
Tate. Purchased with assistance from the National Lottery through the Heritage Lottery Fund, the Art Fund and a group of anonymous donors in memory of Mario Tazzoli 1998
Page 38

Figure with Left Arm Raised, No. 2, ca. 1957–61
Oil on paper
34 x 27 cm (13⅜ x 10⅝ in.)
Tate. Purchased with assistance from the National Lottery through the Heritage Lottery Fund, the Art Fund and a group of anonymous donors in memory of Mario Tazzoli 1998
Page 39

Reclining Figure, No. 1, ca. 1961
Oil and ink on paper
23.8 x 15.6 cm (9⅜ x 6⅛ in.)
Tate. Purchased with assistance from the National Lottery through the Heritage Lottery Fund, the Art Fund and a group of anonymous donors in memory of Mario Tazzoli 1998
Page 40

Reclining Woman, 1961
Oil on canvas
198.8 x 141.6 cm (78¼ x 55¾ in.)
Tate. Purchased 1961
Page 41

Portrait of George Dyer Riding a Bicycle, 1966
Oil on canvas
198 x 147.5 cm (77¹⁵⁄₁₆ x 58¹⁄₁₆ in.)
Beyeler Museum AG, Riehen/Basel, 87.1
Page 43

Portrait of Isabel Rawsthorne, 1966
Oil on canvas
81.3 x 68.6 cm (32 x 27 in.)
Tate. Purchased 1966
Page 44

Study for Head of Lucian Freud, 1967
Oil on canvas
35.5 x 30.5 cm (14 x 12 in.)
Private collection
Page 45

Triptych August 1972, 1972
Oil and sand on canvas
Three panels, 198.1 x 147.3 cm (78 x 58 in.) each
Tate. Purchased 1980
Pages 46–47

LUCIAN FREUD

Man with a Thistle (Self-Portrait), 1946
Oil on canvas
61 x 50.2 cm (24 x 19¾ in.)
Tate. Purchased 1961
Page 50

Girl with a Fig Leaf, 1947
Etching on paper
29.8 x 23.8 cm (11¾ x 9⅜ in.)
Tate. Purchased 1988
Page 51

Girl with a Kitten, 1947
Oil on canvas
41 x 30.7 cm (16⅛ x 12⅛ in.)
Tate. Bequeathed by Simon Sainsbury 2006, accessioned 2008
Page 52

Narcissus, 1948
Ink on paper
21 x 13.7 cm (8¼ x 5⅜ in.)
Tate. Bequeathed by Pauline Vogelpoel, Director of the Contemporary Art Society, 2002, accessioned 2004
Page 53

Boy Smoking, 1950–51
Oil on copper
15.5 x 11.5 cm (6⅛ x 4½ in.)
Tate. Bequeathed by Simon Sainsbury 2006, accessioned 2008
Page 54

Girl with a White Dog, 1950–51
Oil on canvas
76.2 x 101.6 cm (30 x 40 in.)
Tate. Purchased 1952
Page 55

Naked Portrait, 1972–73
Oil on canvas
61 x 61 cm (24 x 24 in.)
Tate. Purchased 1975
Page 57

The Painter's Mother IV, 1973
Oil on canvas
27.3 x 18.6 cm (10¾ x 7 5/16 in.)
Tate. Bequeathed by Simon Sainsbury 2006, accessioned 2008
Page 59

Two Plants, 1977–80
Oil on canvas
149.9 x 120 cm (59 x 47¼ in.)
Tate. Purchased 1980
Page 60

Girl in a Striped Nightshirt, 1983–85
Oil on canvas
29.5 x 25 cm (11⅝ x 9⅞ in.)
Tate. Presented by Mercedes and Ian Stoutzker 2013 and forming part of the Mercedes and Ian Stoutzker Gift to Tate
Page 61

Man Posing, 1985
Etching on paper
69.5 x 54.3 cm (27⅜ x 21⅜ in.)
Tate. Purchased 1987
Page 62

Leigh Bowery, 1991
Oil on canvas
51 x 40.9 cm (20 1/16 x 16⅛ in.)
Tate. Presented anonymously 1994
Page 63

Leigh under the Skylight, 1994
Oil on canvas
269.2 x 119.4 cm (106 x 47 in.)
Private collection, New York
Page 64

Woman Sleeping, 1995
Etching on paper
73 x 59.4 cm (28¾ x 23⅜ in.)
Tate. Presented anonymously 1997
Page 65

Bruce Bernard (Seated), 1996
Oil on canvas
101.6 x 81.3 cm (40 x 32 in.)
Collection of Michael Moritz and Harriet Heyman
Page 66

David Dawson, 1998
Etching on paper
75.8 x 57.4 cm (29⅞ x 22⅝ in.)
Tate. Presented anonymously 1998
Page 67

Naked Portrait, 2001
Oil on canvas
167.6 x 132.1 cm (66 x 52 in.)
Collection of Michael Moritz and Harriet Heyman
Page 68

Self-Portrait Reflection, 2003
Oil on canvas
17.8 x 12.7 cm (7 x 5 in.)
Collection of Michael Moritz and Harriet Heyman
Page 69

David and Eli, 2003–4
Oil on canvas
162.6 x 174 cm (64 x 68½ in.)
Lent from a private collection 2016
Page 71

LEON KOSSOFF

Building Site, Oxford Street, 1952
Crayon, charcoal, and gouache on paper
112 x 133.5 cm (44⅛ x 52 9/16 in.)
Tate. Purchased 1996
Page 75

Man in a Wheelchair, 1959–62
Oil on wood
213.4 x 123.2 cm (84 x 48½ in.)
Tate. Purchased 1963
Page 76

Woman III in Bed, Surrounded by Family, 1965
Oil on board
185.4 x 124.5 cm (73 x 49 in.)
Tate. Purchased 1981
Page 77

Children's Swimming Pool, Autumn Afternoon, 1971
Oil on board
168 x 214 cm (66⅛ x 84¼ in.)
Tate. Purchased 1981
Page 78

Willesden Junction, Morning in October, 1971
Oil on board
91.6 x 183.4 cm (36 1/16 x 72 3/16 in.)
Tate. Lent from a private collection 2006
Page 79

Demolition of the Old House, Dalston Junction, Summer 1974, 1974
Oil on board
160 x 218.4 cm (63 x 86 in.)
Tate. Purchased 1975
Page 80

Father Resting, 1977
Charcoal
77 x 56 cm (30 5/16 x 22 1/16 in.)
Private collection
Page 81

Two Seated Figures II, 1980
Charcoal
79.4 x 56.5 cm (31¼ x 22¼ in.)
Private collection, promised gift to Tate
Page 82

Two Seated Figures No. 2, 1980
Oil on board
243.8 x 182.8 cm (96 x 72 in.)
Tate. Purchased 1983
Page 83

Booking Hall, Kilburn Underground, 1987
Oil on board
198.2 x 182.7 cm (78 x 71 15/16 in.)
Tate. Purchased with assistance from the Friends of the Tate Gallery and the Mail on Sunday through the Friends of the Tate Gallery 1989
Page 84

Christ Church, Spitalfields, Morning, 1990
Oil on board
198.6 x 189.2 cm (78 3/16 x 74½ in.)
Tate. Purchased 1994
Page 85

MICHAEL ANDREWS

A Man Who Suddenly Fell Over, 1952
Oil on hardboard
120.6 x 172.7 cm (47½ x 68 in.)
Tate. Purchased 1958
Page 88

Study for a Man in a Landscape (Digswell), 1959
Oil on canvas
40.6 x 35.9 cm (16 x 14⅛ in.)
Tate. Presented by the executors of the estate of David Wilkie 1993
Page 89

The Deer Park, 1962
Oil on board
214 x 244.5 cm (84½ x 96½ in.)
Tate. Purchased 1974
Page 90

Lights IV: The Pier and the Road, 1973
Acrylic and graphite on canvas
152.4 x 153.5 cm (60 x 60 7/16 in.)
The Metropolitan Museum of Art, New York, Purchase, Mr. and Mrs. Milton Petrie Gift, 1981, 1981.196
Page 91

Melanie and Me Swimming, 1978–79
Acrylic on canvas
182.9 x 182.9 cm (72 x 72 in.)
Tate. Purchased 1979
Page 92

Thames Painting, the Estuary, 1994–95
Oil with sand and ash embedded on canvas
213 x 182.5 cm (83⅞ x 71⅞ in.)
Pallant House Gallery, Chichester, West Sussex
Page 93

FRANK AUERBACH

Portrait of Leon Kossoff, 1951
Oil on board
61.4 x 45.4 cm (24 3/16 x 17⅞ in.)
Tate. Lent from a private collection 2006
Page 96

E.O.W. Nude, 1953–54
Oil on canvas
50.8 x 76.8 cm (20 x 30¼ in.)
Tate. Purchased 1959
Page 97

Self-Portrait, 1958
Charcoal and paper collage
77.2 x 56.5 cm (30⅜ x 22¼ in.)
Courtesy of Daniel Katz Gallery, London
Page 98

Oxford Street Building Site I, 1959–60
Oil on board
198.1 x 153.7 cm (78 x 60½ in.)
Tate. Purchased 1961
Page 99

Head of E.O.W., 1959–60
Charcoal, paper, and watercolor on paper
78.7 x 58.1 cm (31 x 22⅞ in.)
Tate. Purchased 1976
Page 100

The Sitting Room, 1964
Oil on board
128.2 x 127.7 cm (50½ x 50¼ in.)
Tate. Presented by the Friends of the Tate Gallery 1984
Page 101

Study after Titian II, 1965
Oil on canvas
67.3 x 62.2 cm (26½ x 24½ in.)
Tate. Presented by the executors of the estate of David Wilkie 1993
Page 102

Mornington Crescent with the Statue of Sickert's Father-in-Law, 1966
Oil on panel
122 x 152.5 cm (48 1/16 x 60 1/16 in.)
Courtesy of the Daniel Katz Family Trust, London
Page 103

The Origin of the Great Bear, 1967–68
Oil on board
114.6 x 140.2 cm (45⅛ x 55 3/16 in.)
Tate. Presented by the executors of the estate of David Wilkie 1993
Page 105

Primrose Hill, 1967–68
Oil on board
121.9 x 146.7 cm (48 x 57¾ in.)
Tate. Purchased 1971
Page 106

Working Drawing for "Primrose Hill," 1968
Chalk and graphite on paper
25.1 x 31.1 cm (9⅞ x 12¼ in.)
Tate. Purchased 1971
Page 107

Working Drawing for "Primrose Hill," 1968
Graphite on paper
26.7 x 31.8 cm (10½ x 12½ in.)
Tate. Purchased 1971
Page 108

Working Drawing for "Primrose Hill," 1968
Graphite on paper
25.1 x 30.5 cm (9⅞ x 12 in.)
Tate. Purchased 1971
Page 109

Working Drawing for "Primrose Hill," 1968
Graphite on paper
22.5 x 26.7 cm (8⅞ x 10½ in.)
Tate. Purchased 1971
Page 110

Working Drawing for "Primrose Hill," 1968
Graphite on paper
22.5 x 26 cm (8⅞ x 10¼ in.)
Tate. Purchased 1971
Page 111

Primrose Hill, 1971
Oil on panel
101.5 x 127 cm (39 15/16 x 50 in.)
Courtesy of the Daniel Katz Family Trust, London
Page 113

J.Y.M. Seated No. 1, 1981
Oil on board
71.1 x 61 cm (28 x 24 in.)
Tate. Purchased 1981
Page 114

To the Studios, 1990–91
Oil on canvas
169.5 x 149.4 cm (66¾ x 58 13/16 in.)
Tate. Purchased 1992
Page 115

Mornington Crescent—Summer Morning, 2004
Oil on canvas
132.7 x 132.3 cm (52¼ x 52⅛ in.)
Tate. Accepted by HM Government in lieu of inheritance tax and allocated to Tate 2015
Page 116

Self-Portrait II, 2010
Graphite
76.5 x 57.5 cm (30⅛ x 22⅝ in.)
Private collection
Page 117

R. B. KITAJ

Erasmus Variations, 1958
Oil on canvas
104.9 x 84.2 cm (41 5/16 x 33 1/8 in.)
Tate. Accepted by HM Government in lieu of inheritance tax and allocated to Tate 2007
Page 120

The Murder of Rosa Luxemburg, 1960
Oil, ink, graphite, and paper on canvas
153 x 152.4 cm (60 1/4 x 60 in.)
Tate. Purchased 1980
Page 121

Isaac Babel Riding with Budyonny, 1962
Oil on canvas
182.9 x 152.4 cm (72 x 60 in.)
Tate. Purchased 1963
Page 122

Boys and Girls!, 1964
Screenprint on paper
52.7 x 41.3 cm (20 3/4 x 16 1/4 in.)
Tate. Presented by Rose and Chris Prater through the Institute of Contemporary Prints 1975
Page 123

The Defects of Its Qualities, 1967–68
Screenprint on paper
90.2 x 61 cm (35 1/2 x 24 in.)
Tate. Presented by Rose and Chris Prater through the Institute of Contemporary Prints 1975
Page 124

The Rise of Fascism, 1975–79
Oil, charcoal, and pastel on paper
85.1 x 158.4 cm (33 1/2 x 62 3/8 in.)
Tate. Purchased 1980
Page 125

Two London Painters: Frank Auerbach and Sandra Fisher, 1979
Pastel and watercolor
56.2 x 78.4 cm (22 1/8 x 30 7/8 in.)
Los Angeles County Museum of Art, Michael and Dorothy Blankfort Bequest, AC1999.34.40
Page 126

Cecil Court, London W.C.2. (The Refugees), 1983–84
Oil on canvas
183 x 183 cm (72 1/16 x 72 1/16 in.)
Tate. Purchased 1985
Page 127

The Wedding, 1989–93
Oil on canvas
182.9 x 182.9 cm (72 x 72 in.)
Tate. Presented by the artist 1993
Page 128

My Cities (An Experimental Drama), 1990–93
Oil on canvas
183.2 x 183.2 cm (72 1/8 x 72 1/8 in.)
Tate. Purchased 1997
Page 129

SELECTED BIBLIOGRAPHY

GROUP EXHIBITION CATALOGUES AND BOOKS

Arnhold, Hermann, ed. *Bare Life: Bacon, Freud, Hockney, and Others; London Artists Working from Life, 1950–80*. Exhibition catalogue. Münster: LWL-Museum für Kunst und Kultur; Munich: Hirmer, 2014. Texts by Andrew Brighton, Eckhart J. Gillen, Lee Hallman, Invar-Torre Hollaus, Catherine Lampert, Lynda Morris, Tanja Pirsig-Marshall, and Colin Wiggins.

Calvocoressi, Richard, and Philip Long, eds. *From London: Bacon, Freud, Kossoff, Andrews, Auerbach, Kitaj*. Exhibition catalogue, Scottish National Gallery of Modern Art, Edinburgh; Musée National d'Histoire et d'Art, Luxembourg; Musée Cantonal des Beaux-Arts, Lausanne, Switzerland; Fundació Catalunya–La Pedrera, Barcelona. London: British Council; Edinburgh: Scottish National Gallery of Modern Art, 1995. Texts by Bruce Bernard, Richard Calvocoressi, and David Cohen.

Eight Figurative Painters: Michael Andrews, Frank Auerbach, Francis Bacon, William Coldstream, Lucian Freud, Patrick George, Leon Kossoff, Euan Uglow. Exhibition catalogue, Yale Center for British Art, New Haven, CT; Santa Barbara Museum of Art, CA. New Haven, CT: Yale Center for British Art, 1981. Texts by Andrew Forge and Lawrence Gowing.

Hicks, Alistair. *The School of London: The Resurgence of Contemporary Painting*. Oxford: Phaidon, 1989.

Hyman, James. *The Battle for Realism: Figurative Art in Britain during the Cold War, 1945–1960*. New Haven, CT: Yale University Press in association with Paul Mellon Centre for Studies in British Art, 2001.

Joachimides, Christos, Norman Rosenthal, and Nicholas Serota, eds. *A New Spirit in Painting*. Exhibition catalogue. London: Royal Academy of Arts, 1981.

Kitaj, R. B. *The Human Clay: An Exhibition*. Exhibition catalogue, Hayward Gallery, London. London: Arts Council of Great Britain, 1976.

Lampert, Catherine. *The Mystery of Appearance: Conversations between Ten British Post-war Painters; Michael Andrews, Frank Auerbach, Francis Bacon, Patrick Caulfield, William Coldstream, Lucian Freud, Richard Hamilton, David Hockney, Leon Kossoff, Euan Uglow*. Exhibition catalogue. London: Haunch of Venison, 2011.

Morphet, Richard. *The Hard-Won Image: Traditional Method and Subject in Recent British Art*. Exhibition catalogue. London: Tate Gallery, 1984.

Ordovas, Pilar, ed. *Crossing the Channel: Friendships and Connections in Paris and London, 1946–1965: Francis Bacon, Lucian Freud, and Alberto Giacometti*. Exhibition catalogue. London: Gagosian Gallery, 2010.

The School of London and Their Friends: The Collection of Elaine and Melvin Merians. Exhibition catalogue. New Haven, CT: Yale Center for British Art, 2001. Texts by Richard Cork, Patrick McCaughey, and Emily M. Weeks.

A School of London: Six Figurative Painters. Exhibition catalogue, Museo d'Arte Moderna Ca' Pesaro, Venice, Italy; Kunstnernes Hus, Oslo; Louisiana Museum of Modern Art, Humlebaek, Denmark; Kunstmuseum Düsseldorf, Germany. London: British Council, 1987. Text by Michael Peppiatt.

The Transformation of Appearance: Andrews, Auerbach, Bacon, Freud, Kossoff. Exhibition brochure, Sainsbury Centre for Visual Arts, Norwich, UK. London: Tate Gallery Publications, 1991. Text by Paul Moorhouse.

Wilcox, Tim, ed. *The Pursuit of the Real: British Figurative Painting from Sickert to Bacon*. Exhibition catalogue. London: Lund Humphries in association with Manchester City Art Gallery, 1990. Texts by Andrew Causey, Lynda Checketts, Michael Peppiatt, and Tim Wilcox.

MICHAEL ANDREWS

Feaver, William, and Paul Moorhouse. *Michael Andrews*. Exhibition catalogue. London: Tate Publishing, 2001.

Michael Andrews. Exhibition catalogue, Hayward Gallery, London; Fruitmarket Gallery, Edinburgh; Whitworth Art Gallery, University of Manchester. London: Arts Council of Great Britain, 1980–81. Texts by Lawrence Gowing, Catherine Lampert, and David Sylvester.

Michael Andrews: Landscapes. Exhibition catalogue. London: James Hyman Fine Art, 2005. Text by Frank Auerbach.

Michael Andrews: Lights. Exhibition catalogue. Madrid: Museo Thyssen-Bornemisza, 2000. Texts by William Feaver and Belén Gopegui.

Michael Andrews: "The Delectable Mountain," the Ayers Rock Series and Other Landscape Paintings. Exhibition catalogue, Whitechapel Art Gallery, London; Fondation Nationale des Arts Graphiques et Plastiques, Paris; Scottish National Gallery of Modern Art, Edinburgh; Grey Art Gallery and Study Center, New York University. London: Trustees of the Whitechapel Art Gallery, 1991. Texts by Bruce Bernard, Catherine Lampert, and Jonathan Raban.

Michael Andrews: The Scottish Paintings. Exhibition catalogue. Edinburgh: Scottish National Gallery of Modern Art, 1991. Text by Richard Calvocoressi.

Wilson, Colin St John. *The Artist at Work: On the Working Methods of William Coldstream and Michael Andrews*. London: Lund Humphries, 1999.

FRANK AUERBACH

Feaver, William. *Frank Auerbach*. New York: Rizzoli, 2009.

Frank Auerbach. Exhibition catalogue, Hayward Gallery, London; Fruitmarket Gallery, Edinburgh. London: Arts Council of Great Britain, 1978. Text by Leon Kossoff and conversation with Catherine Lampert.

Frank Auerbach: Paintings and Drawings, 1977–1985. Exhibition catalogue, British Pavilion, XLII Venice Biennale. London: Fine Arts Dept., British Council, 1986. Text by Catherine Lampert.

Frank Auerbach: Recent Work. Exhibition catalogue. Amsterdam: Rijksmuseum Vincent van Gogh, 1989. Text by Mel Gooding.

Frank Auerbach: Recent Works. Exhibition catalogue. New York: Marlborough Gallery, 1998. Interview with Michael Peppiatt.

Hughes, Robert. *Frank Auerbach*. London: Thames & Hudson, 1990.

Lampert, Catherine, ed. *Frank Auerbach*. Exhibition catalogue, Kunstmuseum Bonn, Germany, and Tate Britain, London. London: Tate Britain, 2015. Text by T. J. Clark and reprint of conversation with Catherine Lampert (1978).

———. *Frank Auerbach: Speaking and Painting*. London: Thames & Hudson, 2015.

Lampert, Catherine, Norman Rosenthal, and Isabel Carlisle. *Frank Auerbach: Paintings and Drawings, 1954–2001*. Exhibition catalogue. London: Royal Academy of Arts, 2001.

Ordovas, Pilar, ed. *Raw Truth: Auerbach—Rembrandt*. Exhibition catalogue, Ordovas, London; Rijksmuseum, Amsterdam. London: Ordovas, 2013. Conversation between Frank Auerbach, Taco Dibbits, Pilar Ordovas, and Geoffrey Parton.

Wiggins, Colin. *Frank Auerbach at the National Gallery: Working after the Masters*. Exhibition catalogue. London: National Gallery Publications, 1995. Texts by Lucian Freud and Colin Wiggins.

Wright, Barnaby, ed. *Frank Auerbach: London Building Sites, 1952–62*. Exhibition catalogue. London: Courtauld Gallery and Paul Holberton, 2009. Texts by Margaret Garlake, Paul Moorhouse, and Barnaby Wright.

FRANCIS BACON

Ades, Dawn, and Andrew Forge. *Francis Bacon*. Exhibition catalogue. London: Tate Gallery and Thames & Hudson, 1985.

Alley, Ronald, and John Rothenstein. *Francis Bacon*. New York: Viking, 1964.

Brighton, Andrew. *Francis Bacon*. London: Tate Gallery, 2001.

Deleuze, Gilles. *Francis Bacon: The Logic of Sensation*. Translated by Daniel W. Smith. Minneapolis: University of Minnesota Press, 2004.

Farson, Daniel. *The Gilded Gutter Life of Francis Bacon*. New York: Pantheon, 1993.

Francis Bacon. Exhibition catalogue, Centre Georges Pompidou, Paris. Paris: Connaissance des Arts, 1996. Texts by Michael Gibson, Fabrice Hergott, David Sylvester, and René Viau.

Gale, Matthew, and Chris Stephens, eds. *Francis Bacon*. Exhibition catalogue, Tate Britain, London; Museo Nacional del Prado, Madrid; Metropolitan Museum of Art, New York. London: Tate Publishing, 2008.

Geitner, Amanda, Thierry Morel, and Calvin Winner. *Francis Bacon and the Masters*. Exhibition catalogue, Sainsbury Centre for Visual Arts, University of East Anglia. London: Fontanka, 2015.

Gowing, Lawrence, and Sam Hunter. *Francis Bacon*. Exhibition catalogue, Hirshhorn Museum and Sculpture Garden, Washington, DC; Los Angeles County Museum of Art; Museum of Modern Art, New York. New York: Thames & Hudson, 1989.

Harrison, Martin. *In Camera: Francis Bacon; Photography, Film, and the Practice of Painting*. New York: Thames & Hudson, 2005.

———, ed. *Francis Bacon: Catalogue Raisonné*. 5 vols. London: Estate of Francis Bacon, 2016.

———, ed. *Francis Bacon: New Studies*. Göttingen: Steidl, 2009.

Peppiatt, Michael. *Francis Bacon: Anatomy of an Enigma*. London: Weidenfeld & Nicolson, 1996.

———. *Francis Bacon in Your Blood: A Memoir*. New York: Bloomsbury, 2015.

Russell, John. *Francis Bacon*. Rev. ed. New York: Thames & Hudson, 1993.

Sinclair, Andrew. *Francis Bacon: His Life and Violent Times*. New York: Crown, 1993.

Sylvester, David. *Interviews with Francis Bacon: The Brutality of Fact*. 3rd ed. New York: Thames & Hudson, 1988.

LUCIAN FREUD

Calvocoressi, Richard. *Lucian Freud: Early Works*. Exhibition catalogue. Edinburgh: Scottish National Gallery of Modern Art, 1997.

Dawson, David. *A Painter's Progress: A Portrait of Lucian Freud*. London: Jonathan Cape, 2014.

Feaver, William. *Lucian Freud*. Exhibition catalogue, Tate Britain, London; Fundació La Caixa, Barcelona; Museum of Contemporary Art, Los Angeles. London: Tate Publishing, 2003.

———. *Lucian Freud*. New York: Rizzoli, 2007.

Figura, Starr. *Lucian Freud: The Painter's Etchings*. Exhibition catalogue. New York: Museum of Modern Art, 2007.

Gayford, Martin. *Man with a Blue Scarf: On Sitting for a Portrait by Lucian Freud*. London: Thames & Hudson, 2010.

Gowing, Lawrence. *Lucian Freud*. London: Thames & Hudson, 1982.

Haag, Sabine, and Jasper Sharp, eds. *Lucian Freud*. Exhibition catalogue, Kunsthistorisches Museum, Vienna. Munich: Prestel, 2013. Texts by Pierre Rosenberg, Mark Evans, and Guido Messling.

Howgate, Sarah, with Michael Auping and John Richardson. *Lucian Freud: Portraits*. Exhibition catalogue, National Portrait Gallery, London, and Modern Art Museum of Fort Worth, Texas. New Haven, CT: Yale University Press, 2012.

Hughes, Robert. *Lucian Freud: Paintings*. Exhibition catalogue, Hirshhorn Museum and Sculpture Garden, Smithsonian Institution, Washington, DC; Musée National d'Art Moderne, Paris; Hayward Gallery, London; Neue Nationalgalerie, Berlin. Organized by the British Council. London: Thames & Hudson, 1987.

Lampert, Catherine, ed. *Lucian Freud*. Exhibition catalogue, Irish Museum of Modern Art, Dublin; Louisiana Museum of Modern Art, Humlebaek, Denmark; Gemeentemuseum Den Haag, The Hague. Dublin: Irish Museum of Modern Art, 2007. Texts by Martin Gayford, Catherine Lampert, and Frank Paul.

———. *Lucian Freud: Recent Work*. Exhibition catalogue, Whitechapel Art Gallery, London; Metropolitan Museum of Art, New York; Museo Nacional Centro de Arte Reina Sofía, Madrid. New York: Rizzoli, 1993.

Lucian Freud: The Studio. Exhibition catalogue, Centre Georges Pompidou, Paris. Munich: Hirmer, 2010. Texts by Laurence de Cars, Jean Clair, Philippe Comar, Éric Darragon, and Richard Shiff.

Lucian Freud: Works on Paper. Exhibition catalogue, Ashmolean Museum, Oxford; Fruitmarket Gallery, Edinburgh; Ferens Art Gallery, Hull; Walker Art Gallery, Liverpool; Royal Albert Memorial Museum, Exeter; California Palace of the Legion of Honor, Fine Arts Museums of San Francisco. New York: Thames & Hudson, 1988. Texts by Robert Flynn Johnson and Nicholas Penny.

R. B. KITAJ

Aulich, James, and John Lynch, eds. *Critical Kitaj: Essays on the Work of R. B. Kitaj*. Manchester: Manchester University Press, 2000.

Kugelmann, Cilly, Eckhart Gillen, and Hubertus Gassner. *Obsessions: R. B. Kitaj, 1932–2007*. Exhibition catalogue, Jüdisches Museum, Berlin; Jewish Museum, London; Pallant House, Chichester; Hamburger Kunsthalle, Hamburg. Bielefeld: Kerber; Berlin: Jewish Museum, 2012.

Lambirth, Andrew. *Kitaj*. London: PWP Contemporary Art, 2004.

Livingstone, Marco. *Kitaj*. 4th ed. London: Phaidon, 2010.

———, ed. *R. B. Kitaj: An American in Europe*. Exhibition catalogue, Astrup Fearnley Museet for Moderne Kunst, Oslo; Museo Nacional Centro de Arte Reina Sofía, Madrid; Jüdisches Museum der Stadt Wien, Vienna; Sprengel Museum, Hannover, Germany. Hannover: Sprengel Museum, 1998.

Morphet, Richard, ed. *R. B. Kitaj: A Retrospective*. Exhibition catalogue, Tate Gallery, London; Los Angeles County Museum of Art; Metropolitan Museum of Art, New York. London: Tate Gallery, 1994. Texts by Richard Morphet and Richard Wollheim.

Ramkalawon, Jennifer. *Kitaj Prints: A Catalogue Raisonné*. London: British Museum Press, 2013.

R. B. Kitaj. Exhibition catalogue, Hirshhorn Museum and Sculpture Garden, Smithsonian Institution, Washington, DC; Cleveland Museum of Art; Städtische Kunsthalle Düsseldorf. Washington, DC: Smithsonian Institution Press, 1981. Texts by John Ashbery, Jane Livingston, and Joe Shannon.

R. B. Kitaj: A Survey, 1958–2007. Exhibition catalogue. London: Marlborough Fine Art, 2015. Text by Robert Storr.

Ríos, Julián. *Kitaj: Pictures and Conversations*. London: Hamish Hamilton, 1994.

LEON KOSSOFF

Kendall, Richard. *Drawn to Painting: Leon Kossoff Drawings and Prints after Nicolas Poussin*. Exhibition catalogue, Los Angeles County Museum of Art; J. Paul Getty Museum, Los Angeles. London: Merrell, 2000.

Kossoff: Selected Paintings, 1956–2000. Exhibition catalogue. Humlebaek, Denmark: Louisiana Museum of Modern Art; Lucerne, Switzerland: Kunstmuseum Luzern, 2005. Text by Anders Kold.

Leon Kossoff: London Landscapes. Exhibition catalogue. London: Annely Juda Fine Art; New York: Mitchell-Innes & Nash; Los Angeles: L.A. Louver, 2013. Text by Andrea Rose.

Leon Kossoff: Paintings from a Decade, 1970–1980. Exhibition catalogue, Museum of Modern Art, Oxford; Graves Art Gallery, Sheffield, UK. Oxford: Museum of Modern Art, 1981. Text by David Elliott.

Leon Kossoff: Recent Paintings. Exhibition catalogue. London: Whitechapel Art Gallery, 1972. Text by David Mercer.

Leon Kossoff: Recent Paintings. Exhibition catalogue, British Pavilion, XLVI Venice Biennale; Stedelijk Museum, Amsterdam. London: British Council, 1995. Texts by Rudi Fuchs, Leon Kossoff, Andrea Rose, and David Sylvester.

Moorhouse, Paul. *Leon Kossoff*. Exhibition catalogue. London: Tate Gallery; New York: Thames & Hudson, 1996.

Wiggins, Colin, with Philip Conisbee and Juliet Wilson-Bareau. *Leon Kossoff: Drawing from Painting*. Exhibition catalogue. London: National Gallery, 2007.

ILLUSTRATION CREDITS

Every effort has been made to contact the owners and photographers of objects reproduced here whose names do not appear in the captions or in the illustration credits. Anyone having further information concerning copyright holders is asked to contact Getty Publications so this information can be included in future printings.

Fig. 1. Image: John Deakin Archive / Getty Images

Fig. 2, page 93. Art: © The Estate of Michael Andrews, courtesy James Hyman Gallery, London / Image: Bridgeman Images

Fig. 3. Art: © Trustees of the Stanley Spencer Estate / Bridgeman Copyright Service

Fig. 4, pages 66, 68–69, 71. Art: © Lucian Freud Archive / Bridgeman Copyright Service / Image: Bridgeman Images

Fig. 5. Image: © Tate, London 2016

Fig. 6, pages 33, 55. Art and image: © Tate, London 2016

Fig. 7. Art: © The Estate of Sir William Coldstream. All Rights Reserved 2010 / Bridgeman Art Library / Image: © Tate, London 2016

Fig. 8. Art: © 2016 Alberto Giacometti Estate / Licensed by VAGA and Artist Rights Society (ARS), New York, NY / Image: Bridgeman Images

Fig. 9. Art: © 2016 The Willem de Kooning Foundation / Artists Rights Society (ARS), New York / Image: © The Museum of Modern Art / Licensed by SCALA / Art Resource, NY

Fig. 10. Image: Erich Lessing / Art Resource, NY

Fig. 11, page 45. Art: © The Estate of Francis Bacon. All Rights Reserved / DACS, London / Artists Rights Society (ARS), NY 2016

Fig. 12. Art: © Jasper Johns and ULAE / Licensed by VAGA, New York, NY. Published by Universal Limited Art Editions / Image: © The Museum of Modern Art / Licensed by SCALA / Art Resource, NY

Page 30. Art: © The Cecil Beaton Studio Archive at Sotheby's

Pages 32, 34, 36–41, 44, 46–47. Art: © The Estate of Francis Bacon. All Rights Reserved / DACS, London / Artists Rights Society (ARS), NY 2016 / Image: © Tate, London 2016

Page 35. Art: © The Estate of Francis Bacon. All Rights Reserved / DACS, London / Artists Rights Society (ARS), NY 2016 / Photography: © The Art Institute of Chicago

Page 43. Art: © The Estate of Francis Bacon. All Rights Reserved / DACS, London / Artists Rights Society (ARS), NY 2016 / Image: Peter Schibli, Basel

Page 48. Image: © National Portrait Gallery, London

Pages 50–54, 57, 59–65, 67. Art: © Lucian Freud Archive / Bridgeman Copyright Service / Image: © Tate, London 2016

Page 72. Art: © Mark Gerson / Image: Bridgeman Images

Pages 75–80, 83–85. Art: © Leon Kossoff / Image: © Tate, London 2016

Page 81. Art: © Leon Kossoff / Image: Todd-White Art Photography, London

Page 82. Art: © Leon Kossoff / Image: Prudence Cuming Associates Ltd.

Pages 86, 94, 118. Art: © The Lewinski Archive at Chatsworth / Image: Bridgeman Images

Pages 88–90, 92. Art: © The Estate of Michael Andrews, courtesy James Hyman Gallery, London / Image: © Tate, London 2016

Page 91. Art: © The Estate of Michael Andrews, courtesy James Hyman Gallery, London / Image: © The Metropolitan Museum of Art / Art Resource, NY

Pages 96–97, 99–102, 105–11, 114–16. Art: © Frank Auerbach, courtesy Marlborough Fine Art / Image: © Tate, London 2016

Pages 98, 103, 113, 117. Art: © Frank Auerbach, courtesy Marlborough Fine Art

Pages 120–25, 127–29. Art: © R. B. Kitaj Estate, courtesy Marlborough Fine Art / Image: © Tate, London 2016

Page 126. Art: © R. B. Kitaj Estate, courtesy Marlborough Fine Art / Image: © 2016 Museum Associates / LACMA / Licensed by Art Resource, NY

INDEX

Page numbers in *italics* refer to illustrations.